PHONETICS IN ENGLISH

PHONETICS IN ENGLISH

Sonu Marwah

ANMOL PUBLICATIONS PVT. LTD.
NEW DELHI-110 002 (INDIA)

ANMOL PUBLICATIONS PVT. LTD.
Regd. Office: 4360/4, Ansari Road, Daryaganj,
New Delhi-110002 (India)
Tel.: 23278000, 23261597, 23286875, 23255577
Fax: 91-11-23280289
Email: anmolpub@gmail.com
Visit us at: www.anmolpublications.com

Branch Office: No. 1015, Ist Main Road, BSK IIIrd Stage
IIIrd Phase, IIIrd Block, Bangalore-560 085 (India)
Tel.: 080-41723429 • Fax: 080-26723604
Email: anmolpublicationsbangalore@gmail.com

Phonetics in English

First Edition, 2010

ISBN 978-81-261-4590-4

PRINTED IN INDIA

Printed at Balaji Offset, Delhi.

Contents

Preface

Speech is an exceedingly complex human activity, and it took a great deal of scientific exploration, experimentation, development, as well as considerable computational power to deal successfully with speech. Moreover, the challenge hasn't been fully met yet. Change the way you pronounce your commands ever so subtly.

Or put even good computer speech and human speech side by side, and most listeners will still show a clear preference for human speech. As a result, the race is on to improve computer speech interfaces, a race that has recently been joined by some of the world's major computer firms. It can be expected that over the next ten years, major efforts will be launched to create competing products, and to improve on existing software.

Moreover, the world is a multilingual place, and at least the synthesis side of speech will have a distinctly international flavour. The recognition side may initially be handled in language-independent fashion, but in the long run, even in this area, "one size may not fit all". Increasingly, the aim will be to create and understand natural, error-free and truly pronounce speech.

Author

Chapter 1

English Phonetics

OVERVIEW

Phonetics is the study of speech sounds. Although language is obviously composed of sound, speech sounds came to be the main focus of linguistic investigation only in the 20th century.

19th century linguists were more interested in written rather than spoken language. Only with the work of Swiss linguist Ferdinand de Saussure in the early 20th century did linguists recognize the primacy of sound in human language and the secondary, superficial nature of writing.

- Acoustic phonetics is the study of the physical properties of sounds, the air wave frequencies of which sounds consist. The frequency of vibrations measured in hertz; volume of sound measured in decibels. Instruments used to measure and record speech sounds include the sound spectrograph, which produces readouts called sound spectrograms.
- Auditory phonetics is the study of how sounds are perceived by the human ear or recognized by the brain. (Mention Oronyms, Mondegreens.)
- Articulatory phonetics is the study of how sounds are produced by the vocal apparatus. The flow of sound during any given speech act can be divided into units of sound that recur in the flow of other speech acts. In phonetic transcription using the IPA, these separate sounds, called phones, are customarily enclosed in square brackets to distinguish them from

letters: [o] = the sound of the vowel in the word *rope,* not the letter o.

The division of the speech continuum into separate sounds, or phones, is made on the basis of both articulatory and acoustic data. Auditorily, the sounds seem to the ear to change at a particular point. Acoustically, this change can be seen on a sound spectrogram. Auditorily, the change of one sound to another is the result of measurable changes in the movement of the speech organs.

Data from all three branches of phonetics have revealed another important point about speech sounds. The phone is not the smallest formal unit in language. Listen to the phones [v] and [u]. Auditorily, we perceive a single unit of sound. Articulatorily, however, more than one part of the vocal apparatus is at work making the sound (cf. f/v or i/u).

This fact only became apparent during the work of the Prague School linguists in the earlier part of this century. Nikolai Trubetskoi noticed that each speech sound or phone is a complex entity. He called each component of a sound aphonetic feature (voicing, lip rounding are phonetic features). These features are produced more or less simultaneously rather than consecutively, which is why we tend to hear them all together as a single unit.

After the Second World War, when sound spectrographs came into general use, the phonetic features posited by the Prague School linguists actually became visible. They appear as separate formants in the spectrogram of each sound ([v] has voicing and high static; [u] has a higher first formant and lower second formant, [i] has a higher second formant and lower first formant). Thus, not all sounds are equally different, some share virtually no phonetic features, while others differ in only a single feature. Sounds sharing a given phonetic feature can be grouped together into what are called natural classes (vowels, consonants, nasals, voiced sounds, etc.).

It has been found that a relatively small number of phonetic features were all that was necessary to describe all the sound in any given language. Notice that there are less than half the number of phonetic features as there are sounds in English. Phonetic features are usually based on articulatory and sometimes acoustic details (strident vs. non-strident).

One of the Prague linguists, Roman Jakobson, was intrigued by how few phonetic features there seemed to be in relation to speech sounds in the world's languages. He tried to come up with a set of universal phonetic features that could be used as tools to describe any sound in any language of the world. His theory of universal phonetic features failed, however, because as more languages were described, the number of features kept increasing. In this class, we will concentrate on the natural classes of sounds rather than on the phonetic features. We will also learn the IPA alphabet, a special phonetic alphabet linguists use to write speech sounds.

THE IPA

Before launching into our discussion of articulatory phonetics, it would be useful to discuss the IPA and its use for transcribing English.

Writing uses graphic symbols to represent speech sounds. All systems of writing in use today represent the sounds of language. This connection can be viewed in two ways.

- From sound to writing. Every written language has a system of rules for how to spell the spoken word. These rules are called the orthography, the writing rules of the language.
- From writing to sound. Every written language has a system of rules for pronouncing correctly what is written. These rules are called orthoepy, or pronouncing rules.

Some writing systems come close to achieving a one-to-one correspondence between sound and written symbol. In Spanish, for instance, the rules of orthography and orthoepy are extremely simple. Once you have learned the Spanish alphabet, spelling and reading Spanish words is relatively unproblematical. Nearly every letter has one basic pronunciation, and most basic sounds can be written with one and only one letter (exceptions being the sound [s], which may be written s, c, z).

The Georgian writing system comes even closer to perfect economy. There are 33 different sounds in Georgian and only 33 different letters in the Georgian alphabet. Whenever you hear a new Georgian word, you know exactly how to write it. And whenever you meet a new word in reading a Georgian text, you know exactly how it should be pronounced; and whenever you hear a new Georgian word pronounced, you know exactly how to write it. Other languages, such as English, show far less economy of correspondence between sound and written symbol. The English alphabet has only 26 letters. However, English spells one and the same sound with several different letters depending upon the word. Consequently, one letter or group of letters can be read in any one of several possible ways, such as the *gh* in *rough, ghost, night.* The correspondence between sound and letter in English frequently involves meaning as well as sound. Often, one must know the meaning of an English word to pronounce or write it correctly: *meet/meat; through/threw.*

There are hundreds of alphabets and writing systems in use in the world. Many are based on the Latin alphabet, but the system of sound to symbol correspondences are different in each one. (Example, varieties of the Latin alphabet are used for most European languages, but the values of letters is often different: j in Spanish, English, and Hungarian.)

Here are some more striking examples of the variety of writing systems:

English	horse	apple
Russian lowad;	qbloko	
Georgian	cxeni	vawli
Navaho ¬ií'	bilasáana	
Cherokee	ÙÒñ	¥æ

To alleviate the confusion of having so many different writing systems, phoneticians have devised a single, unified phonetic alphabet capable of representing virtually any sound in any language of the world.

This alphabet is called the International Phonetic Alphabet, or the IPA. The IPA tries to and comes close to achieving the ideal one-to-one correspondence between sound and written symbol— not only for a single language, but for all languages. This allows linguists to write about different languages without studying their particular writing systems.

The need for a universal writing system finds an analogy in the development of standardized scientific names for plants and animals. Zoologists and botanists use a universal system of names called scientific names to denote genus and species. This system of scientific names, developed in the mid 18th century by the Swede Carl Linnéus, is based mostly on Greek and Latin (*the Latin Equus denotes the genus "horse" and Malus denotes the genus"apple".)* Because it is universally accepted, this system of scientific names is understandable to scientists all over the world regardless of their native language.

NEED OF AN IPA

Because you will be expected to spend so much time learning and working with the IPA in the next two weeks, I feel the need to explain even more clearly why it is important that you do so. You may ask: Why do we need a special alphabet like the IPA? Why can't we simply use the 26 letters of the English alphabet more systematically to sound out English words as well as words of other languages?

- Well, there is a far greater number of different sounds in the world's languages than there are letters in the English alphabet. Let's transcribe the sounds given above.

English	[hOrs]	[œpl¢]
Russian	[lOS′t′]	[jAbl′k′]
Georgian	[tsxEni]	[vASli]
Navaho	[:i!…≥]	[bilAsA!…nA]
Cherokee	[sokwili]	[s′&tA]

Notice that to avoid confusion between the IPA transcription and other writing systems, IPA transcription is enclosed in square brackets. We write with the English alphabet; we transcribe with the IPA. If linguists didn't have the IPA, they would have to resort to using the writing system of each individual language, as we did earlier. This would be quite difficult. There are 14 major writing systems in use, and some, such as the Latin alphabet, have hundreds of variants each using a somewhat different set of correspondences between sound and symbol. Also, many hundreds of languages are still not written at all.

Notice that an unmodified English alphabet could not be used to transcribe the many non-English sounds that occur in other languages. Using English letters to convey words of other languages is awkward and has in the past resulted in gross distortions of the pronunciation of foreign words: *Peking, Ceylon, Cherokee.*

- To see how difficult it can be to write non-English words with the English alphabet, try to write the following words using English letter combinations: Georgian tsqali, *water*, ghori *pig*; Sahaptin huq'huq' *pig*; Navaho líí', *horse*; Cherokee vtla, *no.*
- The second question you may ask is this: While it is obvious why we need an IPA to transcribe other languages, can't we at least just use the English alphabet more systematically to write English? In fact, there are quite a few more sounds in English than there are in the English alphabet. There are 26 different letters, but something like 34 different sounds.

Obviously, we need some sort of phonetic alphabet to explain the pronunciation of the extra sounds in English.

We have seen that:

- One English letter is often equivalent to more than one different sound:

  fat/father/fate book/boot this/thistle
- The same sound may be represented by different letters

  ship/education/fissure oat/note/owe

And the problem with English orthography and orthoepy cannot be solved simply by basic education. Even most highly educated people would need to be warned how to pronounce such toponyms as *Puyallup, Sequim, Spokane.* Or last names such as *Vajda*. A phonetic alphabet is necessary for dictionaries and guides to help English speakers pronounce their own language. Furthermore, a standard phonetic transcription is essential when describing different English dialects. Not every speaker of English pronounces the same word in the same way.

cat/cot/caught *father/farther* *bird*

It is obvious that some sort of phonetic transcription is necessary as a guide to pronouncing unfamiliar English words as well as a means of transcribing English dialects.

Although we will discuss un-English sounds found in languages, you will only be responsible for knowing the IPA symbols used in English. These are listed on pp 208-209 and again on the inside cover of you textbook. Notice the symbols for the vowels in cot/caught.

Notice that, like the system of scientific names, the IPA also uses Latin as a base, adding extra symbols ordiacritic marks for various modifications of the basic sounds. Because each IPA symbol stands for one basic sound regardless of the language being transcribed, it differs from the actual Latin alphabet, which often use the same symbol for different sounds in different languages (cf."j" in Engl., Sp, Fr., Germ. Hungarian). Although it looks like English or Latin, the IPA is not truly biased in favour of English or of any other language. The phonetic transcription of English words may also differ radically from conventional English spelling: cf. the transcription of"thigh,""phrase."

Before the IPA gained wide acceptance, American linguists employed a somewhat different set of symbols to transcribe English. The difference between IPA symbols and those used by many American linguists for several sounds can be found on p 185. The symbol used in your book for the sound [r] also differs from the IPA. You may use either symbol for these sounds, but the IPA variants are best.

Also, your book mixes dialects in its transcription. (Explain [O] and [A]; [A] and [a].) You should transcribe English words as you pronounce them in your dialect. Although some of the IPA symbols are not yet accepted by all linguists (witness the choice of symbols for several American sounds), and although new sounds will no doubt be discovered that require new symbols, the IPA is still the most versatile writing system ever devised. Therefore, all linguists and linguistics students should learn and use it.

LIMITATIONS OF THE IPA

Aside from the temporary, logistic problems of getting everyone to use the IPA, there is another more intrinsic limitation inherent to this or any other universal writing system. At the present time it is true that all sounds which contrast to reflect differences in meaning in any known language are represented in the IPA. It is also true that new symbols can easily be added to accommodate the discoveries of new sounds.

The permanent, intrinsic problem with the IPA is that real sounds are infinitely variable. Sound spectrogramsshow that a single sound varies slightly each time it is pronounced. Thus, the IPA could only capture a part of each individuals unique accent, or way of speaking (called an idiolect)

The differences here, of course, are not meaningful. But when comparing sounds across languages, the minute differences become more important. What seems to be the same sound in different languages may actually vary in minute degrees. (cf. the degrees of aspiration in the sound "t" in English, German, Georgian, Mongolian; or the degree or type of glottalization in the sound "t" in Georgian, Navajo or even in English *hatbox*.. Even [m] differs in English and Russian in slight ways that the IPA does not distinguish. Thus, the IPA would not be able to transcribe all the phonetic detail of, say, a Russian accent in English.

The IPA ignores minute differences between sounds if those differences never contrast with one another in any single language. The IPA symbols, therefore, are generalizations. The sounds of speech, however, are more complicated.

Thus, when comparing nearly identical sounds from language to language one must be aware that the IPA is only accurate up to a point. To get a complete picture of native pronunciation, one must fill in the tiny phonetic details left out by the IPA. There is no real solution for this problem. One could invent a slightly different symbol for all the different examples of, say, aspirated "t" or glottal "t," but inventing different symbols for extremely similar sounds in each language would defeat the very purpose for which the IPA was invented. The ultimate uniqueness of sounds in each individual language renders the IPA an imperfect and incomplete alphabet, despite the fact that it is the closest thing to an ideal alphabet we will probably ever have. This inevitable problem derives from the very nature of speaking and writing. Sound can only be depicted with discrete graphic units to a certain degree of precision. The only thing more complete and accurate would be the use of sound spectrograms instead of symbols to denote actual sounds.

Because similar sounds are in reality minutely variable from language to language, the IPA is not a truly perfect alphabet. Because of the nature of language, no alphabet can truly be perfect—the more so if applied across languages. With a finite set of symbols an alphabet can only approximate the infinite number of actual sound variations in speech. Once again, a universal linguistic descriptive device cannot claim to be as accurate and universal as Mendeleyev's Periodic Table of Elements, where a finite number of units (the elements) actually can be used to describe an almost infinite number of combinations. This discrepancy, once again, illustrates the unique nature of human language.

Even if linguists devised a complete set of transcriptions symbols—perhaps based on sound spectograph readings rather than on the Latin alphabet—the phonetician's task would still be incomplete. This is because languages change over time, and new symbols would have to be devised as sounds changed. All human languages change over time—some quickly, others more slowly. Language is changing even now: your grandparents said [hw]; now most of you say [w]. The reasons for such changes are not always clear: language mixing (French borrowings caused the sounds v and z to become initial consonants; f into Slavic from Greek after 988).

Languages isolated from contact with other languages tend to change more slowly, but change they do. Not all language change can by any means be traced to the interaction with different languages ([hw] to [w], for instance) [sk] became sh in Engl. from 5-6 cent AD. Words borrowed during that time, such as Latin disk, become dish.

After 600 AD the rule stopped working, the new remained, but new words coming into the language retained sk. Large number of Danish borrowings occurred circa 700AD: *sky, skull, ski*. The Danish intrusion resulted in some interesting doublets: *ship/skipper, shirt/skirt,* (meanings change over time also).

HISTORY

Phonetics is the study of the sounds of language. These sounds are called phonemes. There are literally hundreds of them used in different languages. Even a single language like English requires us to distinguish about 40! The key word here is distinguish. We actually make much finer discriminations among sounds, but English only requires 40. The other discriminations are what lets us detect the differences in accents and dialects, identify individuals, and differentiate tiny nuances of speech that indicate things beyond the obvious meanings of the words.

VOCAL TRACT

In order to study the sounds of language, we first need to study the vocal tract. Speech starts with the lungs, which push air out and pull it in. The original purpose was, of course, to get oxygen and eliminate carbon dioxide. But it is also essential for speech. There are phonemes that are little more than breathing: the h for example.

Next, we have the larynx, or voice box. It sits at the juncture of the trachea or windpipe coming up from the lungs and the esophagous coming up from the stomach. In the larynx, we have an opening called the glottis, an epiglottis which covers the glottis when we are swallowing, and the vocal cords.

The vocal cords consist of two flaps of mucous membrane stretched across the glottis, as in this photograph:

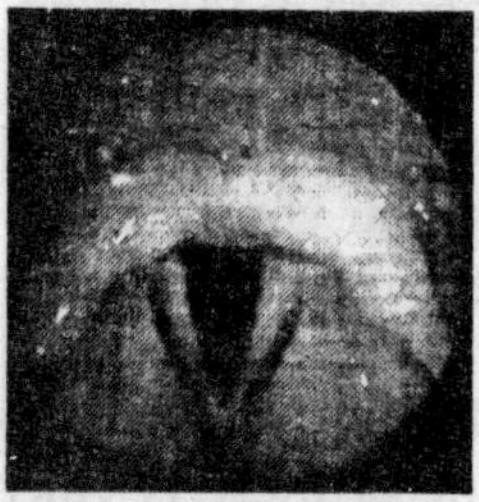

The vocal cords can be tightened and loosened and can vibrate when air is forced past them, creating sound. Some phonemes use that sound, and are calledvoiced. Examples include the vowels (a, e, i, o, and u, for example) and some of the consonants (m, l, and r, for example). Other phonemes do not involve the vocal cords, such as the consonants h, t, or s, and so are called unvoiced.

The area above the glottis is called the pharynx, or upper throat. It can be tightened to make phryngeal consonants. English doesn't have any of these, but they sound like when you try to get a piece of food back up out of your throat.

At the top of the throat is the opening to the nasal passages (called the nasopharynx, in case you are interested). When we allow air to pass into the nose while speaking, the sounds we make are called nasal. Examples include m, n, and the ng sound of sing.

Much of the action during speech occurs in the mouth, of course, especially involving the interaction of the tongue with the roof of the mouth. The roof of the mouth has several specific areas: At the very back, just before the nasal passage, is that little bag called the uvula.

Its major function seems to be moisturizing the air and making certain sounds called, obviously, uvular. The best known is the kind of r pronounced in the back of the mouth by some French and German speakers. Uvular, pharyngeal, and glottal sounds are often refered to as gutterals. Next, we have the soft palate, called the velum. If you turn your tongue back as far as it will go and press up, you can feel how soft it is. When you say k or g, you are using the velum, so they are called velar consonants. Further forward is the hard palate. Quite a few consonants are made using the hard palate, such as s, sh, n, and l, and are called palatals. Just behind the teeth is the dental ridge or alveolus. Here is where many of us make our t's and d's — alveolar consonants.

At the very outer edge of the mouth we have the teeth and the lips. Dental consonants are made by touching the tongue to the teeth. In English, we make the two th sounds like this. Note that one of these is voiced (the th in the) and one is unvoiced (the th in thin). At the lips we can make several sounds as well. The simplest, perhaps, are the bilabial sounds, made by holding the lips together and then releasing the sound, such as p and b, or by keeping them together and releasing the air through the nose, making the bilabial nasal m. We can also use the upper teeth with the lower lip, forlabiodental sounds. This is how we make an f, for example. Incidentally, we also have two names for the parts of the tongue used with these various parts of the mouth: The front edge is called the corona, and the back is called the dorsum. Sounds like t, th, and s are made with the corona, while k, g, and ng are made with the dorsum.

CONSONANTS

Consonants are sounds which involve full or partial blocking of airflow. In English, the consonants are p, b, t, d, ch, j, k, g, f, v, th, dh, s, z, sh, zh, m, n, ng, l, r, w, and y. They are classified in a number of different ways, depending on the vocal tract details we just discussed.

- Stops, also known as plosives. The air is blocked for a moment, then released. In English, they are p, b, t, d, k, and g.
  - *Bilabial plosives*: p (unvoiced) and b (voiced)
  - *Alveolar plosives*: t (unvoiced) and d (voiced)
  - *Velar plosives*: k (unvoiced) and g (voiced)

In other languages, we find labiodental, palatal, uvular, pharyngeal, and glottal plosives as well, and retroflex plosives, which involve reaching back to the palate with the corona of the tongue. In many languages, plosives may be followed by aspiration, that is, by a breathy sound like an h. In Chinese, for example, there is a distinction between a p pronounced crisply and an aspirated p. We use both in English (pit vs poo), but it isn't a distinction that separates one meaning from another.

- Fricatives involve a slightly resisted flow of air. In English, these include f, v, th, dh, s, z, sh, zh, and h.
  - *Labiodental fricatives*: f (unvoiced) and v (voiced)
  - *Dental fricatives*: th (as in thin — unvoiced) and dh (as in the — voiced)
  - *Alveolar fricatives*: s (unvoiced) and z (voiced)
  - *Palatal fricatives*: sh (unvoiced) and zh (like the s in vision — voiced)
  - *Glottal fricative*: h (unvoiced)
- Affricates are sounds that involve a plosive followed immediately by a fricative at the same location. In English, we have ch (unvoiced) and j (voiced). Many consider these as blends: t-sh and d-zh.
- Nasals are sounds made with air passing through the nose. In English, these are m, n, and ng.
  - *Bilabial nasal*: m
  - *Alveolar nasal*: n
  - *Velar nasal*: ng
- Liquids are sounds with very little air resistance. In English, we have l and r, which are both alveolar, but differ in the shape of the tongue. For l, we touch the tip to the ridge of the teeth and let the air go around both sides. For the r, we almost block the air on both sides and let it through at the top. Note that there are many variations of l and r in other languages and even within English itself!
- Semivowels are sounds that are, as the name implies, very nearly vowels. In English, we have w and y, which you can see are a lot like vowels such as oo and ee, but with the lips almost closed for w (a bilabial) and the tongue almost touching the palate for y (a palatal). They are also called glides, since

they normally "glide" into or out of vowel positions (as in woo, yeah, ow, and oy).

In many languages, such as Russian, there is a whole set of palatalized consonants, which means they are followed by a y before the vowel. This is also called anon-glide.

VOWELS

There are about 14 vowels in English. They are the ones found in these words: beet, bit, bait, bet, bat, car, pot (in British English), bought, boat, book, boot, bird, but, and the a in ago. There are also three diphthongs or double vowels: bite, cow, and boy. Diphthongs involve off-glides.: You can hear the y in bite and boy, and the w in cow. Actually, the sounds in bait and boat are also diphthongs (with y and w off-glides, respectively), but the first parts of the diphthongs are different from the nearby sounds in bet and bought.

Vowels are classified in three dimensions:

1. *The height of the tongue in the mouth*: low, mid, or high
   - High are beet, bit, boot, and book
   - Mid are bait, bet, but, boat, bought, bird and a in ago
   - Low are bat, car, and british pot
2. *How far forward or backward in the mouth the tongue rises*: front, centre, or back
   - Front are beet, bit, bait, bet, and bat
   - Centre are but, bird, and a in ago
   - Back are boot, book, boat, bought, and british pot
3. How rounded or unrounded the lips are
   - The front vowels are unrounded
   - The centre and back vowels are rounded

The rounding idea may seem unnecessary until you realise that many languages have rounded front vowels — such as the German ü and ö and the French u and eu -- and many have unrounded back vowels — such as the Japanese u. If you took French in high school, you may remember the teacher telling you to say tea with your lips rounded for French tu. It isn't the best way to teach the sound, but it shows you where it fits in the scheme.

There is one more dimension that doesn't have much to do with English, but is essential in many languages, and that is vowel length. Vowels can be short or long, and it is just a matter of how long you continue the sound. The closest we get in English is that the vowel in beet is longer (as well as higher) than the vowel in bit. The same goes for boot and book, and for caught and the British pot.

In some languages, such as French, there is another quality to vowels, and that is nasality. Some vowels are pronounced with airflow through the nose as well as the mouth. Originally, these were simply vowels followed by nasal consonants. But over time, the French blended the vowels and the nasals into one unit.

DISCOVERY OF IPA

Over the years, linguists have developed a complex chart of phonemes for transcribing the sounds of all languages around the world. It is called the International Phonetic Alphabet, and much of it is in the charts below. If you get question marks or little squares, that means your computer isn't equipt with unicode, in which case you will have to look elsewhere for charts like this.

Vowels

	Front	Central	Back
High	i y	ɨ ʉ	ɯ u
	ɪ ʏ		ʊ
Middle	e ø	ɜ ə ɵ	ɤ o
	ɛ œ	ɐ ʌ	ɔ
Low	æ a		ɑ ɒ

Vowel length is marked with a colon after the vowel, e.g. i:

Nasal vowels are shown by placing a tilde over the vowel, e.g. ã There are dozens more phonemes beyond the ones in the preceding charts, but one set is particularly interesting: Clicks are sounds made by creating a vacuum with the tongue and then suddenly snapping the tongue away. We use these ourselves, though not as parts of words: When we "tsk tsk," when we make clucking sounds, and when we make a click in the side of our mouths when we tell a horse to get a move on. Clicks are used in the Bushman languages and in the Bantu languages that had prolonged contact with them. The best known is the Bantu language Khosa, because of the famous South African singer Miriam Makeba.

Consonants

		Bilabial	Labio-dental	Dental	Alveolar	Retroflex	Palato-alveolar	Palatal	Velar	Uvular	Glottal
Plosives	uv.	P			t	ʈ		c	k	q	ʔ
	v.	B			d	ɖ		ɟ	g	ɢ	
Fricatives	uv.	ɸ	f	θ	s	ʂ	ʃ	ç	x	χ	h
	v.	B	v	ð	z	ʐ	ʒ	ʝ	ɣ	ʁ	ɦ
Nasals		M	ɱ		n	ɳ		ɲ	ŋ	ɴ	
Semivowels	uv.	ʍ									
	v.	W	ʋ		ɹ	ɻ		j			
Rolled/ Trilled		B			r					ʀ	
Tapped/ Flapped					ɾ	ɽ					
Laterals					l	ɭ		ʎ	L		
Lateral -fricatives	uv.				ɬ						
	v.				ɮ						

STRESS AND TONES

In many languages around the world, including English, words are differentiated by means of stress. One syllable is usually given a higher pitch ("up" the musical scale) and sometimes a bit more force. This is how we differentiate af-fect (as in influence) and af-fect (as in emotion), for example. In longer words, there may even be a second semi-stressed syllable, as in math-e-mat-ics: mat has the primary stress, math has the secondary stress. In IPA, primary stress is indicated by preceding the syllable with a high vertical line, secondary with a low vertical line.

Note that even when we do not need to use stress to differentiate words, we use it anyway. Sometimes we can tell where a person is from by how they use stress: insurance is usually stressed on the sur; southerners stress it on the in. But many languages do not use stress at all. To our ears, they sound rather monotone. Some other languages use dynamic stress or tones. Swedish is an example. This means that there is actual change of stress within syllables. In Swedish, there are two tones: The single tone starts high and goes down. If a single toneword has a second syllable, that syllable is unstressed. Single tone words don't sound very unusual to English speakers. The double tone is only found in two syllable words. The first pitch starts in the middle range of pitch and the second tone starts high and goes down. If there is a third syllable, it is unstressed. The double tone gives the word a sing-song quality to English speakers. These tones differentiate many words in Swedish. In the single tone, anden, tomten, biten, and slaget mean the duck, the building, the bit, and the battle, respectively. In the double tone, they mean the spirit, the elf, bitten, and beaten, respectively! English uses dynamic stress or tones also, but only one whole phrases, such as the rising pitch at the end of questions.

But many languages in Africa and Asia use far more complex tones, and in fact are called tonal languages. Chinese is the best known example. Although words are often more than one syllable in length, each syllable has a particular meaning. And Chinese uses a very limitied number of phonemes. It is the tones that prevent every syllable from having hundreds of meanings.

There are five of them:

- *Tone* 1: High and level (as in hey!)
- *Tone* 2: Middle, then rising (as in was it you?)
- *Tone* 3: Middle, falling, then rising (as in mom!? spoken by a whining teenager)
- *Tone* 4: High, then falling (as in Tom spoken by a disappointed mom)

For example, the simple syllable yi can mean many different things. With tone 1 it means cloth, with tone 2 it means to suspect, with tone 3 it means chair, and with tone 4 it means meaning. The syllable wu means house, none, five, and fog, respectively. And ma means mother, hemp, horse, and scold. In the official transcription, the four tones are indicated by ¯, ´, ˇ, *Thai has five tones*: high, middle, low, rising, and falling. The African language Katamba has six, adding a falling, then rising tone. Cantonese has nine tones: high long, high short, middle long, middle short, low long, low short, high falling, middle falling, and low rising.

We don't know how tonal languages arise. Many believe that it has to do with phonemes or even whole syllables that have been lost, but influenced the pronounciation anyway. But this makes it hard to explain that Cantonese, which has kept many old consonant endings, has nine tones, while its relative Mandarin Chinese, which has lost those endings, only has four. Of course a linguist from China might ask how non-tonal languages lost their tones!

One interesting tidbit is that tonality often crosses family lines. In Asia, for example, tonality is found in Chinese, Thai, and Vietnamese — which are unrelated languages. On the other hand, Tibetan and Burmese are related to Chinese, but are not tonal; neither is Khmer, a relative of Vietnamese. Most African languages are tonal, but Swahili is not. Hausa, spoken in Nigeria, is tonal, but relatives like Arabic are not. It is possible that one or another language family influenced others around it, or was original to an area before being invaded by speakers of another language.

PHONETIC ALPHABET

THE SOUNDS OF ENGLISH AND THE INTERNATIONAL PHONETIC ALPHABET

This chart contains all the sounds (phonemes) used in the English language.

For each sound, it gives:

- The *symbol* from the International Phonetic Alphabet (IPA), as used in phonetic transcriptions in modern dictionaries for English learners — that is, in A. C. Gimson's phonemic system with a few additional symbols.

The chart represents British and American phonemes with one symbol. One symbol can mean two different phonemes in American and British English. See the footnotes for British-only and American-only symbols.

- Two English *words* which use the sound. The underline shows where the sound is heard.
- The links labeled *Amer* and *Brit* play sound recordings (you need Flash 9 or higher) where the words are pronounced in American and British English. The British version is given only where it is very different from the American version.

Vowels

1 In some (not many) dictionaries, the e phoneme is written as ɛ (do not confuse with 3:), which is actually more appropriate, because e in the IPA does *not* correspond to the sound in *met* and ***bed***. The same goes for eə but not ei.

2 In ə[r] and 3:[r] the r is not pronounced in BrE, unless the sound comes before a vowel (as in *answering, answer it*). In AmE, the r is always pronounced, and the sounds are sometimes written as əʹ and 3ʹ.

3 In AmE, a: and ɒ are one vowel, so ***calm*** and *cot* have the same vowel. In American transcriptions, *hot* is written as hɑ:t

4 About 40% of Americans pronounce ɔ :the same way

as ɑ: so that *caught* and *cot* have the same vowel. *cot-caught merger.*

5 In American transcriptions, ɔ: is often written as ɒ: (e.g. *law* = lɒ:), unless it is followed by r, in which case it remains an ɔ:.

	Words		IPA	words	
IPA					
^	cup, luck		f	find, if	
ɑ:	arm, father		g	give, flag	
æ	cat, black		h	how, hello	
e	met, bed	1	j	yes, yellow	
ə	away, cinema	2	k	cat, back	
ɜ:^{r}	turn, learn	2	l	leg, little	
ɪ	hit, sitting		m	man, lemon	
i:	see, heat		n	no, ten	
ɒ	hot, rock	3	ŋ	sing, finger	
ɔ:	call, four	4 5	p	pet, map	
ʊ	put, could		r	red, try	
u:	blue, food		s	sun, miss	
aɪ	five, eye		ʃ	she, crash	
aʊ	now, out		t	tea, getting	8
eɪ	say, eight		tʃ	check, church	
oʊ	go, home	6	θ	think, both	
ɔɪ	boy, join		ð	this, mother	
eə^r	where, air	1 7	v	voice, five	
ɪə^r	near, here	7	w	wet, window	
ʊə^r	pure, tourist	7	z	zoo, lazy	
b	bad, lab		ʒ	pleasure, vision	
d	did, lady		dʒ	just, large	

6 Most British dictionaries represent ou as ə u. For some BrE speakers, ou is more appropriate (they use a rounded vowel) — for others, the proper symbol is ə u. For American speakers, ou is usually more accurate.

7 In eə^r iə^r ua^r the r is not pronounced in BrE, unless the sound comes before a vowel (as in *dearest, dear Ann*). In AmE, the r is always pronounced, and the sounds are often written as er ir ur.

8 In American English, t is often pronounced as a "flap t", which sounds like d or (more accurately) like the quick, hard *r* heard e.g. in the Spanish word *pero*. For example:*letter*.

Table. Special Symbols

IPA	What it means
'	The apostrophe symbol (') is used to show word stress. Usually, it is placed before the stressed syllable in a word. For example, **/'kɒntrækt/** is pronouncedlike this, and **/kən trækt'/** like that. Word stress is explained in our article about phonetic transcription.
R	**r** is not a sound — it is a short way of saying that an **r** is pronounced only in American English. For example, if you write that the pronunciation of *bar* is**/ba:ʳ/**, you mean that it is **/ba:r/** in American English, and **/ba: /** in British English. However, in BrE, **r** will be heard if **r** is followed by a vowel. For example, *far gone*is pronounced **/'fa:' gɒ n/** in BrE, but *far out* is pronounced **/'fa:' raut/**.
I	**i** is usually pronounced like a shorter version of **i:**, but sometimes (especially in an old-fashioned British accent) it can sound like **i**. Examples: *very* **/'veri/**, *create***/kri' eit/**, *previous* **/'pri:visə /**, *ability* **/ə:bilti/**.
əl	**əl** means that the consonant **l** is pronounced as a separate syllable (the *syllabic l*, which sounds like a vowel), or that there is a short **ə** sound before it. Examples:*little* **/'litə l/**, *uncle* **/ 'ʌŋkə l/**. Instead of the **əl** symbol, some dictionaries use the *syllabic l* symbol **l̩**, as in/**'lɪtl̩**/, or simply **l**, as in /**'lɪtl**/.
ən	**ən** means that the consonant **n** is pronounced as a separate syllable (the *syllabic n*, which sounds like a vowel), or that there is a short **ə** sound before it. Examples: *written* **/'ritə n/**, *listen* **/'lisə n/**. Instead of the **ən** symbol, some dictionaries use the *syllabic n* symbol **n**, as in**/ritn/**, or simply **n**.

For example, list the"regular t" (heard in this pronunciation of letter) and the"flap t" (heard in this one) with separate symbols. It groups them under a single symbol: t. (In other words, it groups a number of similar sounds under a singlephoneme, for simplicity. To understand how sounds are grouped into phonemes, read the article on phonemic transcription.)

The lists of phonemes (groups of sounds), not individual sounds. Each symbol in the chart can correspond to many different (but similar) sounds, depending on the word and the speaker's accent. Take the phoneme p in the above chart. It occurs in the phonemic transcriptions of pin/pin/and spin/ spin/. In pin, this phoneme is pronounced with aspiration (breathing). This"aspirated p" sound has its own special symbol in the IPA: ph. In spin, the phoneme is pronounced "normally"; the"normal p" sound is represented by p in the IPA. So the pphoneme represents two sounds: p and ph. (This can be confusing, because p can mean both the p phoneme and the p sound.)

PHONETIC SYMBOLS

You won't find phonetic symbols on your computer's keyboard. How do you type them in a Word document, e-mail message, or SuperMemo collection?

There are two solutions:

- You can go to the IPA phonetic keyboard at ipa.typeit.org, type your transcriptions, and copy & paste them to your document.
- You can use the ASCII Phonetic Alphabet, which replaces IPA symbols with characters that you can type on your keyboard.

ENGLISH PHONETIC SPELLING

When speaking on the telephone, it is sometimes useful to spell a word using English Phonetic Spelling. To spell"Club", for example, you would say:"C for Charlie, L for Lima, U for Uniform, B for Bravo."

It is very easy to learn English Phonetic Spelling. Start by spelling your name, then your company or address. Soon, you will know the whole alphabet.

It also helps to remember that there are several groups of words that go together:

Dances: Foxtrot, Tango

- *Shakespeare*: Romeo & Juliet
- *Men's first names*: Charlie, Mike, Oscar, Victor
- *Cities*: Lima, Quebec

A	Alpha	**B**	Bravo
C	Charlie	**D**	Delta
E	Echo	**F**	Foxtrot
G	Golf	**H**	Hotel
I	India	**J**	Juliet
K	Kilo	**L**	Lima
M	Mike	**N**	November
O	Oscar	**P**	Papa
Q	Quebec	**R**	Romeo
S	Sierra	**T**	Tango
U	Uniform	**V**	Victor
W	Whisky	**X**	X-ray
Y	Yankee	**Z**	Zulu

According to the International Phonetic Association, the above list is sometimes wrongly called the "International Phonetic Alphabet".

ENGLISH

English is a West Germanic language related to Dutch, Frisian and German with a significant amount of vocabulary from French, Latin, Greek and many other languages.

English evolved from the Germanic languages brought to Britain by the Angles, Saxons, Jutes and other Germanic tribes, which are known collectively as Anglo-Saxon or Old English. Old English began to appear in writing during the early 8th century AD. Approximately 341 million people speak English as a native language and a further 267 million speak it as a second language in over 104 countries including the UK, Ireland, USA, Canada, Australia, New Zealand, South Africa, American Samoa, Andorra, Anguilla, Antigua and Barbuda, Aruba, Bahamas, Barbados, Belize, Bermuda, Botswana, British Indian Ocean Territory, British Virgin Islands, Brunei, Cameroon, Canada, Cayman Islands, Cook Islands and Denmark.

ENGLISH ALPHABET

Aa	Bb	Cc	Dd	Ee	Ff	Gg	Hh	Ii	Jj	Kk	Ll	Mm
a	bee	cee	dee	e	ef	gee	(h)aitch	i	jay	kay	el	em
[eɪ]	[biː]	[siː]	[diː]	[iː]	[ɛf]	[dʒiː]	[(h)eɪtʃ]	[aɪ]	[dʒeɪ]	[keɪ]	[ɛl]	[ɛm]
Nn	**Oo**	**Pp**	**Qq**	**Rr**	**Ss**	**Tt**	**Uu**	**Vv**	**Ww**	**Xx**	**Yy**	**Zz**
en	o	pee	cue	ar	ess	tee	u	vee	double-u	ex	wy(e)	zed/zee
[ɛn]	[oʊ]	[piː]	[kjuː]	[ɑː/ɑr]	[ɛs]	[tiː]	[juː]	[viː]	[ˈdʌbəljuː]	[ɛks]	[waɪ]	[zɛd/ziː]

PRONUNCIATION

The sounds represented here are those of British English spoken with an R.P. (Received Pronounciation) accent. Other varieties of English differ considerably in pronunciation, especially the vowels and diphthongs.

VOWELS AND DIPHTHONGS

	AmE	AuE	BrE	CaE	IrE	NZE	SAE	ScE	WeE
ash	æːʃ	æʃ	æʃ	aːʃ	ɛ·ʃ	æ·ʃ	æ·ʃ	ɐ̥·ʃ	äʃ
all	ɑːɫ	ɔːɫ	ɔːɫ	ɒːɫ	ɔːɫ	ɔːɫ	ɔ̣ːɫ	ɔːɫ	ɔ̣ːɫ
father	ˈfäðɚ	ˈfäːðɜ	ˈfɑːð̣ə	ˈfɑ·ðɹ̣	ˈfɑ̈ːðɚ	ˈfäːðə	ˈfɑ·ðë	ˈfä·ðəɹ	ˈfɑ̣ːðɜ
better	ˈbɛɾɚ	ˈbe̞ɾɜ	ˈbɛtə	ˈbɛɾɹ̣	ˈbɛt͡ʔɚ	ˈbɪɾə	ˈbe̞tɜ	ˈbɛtʰəɹ	ˈbɛtɜ
day	de̞ɪ	dɛɪ	de̞ɪ	de̞ɪ	deː	dɛɪ	de̞·e̞	deː	de̞ɪ
earth	ɚ·θ	ɜ̝ːθ	ɜːθ	ɚːθ	ɚ·θ	ø̞̈·θ	ɜ̝·θ	ɛ̝ɹθ	œ̈ːθ
drink	dɹ̣ɪŋkʰ	dʒ̱ɹɪŋk	dɹɪŋkʰ	dɹɪŋk˺	dɹ̈ɪŋk̟ʰ	dʒɹɪŋk	dɹ̠ɪŋk̟ʰ	dɾɪŋk̟ʰ	dɹɪŋk
eat	iːtʰ	ɪit	iːtʰ	iːt	it	ɪit	iːtʰ	itʰ	iːt
top	tʰɑ̝p	tʰɒ̝p	tʰɔ̝p	tʰɒp˺	tʰɔːp	tʰɒ̝p	tʰɒp	tʰɔpʰ	tʰɒp
four	fo̞ːɹ	fɔː	fɔː	fo̞ːɹ	fo·ɚ	fɔ̝·ə	fɔː	fo̞·əɹ	fɔː
foot	fʊt	fʊt	fʊtʰ	fʊt	fɤ̈t	fʊt	fʊtʰ	fʉtʰ	fʏ̞t
goose	gʊus	gÿ·s	gu·s	gəʊs	gʏs	gʉ·s	gʉ̝·s	gʉs	gu·s
blood	bɫʌ̣d	blɐ̱d	blɐ̱d	bɫʌ̈d	bɫʌ̣d	blɐ̱d	blə̣d	blʌ̈d	bləd
bone	bʌ̣·ʊn	bɜ̱ʉ̯n	bəʊn	boʊn	boːn	bɜ̱ʉn	bɘʉn	bo̞ən	boːn
cow	kʰæ·ʊ	kʰæ·ʊ	kʰaʊ	kʰaʊ	kʰɐɤ·	kʰaʊ	kʰɐ̝·ö̞	k̟ʰɐu·	kʰɐu·
nail	ne·ʌ̈ɫ	nɛɪəɫ	ne̞ɪɫ	ne·əɫ	ne·əɫ	nɐɪʊ	ne·əɫ	ne·ʌ̈ɫ	neːl
bite	bäitʰ	bɑ̈ɪ̱t	bäɪtʰ	bʌ̈ɪt	bɐit	bɑ̈ɪt	bäetʰ	bʌ̣ɪtʰ	bɐit
ear	i·ɚ	i·ɜ	ɪ̞ə	i·ɹ̣	i·ɚ	i·ɛ̈	iɛ̈·	i·əɹ	jœ̈ː

AmE = American English (General American), AuE = Australian English, BrE = British English (RP), CaE = Canadian English, IrE = Irish English, NZE = New Zealand English, SAE = South African English, ScE = Scottish English, WeE = Welsh English

PHONETIC ALPHABET FOR ENGLISH PRONUNCIATION

This page presents the ASCII Phonetic Alphabet for English Pronunciation. It is a way of writing phonetic transcription of English pronunciation by means of ASCII characters available on all keyboards. This phonetic alphabet can be used to represent English pronunciation in email messages, in posts to discussion forums, on HTML pages, etc. - with the same degree of precision as the usual graphic IPA-based phonetic alphabet used in paper dictionaries or in some electronic dictionaries. Phonetic transcription on this page is written in such a way as to cover both British and American pronunciation. If you remove (r) from these transcriptions you will get transcription for British pronunciation, and if you treat it as r you get American pronunciation. Another unifying symbol is [@:] - which stands for the choice between [a:] in British English and [@] in American English. Thus this system of notation represents the "unified English pronunciation" - demonstrating that British pronunciation and American pronunciation are in fact two forms of the same thing: English pronunciation.

If you want to use this phonetic alphabet to represent American pronunciation only, you can do so by changing "(r)" into "r" and introducing other modifications that you seem would be appropriate. It is true that this alphabet is based on the way British pronunciation is usually transcribed in English dictionaries but it can well serve to depict American pronunciation if one understands the symbols with appropriate phonetic awareness.

We are aware that the terms "British pronunciation" and "American pronunciation" or even "English pronunciation" are not precise and that they are used differently by various authors. If you are an expert on English pronunciation who can distinguish between more kinds of spoken English than just British and American please don't complain about our usage of these terms. Try to understand that many English learners use phrases like "I want to learn British pronunciation", "I want to learn American pronunciation", "I want to have an American accent", or "I want to have a British accent" to organize their thoughts when they are thinking about developing their English accent.

abilities	[.. 'bi l(i) ti(:)z]
ability	[.. 'bi l(i) ti(:)]
able	['ei b.l]
about	[.. 'baut]
abroad	[.. 'bro:d]
absence	['@b s.ns]
accept	[..k 'sept]
accepted	[..k 'sep tid]
accepting	[..k 'sep tiN]
accepts	[..k 'septs]
acceptable	[..k 'sep t.. b.l]
accident	['@k s(i) d.nt]
accidents	['@k s(i) d.nts]
accordance	[.. 'ko:(r) d.ns]
according	[.. 'ko:(r) diN]
account	[.. 'kaunt]
accounts	[.. 'kaunts]
accounted	[.. 'kaun tid]
accounting	[.. 'kaun tiN]
accustom	[.. 'k^s t..m]
accustomed	[.. 'k^s t..md]
accustoms	[.. 'k^s t..mz]
ache	[eik]
ached	[eikt]
aching	['ei kiN]
aches	[eiks]
acid	['@ sid]
acids	['@ sidz]
across	[.. 'kro(:)s]

act	[@kt]
acted	['@k tid]
acting	['@k tiN]
acts	[@kts]
action	['@k S.n]
actions	['@k S.nz]
active	['@k tiv]
actively	['@k tiv li(:)]
activity	[@k 'ti v(i) ti(:)]
activities	[@k 'ti v(i) ti(:)z]
actor	['@k t..(r)]
actors	['@k t..(r)z]
actress	['@k tr(i)s]
actresses	['@k tr(i) siz]
actual	['@k tSu..l]
actually	['@k tS.. li(:)]
add	[@d]
added	['@ did]
adds	[@dz]
adding	['@ diN]
addition	[.. 'di S.n]
additions	[.. 'di S.nz]
unacceptable	[^n..k 'sep t.. b.l]
adjective	['@ dZ(i)k tiv]
additional	[.. 'di S.. n.l]
additionally	[.. 'di S.. n.l i(:)]
adjectives	['@ dZ(i)k tivz]
adjectival	[@ dZ(i)k 'tai v.l]
admiration	[@d m.. 'rei S.n]
admire	[..d 'mai..(r)]
admired	[..d 'mai..(r)d]
admires	[..d 'mai..(r)z]
admirable	['@d m.. r.. b.l]
admiring	[..d 'mai (..) riN]
admiringly	[..d 'mai (..) riN li(:)]
admirer	[..d 'mai (..) r..(r)]
admirers	[..d 'mai (..) r..(r)z]
admit	[..d 'mit]

admitted	[..d ‘mi tid]
admittedly	[..d ‘mi tid li(:)]
admitting	[..d ‘mi tiN]
admits	[..d ‘mits]
admittance	[..d ‘mi t.ns]
advance	[..d ‘v@:ns]
advanced	[..d ‘v@:nst]
advancing	[..d ‘v@:n siN]
advances	[..d ‘v@:n siz]
advancement	[..d ‘v@:ns m..nt]
advantage	[..d ‘v@:n tidZ]
advantages	[..d ‘v@:n ti dZiz]
disadvantage	[di s..d ‘v@:n tidZ]
disadvantages	[di s..d ‘v@:n ti dZiz]
advantageous	[@d v..n ‘tei dZ..s]
advantageously	[@d v..n ‘tei dZ..s li(:)]
disadvantageous	[dis @d v..n ‘tei dZ..s]
adventure	[..d ‘ven tS..(r)]
adventures	[..d ‘ven tS..(r)z]
adventurous	[..d ‘ven tS.. r..s]
adverb	[‘@d ve:(r)b]
adverbs	[‘@d ve:(r)bz]
advertise	[‘@d v..(r) taiz]
advertised	[‘@d v..(r) taizd]
advertising	[‘@d v..(r) tai ziN]
advertiser	[‘@d v..(r) tai z..(r)]
advertisers	[‘@d v..(r) tai z..(r)z]
advice	[..d ‘vais]
advise	[..d ‘vaiz]
advises	[..d ‘vai ziz]
advised	[..d ‘vaizd]
advising	[..d ‘vai ziN]
adviser	[..d ‘vai z..(r)]
advisers	[..d ‘vai z..(r)z]
affair	[.. ‘fe..(r)]
affairs	[.. ‘fe..(r)z]
afford	[.. ‘fo:(r)d]
afforded	[.. ‘fo:(r) did]

affording [.. 'fo:(r) diN]
affords [.. 'fo:(r)dz]
affordable [.. 'fo:(r) d.. b.l]
acceptability [..k sep t.. 'bi l(i) ti(:)]
affraid [.. 'freid]
after ['@:f t..(r)]
afternoon [@:f t..(r) 'nu:n]
afternoons [@:f t..(r) 'nu:nz]
afterwards ['@:f t..(r) w..(r)dz]
again [.. 'gen]
against [.. 'genst]
age [eidZ]
ages ['ei dZiz]
ago [.. 'gOu]
agree [.. 'gri:]
agreed [.. 'gri:d]
agreeing [.. 'gri: iN]
agrees [.. 'gri:z]
agreement [.. 'gri: m..nt]
agreements [.. 'gri: m..nts]
agreeable [.. 'gri:.. b.l]
disagree [di s.. 'gri:]
disagreed [di s.. 'gri:d]
disagreeing [di s.. 'gri: iN]
disagreement [di s.. 'gri: m..nt]
disagreeable [di s.. 'gri:.. b.l]
ahead [.. 'hed]
Aim [eim]
aimed [eimd]
aiming ['ei miN]
aims [eimz]

ENGLISH IRREGULAR VERBS WITH PHONETIC TRANSCRIPTION

beat	/bi:t/	**beat**	/bi:t/	**beaten**	/'bi:tn/
become	/bɪ 'kʌm/	**became**	/bɪ 'keɪm/	**become**	/bɪ 'kʌm/
begin	/bɪ 'gɪn/	**began**	/bɪ 'gæn/	**begun**	/bɪ 'gʌn/
bend	/bend/	**bent**	/bent/	**bent**	/bent/

bind	/baɪnd/	**bound**	/baʊnd/	**bound**	/baʊnd/
bite	/baɪt/	**bit**	/bɪt/	**bitten**	/ˈbɪtn/
bleed	/bli:d/	**bled**	/bled/	**bled**	/bled/
blow	/blou/	**blew**	/blu:/	**blown**	/bloun/
break	/breɪk/	**broke**	/brouk/	**broken**	/ˈbroukən/
bring	/brɪŋ/	**brought**	/brɔ:t/	**brought**	/brɔ:t/
build	/bɪld/	**built**	/bɪlt/	**built**	/bɪlt/
burn	/bɜ:rn/	**burnt**	/bɜ:rnt/	**burnt**	/bɜ:rnt/
burn	/bɜ:rn/	**burned**	/bɜ:rnd/	**burned**	/bɜ:rnd/
buy	/baɪ/	**bought**	/bɔ:t/	**bought**	/bɔ:t/
catch	/kætʃ/	**caught**	/kɔ:t/	**caught**	/kɔ:t/
choose	/tʃu:z/	**chose**	/tʃouz/	**chosen**	/ˈtʃouzən/
come	/kʌm/	**came**	/keɪm/	**come**	/kʌ n/
cost	/kɒst/	**cost**	/kɒst/	**cost**	/kɒst/
cut	/kʌt/	**cut**	/kʌt/	**cut**	/kʌt/
dig	/dɪg/	**dug**	/dʌg/	**dug**	/dʌg/
do	/du:/	**did**	/dɪd/	**done**	/dʌn/
draw	/drɔ:/	**drew**	/dru:/	**drawn**	/drɔ:n/
dream	/dri:m/	**dreamt**	/dremt/	**dreamt**	/dremt/
dream	/dri:m/	**dreamed**	/dri:md/	**dreamed**	/dri:md/
drink	/drɪŋk/	**drank**	/dræŋk/	**drunk**	/drʌŋk/
drive	/draɪv/	**drove**	/drouv/	**driven**	/ˈdrɪvən/
eat	/i:t/	**ate**	/eɪt, et/	**eaten**	/ˈi:tn/
fall	/fɔ:l/	**fell**	/fel/	**fallen**	/ˈfɔ:lən/
feed	/fi:d/	**fed**	/fed/	**fed**	/fed/
feel	/fi:l/	**felt**	/felt/	**felt**	/felt/
fight	/faɪt/	**fought**	/fɔ:t/	**fought**	/fɔ:t/
find	/faɪnd/	**found**	/faʊnd/	**found**	/faʊnd/
fly	/flaɪ/	**flew**	/flu:/	**flown**	/floun/
forget	/fər ˈget/	**forgot**	/fər ˈgɒt/	**forgotten**	/fər ˈgɒtn/
forgive	/fər ˈgɪv/	**forgave**	/fər ˈgeɪv/	**forgiven**	/fər ˈgɪvən/
freeze	/fri:z/	**froze**	/frouz/	**frozen**	/ˈfrouzən/
get	/get/	**got**	/gɒt/	**got**	/gɒt/
get	/get/	**got**	/gɒt/	**gotten**	/ˈgɒtn/
give	/gɪv/	**gave**	/geɪv/	**given**	/ˈgɪvən/

go	/gou/	went	/went/	gone	/gɒn/
grow	/grou/	grew	/gru:/	grown	/groun/
hang	/hæŋ/	hung	/hʌŋ/	hung	/hʌŋ/
have	/hæv/	had	/hæd/	had	/hæd/
hear	/hɪər/	heard	/hɜ:rd/	heard	/hɜ:rd/
hide	/haɪd/	hid	/hɪd/	hidden	/'hɪdn/
hit	/hɪt/	hit	/hɪt/	hit	/hɪt/
hold	/hould/	held	/held/	held	/held/
hurt	/hɜ:rt/	hurt	/hɜ:rt/	hurt	/hɜ:rt/
keep	/ki:p/	kept	/kept/	kept	/kept/
know	/nou/	knew	/nu:/	known	/noun/
lay	/leɪ/	laid	/leɪd/	laid	/leɪd/
lead	/li:d/	led	/led/	led	/led/
learn	/lɜ:rn/	learnt	/lɜ:rnt/	learnt	/lɜ:rnt/
learn	/lɜ:rn/	learned	/lɜ:rnd/	learned	/lɜ:rnd/
leave	/li:v/	left	/left/	left	/left/
lend	/lend/	lent	/lent/	lent	/lent/
let	/let/	let	/let/	let	/let/
lie	/laɪ/	lay	/leɪ/	lain	/leɪn/
lose	/lu:z/	lost	/lɒst/	lost	/lɒst/
make	/meɪk/	made	/meɪd/	made	/meɪd/
mean	/mi:n/	meant	/ment/	meant	/ment/
meet	/mi:t/	met	/met/	met	/met/
pay	/peɪ/	paid	/peɪd/	paid	/peɪd/
put	/pʊt/	put	/pʊt/	put	/pʊt/
read	/ri:d/	read	/red/	read	/red/
ride	/raɪd/	rode	/roud/	ridden	/'rɪdn/
ring	/rɪŋ/	rang	/ræŋ/	rung	/rʌŋ/
rise	/raɪz/	rose	/rouz/	risen	/'rɪzən/
run	/rʌn/	ran	/ræn/	run	/rʌn/
say	/seɪ/	said	/sed/	said	/sed/
see	/si:/	saw	/sɔ:/	seen	/si:n/
sell	/sel/	sold	/sould/	sold	/sould/
send	/send/	sent	/sent/	sent	/sent/
set	/set/	set	/set/	set	/set/
shake	/ʃeɪk/	shook	/ʃʊk/	shaken	/'ʃeɪkən/
shine	/ʃaɪn/	shone	/ʃoun, ʃɒn/	shone	/ʃoun, ʃɒn/

shoot	/ʃu:t/	shot	/ʃɒt/	shot	/ʃɒt/
show	/ʃou/	showed	/ʃoud/	shown	/ʃoun/
shut	/ʃʌt/	shut	/ʃʌt/	shut	/ʃʌt/
sing	/sɪŋ/	sang	/sæŋ/	sung	/sʌŋ/
sink	/sɪŋk/	sank	/sæŋk/	sunk	/sʌŋk/
sit	/sɪt/	sat	/sæt/	sat	/sæt/
sleep	/sli:p/	slept	/slept/	slept	/slept/
smell	/smel/	smelt	/smelt/	smelt	/smelt/
smell	/smel/	smelled	/smeld/	smelled	/smeld/
speak	/spi:k/	spoke	/spouk/	spoken	/'spoukən/
spell	/spel/	spelt	/spelt/	spelt	/spelt/
spell	/spel/	spelled	/speld/	spelled	/speld/
spend	/spend/	spent	/spent/	spent	/spent/
spill	/spɪl/	spilt	/spɪlt/	spilt	/spɪlt/
spill	/spɪl/	spilled	/spɪld/	spilled	/spɪld/
spit	/spɪt/	spat	/spæt/	spat	/spæt/
spit	/spɪt/	spit	/spɪt/	spit	/spɪt/
split	/splɪt/	split	/splɪt/	split	/splɪt/
spoil	/spoɪl/	spoilt	/spoɪlt/	spoilt	/spoɪlt/
spoil	/spoɪl/	spoiled	/spoɪld/	spoiled	/spoɪld/
stand	/stænd/	stood	/stʊd/	stood	/stʊd/
steal	/sti:l/	stole	/stoul/	stolen	/'stoulən/
strike	/straɪk/	struck	/strʌk/	struck	/strʌk/
swim	/swɪm/	swam	/swæm/	swum	/swʌm/
take	/teɪk/	took	/tʊk/	taken	/'teɪkən/
teach	/ti:tʃ/	taught	/tɔ:t/	taught	/tɔ:t/
tear	/teər/	tore	/tɔr/	torn	/tɔrn/
tell	/tel/	told	/tould/	told	/tould/
think	/θɪŋk/	thought	/θɔ:t/	thought	/θɔ:t/
throw	/θrou/	threw	/θru:/	thrown	/θroun/
understa nd	/ʌndər 'stænd/	underst ood	/ʌndər 'stʊd/	underst ood	/ʌndər 'stʊd/
wake	/weɪk/	woke	/wouk/	woken	/'woukən/
wear	/weər/	wore	/wɔr/	worn	/wɔrn/
win	/wɪn/	won	/wʌn/	won	/wʌn/
write	/raɪt/	wrote	/rout/	written	/'rɪtn/

HOW I LEARNED ENGLISH

My full name is Michal Ryszard Wojcik. I live in Poland and Polish is my native language. I am a mathematician and an enthusiast of English. I learned English very well and now I want to share my experience with other people.

I had my first contact with English when I was six. My dad inspired me to listen to The Beatles. I listened to them every day for the next seven years. In the beginning I could understand nothing of what they were singing. But soon I started to understand individual words, especially the ones which appeared in the titles.

Later I got a book with the words of all the songs. I read the book many times. I learned many songs by heart. I sang the songs to myself. Still, I understood very little of the meaning. It became my dream to learn English so well that I could understand The Beatles. So The Beatles were my first motivation. That is how I started my way toward English.

Today, I can understand The Beatles very clearly. Each time I hear a Beatles song, I am delighted and proud because I have made my childhood dream come true. I listen to many rock bands, all in English, and I listen every day, sometimes for over seven hours a day. I am constantly aware of my success with English because I can understand the lyrics of the songs I listen to. And that gives me pleasure and satisfaction for many hours every day.

When I was 13 years old, I started reading science fiction books. I read in Polish. The books were all American. I could not read the original versions because I did not know English so well. As I read in Polish, I was more and more eager to read the books in English. Somehow I felt that in English the books will be even more interesting and reading will be more exciting. I finally decided that I wanted to read books in English. This decision guided me for many years.

I learned every new English word that I met. With each new word I felt closer to my goal. With each word I felt that my reading ability was increasing. Each word added to my sense of power.

At some point I read my first whole book in English and

I understood it. That moment was a breakthrough in my life. I knew that I had broken a barrier, gotten into a new world. I found that reading is much more exciting in English. When I read in English, I have not only the pleasure of reading, but also the pleasure of using English and the pleasure of learning English. For the last four years I have read books only in English, with very few exceptions.

I have read many pop-science books in English. Some of them are still not available in Polish. My knowledge of English allowed me to get in touch with the current state of evolutionary theory and cognitive science of the mind. Without English, I would not have read the books because there are no Polish translations of them. When I learned English well enough to read pop-science books, I discovered that English is a very important tool for learning science.

Currently I study mathematics. Most of the books I use are in English. In fact, most of the books in my math institute's library are in English. I discovered that my knowledge of English is very important for my learning mathematics. Without English I would be limited to the few books which are in Polish, and there are really few of them. Over a year ago I decided to use English only in mathematical notes. I read and write math materials in English, like most professional mathematicians. I have become part of the international mathematical community. I can read math materials on the Internet and I can publish my own materials, with no language barriers. I feel free!

English has given me so much satisfaction and pleasure and also I find it so useful in my scientific pursuit, that I decided to share my methods and my experience with other people. On Antimoon, I try to help people to learn English with pleasure. I know that it is possible to derive satisfaction from the process of learning English and I want to share it with others.

THE MOST USEFUL VOCABULARY IS RELATIVELY EASY TO LEARN

The defining vocabulary for a dictionary is a small set of

words which are used to define all other words in that dictionary - very useful for English-English dictionaries designed for those learners of English who already know the basics of English and who are thus ready to continue learning English without translating into their native language.

Let us take a look at some properties of such a defining vocabulary:

- *Limited*: It's relatively easy to learn all the defining words in a short time
- *Very expressive*: Practically enough to express everything in the English language
- The most useful selection of words of all the words in English.

You can have a look at the Longman Defining Vocabulary - a list of about 2000 words that can be used to talk about anything and to define all other words.

How to learn the most useful vocabulary in English - easily and quickly.

First get an English-English dictionary for English learners. Then start reading any text in English and look up the words which you don't know. As you read the definitions for those words you will be constantly seeing the defining vocabulary used in practice. Apart from learning the words which you have looked up you will be first of all learning the defining vocabulary. By using an English-English dictionary regularly for learning any words however difficult you will be forced to absorb the most useful English words. It's as simple as that.

This is especially effective when you copy the definitions and example sentences from the dictionary by hand. If you do so you will be actually writing a lot of correct and useful sentences in English. You will be developing good habits and making sure that what you learn is really absorbed into your head. Those definitions will contain ready-made patterns that you can follow to express yourself. You will learn to express yourself correctly and clearly.

In this learning method the actual effort comes down to looking up words in an English-English dictionary and writing them down with their definitions and example sentences. This is really something that you can do. And the time spent using this method is really spent on learning English because you will be constantly reading and writing correct and useful English sentences.

THE VOCABULARY

Here is the list of defining words in the *Longman Dictionary of Contemporary English* (LDOCE). All definitions in the dictionary are written using the words in the defining vocabulary (or words defined elsewhere in the dictionary). The defining vocabulary was chosen using common English frequency lists.

a	
ability	about
above	abroad
absence	absent
accept	acceptable
accident	accordance
according	according to
account	ache
acid	across
act	action
active	activity
actor	actress
actual	add
addition	address
adjective	admiration
admire	admit
admittance	adult
advance	advantage
adventure	adverb
advertise	advertisement
advice	advise
affair	afford
afraid	after
afternoon	afterwards

again
age
agree
ahead
air
airforce
alcohol
alive
allow
alone
aloud
already
although
always
amount
amusement
an
and
angle
animal
annoy
another
ant
anxious
anyhow
anything
apart
appear
apple
approval
arch
argue
arm
arms
around
arrangement
arrive
against
ago
agreement
aim
aircraft
airport
alike
all
almost
along
alphabet
also
altogether
among
amuse
amusing
ancient
anger
angry
ankle
annoyance
answer
anxiety
any
anyone
anywhere
apparatus
appearance
appoint
approve
area
argument
armor
army
arrange
arrival
art

article
artificial
as
ash
ashamed
aside
ask
asleep
association
at
atom
attack
attempt
attend
attendance
attention
attract
attractive
aunt
autumn
average
avoid
awake
away
awkward

b

baby
back
background
backward
backwards
bacteria
bad
bag
bake
balance
ball
banana
band
bank
bar
bare
barrel
base
basket
bath
bathe
battle
be
beak
beam
bean
bear
beard
beat
beautiful
beauty
because
become
bed
bee
beer
before
beg
begin
beginning
behave
behaviour
behind
belief
believe
bell

belong
belt
beneath
beside
best
between
bicycle
bill
bird
birthday
bite
black
blame
bless
block
blow
board
body
bomb
book
border
borrow
bottle
bowels
box
brain
brass
bread
break
breast
breathe
brick
bright
broad
brother
brush
build

below
bend
berry
besides
better
beyond
big
bind
birth
bit
bitter
blade
bleed
blind
blood
blue
boat
boil
bone
boot
born
both
bottom
bowl
boy
branch
brave
breadth
breakfast
breath
breed
bridge
bring
broadcast
brown
bucket
building

bullet	bunch
burial	burn
burst	bury
bus	bush
business	busy
but	butter
button	buy
by	

C

cage	cake
calculate	calculator
call	calm
camera	camp
can	candle
cap	capital
captain	car
card	cardboard
care	careful
careless	carriage
carry	cart
case	castle
cat	catch
cattle	cause
cell	cement
cent	centre
centimetre	central
century	ceremony
certain	chain
chair	chairperson
chalk	chance
change	character
charge	charm
chase	cheap
cheat	check [cheque]
cheek	cheer
cheerful	cheese

chemical
chest
chief
childhood
chimney
chocolate
choose
cigarette
circle
citizen
civilization
class
clean
clerk
cliff
clock
close
clothes
cloud
coal
coat
coin
collar
college
comb
combine
comfort
command
common
company
comparison
competition
complain
complete
computer
concerning
condition

chemistry
chicken
child
children
chin
choice
church
cinema
circular
city
claim
clay
clear
clever
climb
clockwork
cloth
clothing
club
coast
coffee
cold
collect
colour
combination
come
comfortable
committee
companion
compare
compete
competitor
complaint
compound
concern
concert
confidence

confident	confuse
connect	conscience
conscious	consider
consist	consonant
contain	contents
continue	continuous
contract	control
convenient	conversation
cook	cool
copper	copy
cord	corn
corner	correct
cost	cotton
cough	could
council	count
country	courage
course	court
cover	cow
coward	cowardly
crack	crash
cream	creature
creep	cricket
crime	criminal
crop	cross
crowd	cruel
cruelty	crush
cry	cultivate
cup	cupboard
cure	curl
current	curse
curtain	curve
custom	customer
cut	cycle

d

daily	damage
dance	danger
dangerous	dare
daring	dark

date
daughter
day
dead
deal
dear
death
debt
decay
deceit
deceive
decide
decimal
decision
declaration
declare
decorate
decoration
decrease
deep
deer
defeat
defend
defence
degree
delay
delicate
delight
deliver
demand
department
depend
dependent
depth
descend
describe
description
descriptive
desert
deserve
desirable
desire
desk
destroy
destruction
detail
determination
determined
develop
devil
diamond
dictionary
die
difference
different
difficult
difficulty
dig
dinner
dip
direct
direction
dirt
dirty
disappoint
discourage
discouragement
discover
discovery
dish
dismiss
distance
distant
ditch

divide	division
do	doctor
dog	dollar
door	doorway
dot	double
doubt	down
drag	draw
drawer	dream
dress	drink
drive	drop
drown	drug
drum	drunk
dry	duck
dull	during
dust	duty

e

each	eager
ear	early
earn	earth
east	eastern
easy	eat
edge	educate
education	effect
effective	effort
egg	eight
eighth	either
elastic	elbow
elect	election
electric	electricity
elephant	else
employ	employer
employment	empty
enclose	enclosure
encourage	encouragement
end	enemy
engine	engineer
enjoy	enjoyment

enough
enter
entertain
entertainment
entrance
envelope
equal
equality
escape
especially
establish
establishment
even
evening
event
ever
every
everyone
everything
everywhere
evil
exact
examination
examine
example
excellent
except
exchange
excite
excited
exciting
excuse
exercise
exist
existence
expect
expensive
experience
explain
explanation
explode
explosion
explosive
express
expression
extreme
eye
eyelid

---

f

---

face
fact
factory
fail
failure
faint
fair
fairy
faith
faithful
fall
false
fame
familiar
family
famous
fancy
far
farm
farmer
farmyard
fashion

fashionable	fast
fasten	fat
fate	father
fault	favour
favourable	favourite
fear	feather
feed	feel
feeling	feelings
fellow	female
fence	fever
few	field
fierce	fifth
fight	figure
fill	film
find	fine
finger	finish
fire	fireplace
firm	first
fish	fisherman
fit	five
fix	flag
flame	flash
flat	flesh
flight	float
flood	floor
flour	flow
flower	fly
fold	follow
fond	food
fool	foolish
foot	football
footpath	footstep
for	forbid
force	forehead
foreign	foreigner
forest	forget
forgive	fork

form
former
fort
fortune
forwards
fourth
frame
freedom
frequent
friend
frighten
from
fruit
full
funeral
fur
furniture
future

formal
formerly
fortunate
forward
four
fox
free
freeze
fresh
friendly
frightening
front
fulfill
fun
funny
furnish
further

g

gain
garage
garment
gasoline [petrol]
gather
generous
gentleman
gift
give
glass
glue
goat
gold
good
goods
government
graceful
grain

game
garden
gas
gate
general
gentle
get
girl
glad
glory
go
god
golden
good-bye
govern
grace
gradual
gram

grammar	grand
grandfather	grandmother
grass	grateful
grave	gray
great	green
greet	greeting
grief	grieve
ground	group
grow	growth
guard	guess
guest	guidance
guide	guilt
gun	

h

habit	habitual
hair	hairy
half	hall
hammer	hand
handkerchief	handle
hang	happen
happy	hard
harden	hardly
hardship	harm
harmful	harmless
hasty	hat
hate	hatred
have	he
head	health
healthy	hear
heart	heat
heaven	heavy
heel	height
help	helpful
hen	her
here	hers
herself	hide
high	hill

him
himself
hire
his
historical
history
hit
hold
holiday
hollow
holy
home
honest
honesty
honour
honourable
hook
hope
hopeful
hopeless
horizon
horn
horse
hospital
host
hot
hotel
hour
hourly
house
how
human
humour
humourous
hundred
hundredth
hunger
hungry
hunt
hurry
hurt
husband
hut

i

ice
icy
idea
if
ill
image
imaginary
imagination
imagine
importance
important
improve
improvement
in
include
including
income
increase
indoor
indoors
industrial
industry
infect
infection
infectious
influence
influential
inform

information
inner
inquiry
inside
instruct
instrument
insure
intention
interesting
interrupt
into
introduction
invention
invite
iron
it
itself
ink
inquire
insect
instead
instruction
insurance
intend
interest
international
interruption
introduce
invent
invitation
inwards
island
its

j

jaw
jealousy
jewel
job
joint
journey
judge
juice
just
jealous
jelly
jewelry
join
joke
joy
judgment
jump
justice

k

keen
key
kill
kilogram
kind
kingdom
kitchen
kneel
keep
kick
kilo
kilometre
king
kiss
knee
knife

knock	knot
know	knowledge

l

labour	lack
ladder	lady
lake	lamb
lamp	land
language	large
last	late
lately	laugh
laughter	law
lawyer	lay
lazy	lead
lead	leaf
lean	learn
least	leather
leave	left
leg	legal
lend	length
less	lesson
let	letter
level	library
lid	lie
life	lift
light	lightning
like	likely
limb	limit
line	lion
lip	liquid
list	listen
liter	literature
little	live
load	loaf
local	lock
lodging	lodgings
log	lonely

long	look
loose	lord
lose	loss
lot	loud
love	low
lower	loyal
loyalty	luck
lump	lung

m

machine	machinery
mad	magazine
magic	magician
mail	main
make	male
man	manage
manager	manner
many	map
march	mark
market	marriage
marry	mass
master	mat
match	material
matter	may
me	meal
mean	meaning
means	measure
meat	medical
medicine	meet
meeting	melt
member	memory
mend	mention
merry	message
messenger	metal
metre	metric
microscope	middle
might	mile
military	milk

million	millionth
mind	mine
mineral	minister
minute	mirror
miss	mist
mistake	mix
mixture	model
modern	moment
money	monkey
month	monthly
moon	moral
morals	more
morning	most
mother	motor
mountain	mouse
mouth	move
much	mud
multiply	murder
muscle	music
musician	must
my	myself
mysterious	mystery

n

nail	name
narrow	nasty
nation	national
nature	naval
navy	near
nearly	neat
necessary	neck
need	needle
neighbour	neighbourhood
neither	nerve
nervous	nest
net	network
never	new

news	newspaper
next	nice
night	nine
ninth	no
no one	noble
nobleman	noise
none	nonsense
nor	north
northern	nose
not	nothing
notice	noun
now	nowhere
number	nurse
nut	nylon

O

o'clock	obedience
obedient	obey
object	obtain
occasion	ocean
odd	of
off	offend
offense	offensive
offer	office
officer	official
often	oil
old	old-fashioned
on	once
one	oneself
onion	only
open	operate
operation	opinion
opponent	oppose
opposite	opposition
or	orange
order	ordinary
organ	organization

origin
other
otherwise
ought
our
ours
ourselves
out
outdoor
outdoors
outer
outside
over
owe
owing to
own
oxygen

P

---

pack
packet
page
pain
painful
paint
painting
pair
palace
pale
pan
paper
parallel
parcel
parent
park
parliament
part
participle
particular
partner
party
pass
passage
passenger
past
pastry
path
patience
patient
pattern
pause
pay
payment
peace
peaceful
pen
pence
pencil
people
pepper
per
perfect
perform
perhaps
period
permission
permit
person
personal
persuade
pet

photograph
phrase
piano
picture
pig
pilot
pink
pity
plain
plane
plastic
play
please
pleasure
plural
poem
poetry
pointed
poisonous
police
polite
politician
pool
popular
population
position
possession
possible
post
potato
pour
power
practical
praise
prayer
preparation
presence
preserve
photography
physical
pick
piece
pile
pin
pipe
place
plan
plant
plate
pleasant
pleased
plenty
pocket
poet
point
poison
pole
polish
political
politics
poor
popularity
port
possess
possibility
possibly
pot
pound
powder
powerful
practice
pray
precious
prepare
present
president

press
pressure
pretend
pretty
prevent
price
prickly
pride
priest
prince
principle
print
prison
prisoner
private
prize
probability
probable
problem
process
procession
produce
product
production
profession
profit
promise
pronounce
pronunciation
proof
proper
property
protect
protection
protective
proud
prove
provide
provision
provisions
public
pull
pump
punish
punishment
pupil
pure
purple
purpose
push
put

---

q

---

quality
quantity
quarrel
quarter
queen
question
quick
quiet
quite

---

r

---

rabbit
race
radio
railway
rain
raise

range
rapid
rat
rather
reach
ready
really
reasonable
recent
recognition
record
reduce
refusal
regard
related
relative
religious
remark
remind
rent
repeat
report
representative
request
respectful
rest
result
reward
rich
ride
ring
rise
river
rob
rod
roof

rank
rare
rate
raw
read
real
reason
receive
recently
recognize
red
reduction
refuse
regular
relation
religion
remain
remember
remove
repair
reply
represent
republic
respect
responsible
restaurant
return
rice
rid
right
ripe
risk
road
rock
roll
room

root	rope
rose	rough
round	row
royal	rub
rubber	rude
ruin	rule
ruler	run
rush	

S

sad	safe
safety	sail
sale	salt
same	sand
satisfaction	satisfactory
satisfy	save
say	scale
scatter	scene
scenery	school
science	scientific
scientist	scissors
screw	sea
search	season
seat	second
secrecy	secret
secretary	see
seed	seem
seize	sell
send	sensation
sense	senseless
sensible	sensitive
sentence	separate
serious	servant
serve	service
set	settle
seven	seventh
several	severe
sew	sex

sexual
shadow
shall
shape
sharp
sheep
shelf
shelter
shine
shirt
shoe
shop
shore
shot
shoulder
show
sick
sideways
sign
signature
silent
silly
similar
simple
sincere
single
sink
sit
six
size
skillful
skirt
slave
slide
slip
slope
small
smile

shade
shake
shame
share
she
sheet
shell
shield
ship
shock
shoot
shopkeeper
short
should
shout
shut
side
sight
signal
silence
silk
silver
similarity
since
sing
singular
sister
situation
sixth
skill
skin
sky
sleep
slight
slippery
slow
smell
smoke

smooth
snow
soap
society
soft
soldier
solid
somehow
something
somewhere
song
sore
sorry
soul
soup
south
space
spade
spear
specialist
speed
spend
spirit
splendid
spoil
sport
spread
square
stair
stand
star
state
stay
steal
steel
stem
stick
stiff

snake
so
social
sock
soil
solemn
some
someone
sometimes
son
soon
sorrow
sort
sound
sour
southern
spacecraft
speak
special
speech
spell
spin
spite
split
spoon
spot
spring
stage
stamp
standard
start
station
steady
steam
steep
step
sticky
still

sting	stitch
stomach	stone
stop	store
storm	story
straight	strange
stranger	stream
street	strength
stretch	strike
string	stroke
strong	structure
struggle	student
study	stupid
style	subject
substance	subtract
succeed	success
successful	such
suck	sudden
suffer	sugar
suggest	suit
suitable	sum
summer	sun
supper	supply
support	suppose
sure	surface
surprise	surround
swallow	swear
sweep	sweet
swell	swim
swing	sword
sympathetic	sympathy
system	

t

table	tail
take	talk
tall	taste
tax	taxi
tea	teach
team	tear

tear
television
temper
temple
tendency
tennis
tent
terror
than
that
theater
theirs
themselves
there
these
thick
thin
think
thirst
this
those
thought
thousandth
threat
three
through
thumb
thus
tidy
tiger
time
tin
tire
to
today
together

telephone
tell
temperature
tend
tender
tense
terrible
test
thank
the
their
them
then
therefore
they
thief
thing
third
thirsty
thorough
though
thousand
thread
threaten
throat
throw
thunder
ticket
tie
tight
timetable
tire [tyre]
title
tobacco
toe
tomorrow

tongue	tonight
too	tool
tooth	top
total	touch
tour	tourist
towards	tower
town	toy
track	trade
traffic	train
translate	transparent
trap	travel
treat	treatment
tree	tremble
tribe	trick
trip	tropical
trouble	trousers
true	trunk
trust	truth
try	tube
tune	turn
twice	twist
type	typical

u

ugly	uncle
under	understand
undo	uniform
union	unit
unite	universal
universe	university
until	up
upper	upright
upset	upside down
upstairs	urge
urgent	us
use	useful
useless	usual

valley	valuable
value	variety
various	vary
vegetable	vehicle
verb	very
victory	view
village	violence
violent	visit
voice	vote
vowel	voyage

w

wages	waist
wait	waiter
wake	walk
wall	wander
want	war
warm	warmth
warn	wash
waste	watch
water	wave
way	we
weak	wealth
weapon	wear
weather	weave
wedding	week
weekly	weigh
weight	welcome
well	west
western	wet
what	whatever
wheat	wheel
when	whenever
where	whether
which	whichever
while	whip
whisper	whistle

white	who
whoever	whole
why	wicked
wide	widespread
width	wife
wild	will
willing	win
wind	wind
window	wine
wing	winter
wire	wisdom
wise	wish
with	within
without	witness
woman	wonder
wood	wooden
wool	woolen
word	work
world	worm
worry	worse
worship	worst
worth	worthy
worthy of	would
wound	wrap
wreck	wrist
write	wrong
wrongdoing	

y

yard	year
yearly	yellow
yes	yesterday
yet	you
young	your
yours	yourself
youth	zero

SURROUND YOURSELF WITH ENGLISH

The human brain is good at learning languages but it has to be put into real-life situations in order to use its ability. In other words, you have to activate your language learning ability by giving your brain a clear and persistent signai that the English language is an important component of your environment — something that you have to learn in order to survive, or at least in order to be successful.

When you surround yourself with English in your everyday life, you will make it appear to your brain that the English language is something real in your life and that it is vitally important to learn this language. You should then notice that you are unconsciously using learning faculties that have been awakened. Your English learning process should enter a new stage: rapid absorption of every piece of information about the ability to understand English messages, and this should not be especially tiring for you because you will be running on the natural ability to learn languages in real situations.

The failure of many learners to learn a foreign language may often be attributed to their lack of motivation at the deep physiological and psychological level. When learning English is interpreted by your mind as a burdensome duty imposed on you by schools, parents, or ill-understood socio-economic arguments, then you will not find ready resources in your mind to be wasted on something so dubious. But if, on the other hand, your mind sees that learning English is a part of the reality that you live in and that it is a component having influence on your success, then surely you will find that after all you are well-equiped by nature to be a language learner.

Here are a number of ideas for surrounding yourself with the English language:

- use English language version software
- watch English movies in the original language version
- get daily news in English into your mailbox
- if you read the Bible regularly, get an English version

ENGLISH LANGUAGE

If you buy an English learning software it will help you improve your English only if you use it regularly. It is not certain that you will find the motivation to actually spend your time learning English with this software. However, if you buy an English language version of your operating system you will certainly find the time and motivation to use this "English-learning" software. So perhaps it is far better to spend money on English language versions of the computer programmes that you use every day than to buy specialized English learning programmes.

ENGLISH IN ORIGINAL LANGUAGE

If you are a person who regularly watches movies you can use this fact to realise that you have a lot of time for learning English. If you are watching an English movie in the original you are effectively spending time on learning English and having fun at the same time. Moreover, if you manage to understand what's going on in the movie you can feel great satisfaction and you gain a proof for yourself that you can use your English ability in practice.

DAILY ENGLISH

Most people follow the daily news in one way or another. If you sign up for a free newsletter with daily news in English you will be both following the news and learning English at the same time. Again, this is a way of increasing your time spent on learning English without needing extra time.

READING ENGLISH

Those people who regularly spend their time reading the Bible have a lot of time for learning English because they can devote some of this time to reading an English language version of the Bible. Since the Bible is a translation from ancient languages, reading it in some other language than your native language can help you get a better perspective on its content. If you learn English you should also read the Bible in English.

PHONETICS IN LINGUISTIC

Phonetics is the subfield within linguistics that is concerned with the sounds of speech. Broadly speaking, there are three different, but related questions researchers have tried to answer about human speech. First, how do people use their mouths, lungs and other parts of their bodies to make the sounds of speech? How are the motions or positions of the tongue and other parts of the mouth different when we pronounce, say, the *t* in *toe* and the *d* in *doe*? Second, researchers have tried to determine what it is that is distinctive about the sounds themselves. Suppose we were to make a graphic image of the sounds of *toe* and *doe*; how would the sounds of these words differ? Third, researchers have also tried to understand the psychological processes by which people perceive speech. They are striving to understand how the human brain uses the various features and characteristics of a bit of sound to figure out that the speaker meant to be making a *p* sound.

We will be concerned here only with the first question: how do people make the sounds of language. This area is called ARTICULATORY PHONETICS.

This tutorial will review basic facts about how speech sounds are differentiated and how we represent them in print:

1 *The constriction dimension*: Vowels vs Consonants.The most basic dimension that organizes speech sounds has to do with the presence of some sort of constriction in the mouth. Some sounds are made with the mouth fully open in a way that allows air to flow freely out. The vowel sounds we produce in the middle of words like *keep, cop* and *coop* are like this. Notice that if you leave off the consonants at the beginnings and ends of these words you can sing or sustain the vowel sounds by themselves for as long as you have enough breath to continue. Other sounds, however, cannot be sustained at all. The *k* sound at the beginning of these three words is not sustainable (notice it is the same sound despite its being represented in writing by *k* in one word and

by *c* in the other two). You also cannot sustain *p* and *t* sounds. This fact is illustrated in Figure, which shows a recording of the word *apple*. Notice that there is a silent interval in the middle that coincides with articulation of the (single) *p* sound in the middle of this word.

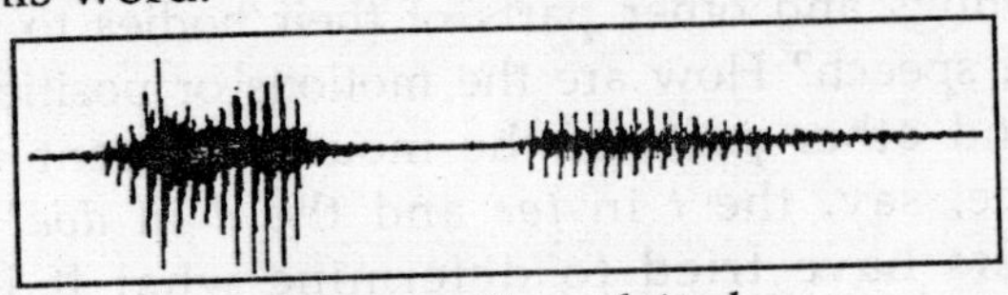

Fig. Recording of *Apple*.

Thus, the most basic way to organize speech sounds is to separate them into two groups according to whether or not they involve significant constriction of the vocal tract. Vowels are those sounds that have little or no constriction, while consonants are all those that involve some degree of constriction, from total to moderate.

If you consider some of the other consonant sounds, you will quickly see that constriction is a matter of degree, not either/or. Producing the *s* in *aspire*involves much more constriction of the vocal tract than is found in vowels, but less than occurs in sounds like *p, t,* and *k*. Even though the tongue mostly blocks the flow of air while producing an *s* sound, still the sound can be sustained, which shows that the blockage is not total. Sounds such as the *r* in *raw* involve still less constriction, even though this degree of constriction is still greater than that for vowels.

2 *Distinguishing one consonant (or vowel) from another*: It is not enough, however, just to be able to distinguish consonants from vowels; we must also be able to capture the differences in articulation from one consonant to another and differences from vowel to vowel. Within the two categories weíve established so far, consonants and vowels, the differences among sounds are described in quite different terms. Among consonants we will rely on three major dimensions

or paràmetres: 1) where the constriction is made in the mouth (e.g., at the lips, against the roof of the mouth, etc.), 2) how much the flow of air is constricted (e.g., a complete blockage of the flow of air, as in *p*, or only a partial blockage, as in *s*), and 3) whether or not the sound involves ìvoicingî.

Since there is little or no constriction for vowels, and vowels are (almost) always voiced, the dimensions that are useful for consonants will be of lıttle help. We will see below that most differences among vowels can be specified in terms of tongue position and degree of lip rounding.

However, before we review a system for describing differences among consonants and vowels, we need to attend to two other matters.

3. *The International Phonetic Alphabet (IPA)*: Unfortunately, the standard spellings of English words are often rather indirect and inconsistent indicators of the typical sounds of those words. For example, the *ph* in *phonetic* denotes the same sound as the *f* in *foam* and the *gh* in *enough*. The *ti* in *national* is associated with the same sound as the *sh* in *show*. The letter *e* may indicate no sound at all, as in *indicate*, and the letter *a* in this same word may represent the same sound as the *ei* in *freight* (which happens to rhyme with *bait*) or the very different vowel in *cat*. In fact, the playwright George Bernard Shaw once noticed that there is a very common English word in which *o* denotes the same vowel sound as appears in *bit*, which led him to suggest that a possible spelling of *fish* in English might be *ghoti*.

These issues obviously arise in English, but there are similar problems that bear on writing systems generally. The most important difficulty is simply that the different symbols are often used to represent the same sound across different languages and there are also many cases where the same symbol represents two or more different sounds across different languages. There are also many languages that have no official writing system at all.

In order for scholars and researchers to study and compare sounds in the worldís languages it is essential that there be a single standardized way of representing sounds. The most widely used system is called the International Phonetic Alphabet. We will use this system, the IPA, in this course, though we will make some minor amendments that are commonly used to make the system more convenient for representing English sounds.

By far the most important requirement for the IPA is that there is a one-for-one relationship between sounds and symbols. Thus, if we were to decide that the symbol for the vowel sound in the name Kate were to be, then we would use this same symbol wherever a word used that sound. Following this strategy, we might write the words Kate, freight, and bait as Kt, frt and bt. (We drop the e from Kate because there is no such thing as a ìsilentî symbol when we are insisting on a one-for-one relation between sounds and symbols. No sound, no symbol.)

For the purposes of a student trying to learn the IPA, it might have been better if the creators of the system had gone on to make up a completely original set of symbols for all the sounds used in the worldís languages. Then when you learned a symbol you could associate that symbol with the one and only sound it was meant to represent. The dark side of this plan, however, would be that anyone learning the IPA would have to learn to recognize and write dozens of new symbols.

Instead, the IPA uses a somewhat eclectic mixture of pre-existing symbols, including many common ìlettersî from the Roman and Greek alphabets, special variations on these, plus various diacritical and accent marks that are used in various languages or that were made up specially. This invites confusion.

Some of the IPA symbols have essentially the same uses in the IPA that they do in ordinary English orthography (ORTHOGRAPHY = system of writing), but some familiar symbols from the English alphabet are used very differently in the IPA. This is especially true for symbols used to represent vowels. While the IPA uses the symbol i, it stands for the vowel sound that appears in the word peek, not for any of the various sounds it is usually associated with in English.

4. *The vocal tract*: The human vocal tract, within which speech sounds are produced, is made up of a number of structures in the head and neck, extending from the lips and nostrils down to the larynx at the top of the trachea. A cross-section of the vocal tract (at the mid-line of the head) is shown in Figure 2. Though all of the structures in the human vocal tract also appear in the vocal tracts of chimpanzees, other apes, and monkeys, the overall layout and arrangement of these structures, especially at the back of the throat, is strikingly different in humans than it is other primates. These differences appear to be related to the uniquely human capacity for speech.

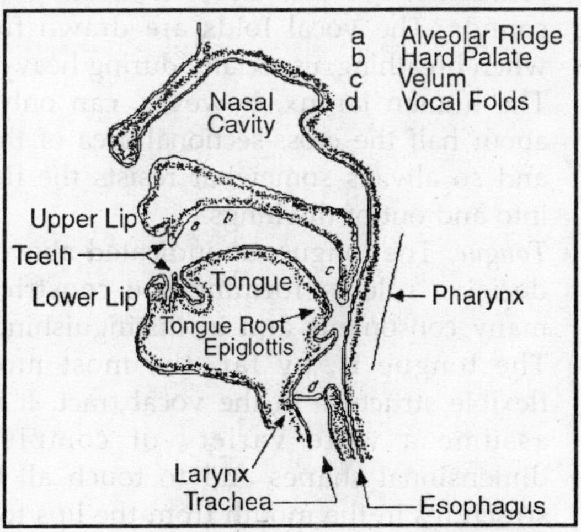

Fig. The human Vocal Tract

The structures that are used to form speech sounds (principally the tongue, teeth and lips) are called articulators. Some of the more important structures in the vocal tract are described below.

A. *Larynx*: The larynx (or voice box) is made mostly of cartilage and sits at the top of the trachea (the ìwind pipeî that connects the nose and mouth with the lungs). The larynx provides a rigid framework within which two bands of muscle, the vocal folds (sometimes called ìvocal chordsî) are stretched across the top of the airway to the lungs. When fully tensed and drawn together, the vocal folds can effectively block the flow of air out of the lungs (or provide a last ditch barrier against food or water that threatens to get into the lungs). In a somewhat more relaxed state, the vocal folds vibrate as air from the lungs is forced between them. This process is characteristic of the production of vowel sounds in all the worldís languages. The vocal folds can be positioned in a variety of ways that are used to produce different vowel qualities in various languages and sometimes are also used in forming consonant sounds. The vocal folds are drawn fully apart when breathing, especially during heavy exertion. The human larynx, however, can only open to about half the cross-sectional area of the trachea and so always somewhat resists the flow of air into and out of the lungs.

B. *Tongue*: The tongue, as indicated above, plays a decisive role in forming the constrictions for many consonants and in distinguishing vowels. The tongue is, by far, the most mobile and flexible structure in the vocal tract. It is able to assume a wide variety of complex three-dimensional shapes and to touch all the other structures in the mouth from the lips to the back wall of the pharynx. In forming many consonant sounds the tongue plays a key role in making the constriction in the vocal tract that characterizes the consonant. Differences in vowel quality are determined largely by shapes the tongue assumes without significantly constricting the vocal tract.

C. *Pharynx*: The pharynx is the open space at the back of the throat that runs from the back of the nasal cavity down to the larynx. A crucial distinguishing feature of this cavity in humans is that the front wall of the oral pharynx (below the velum) is formed by the back (or root) of the tongue. Mostly because of the flexibility of the tongue this means that the shape and size of the pharynx can vary greatly.

D. *Velum*: The velum is the back part of the soft palate, the fleshy part of the roof of your mouth that you can feel with your tongue or finger about half to two-thirds of the way back from your teeth. The velum is a moveable structure that, when pressed up and back, closes the airway from the mouth into the nasal cavity.

E. *Epiglottis*: The epiglottis is the small structure that projects backward into the airway just above the larynx and vocal folds. It helps to keep food and water out of the larynx. The human epiglottis cannot touch the velum, but in other mammals the epiglottis and larynx can make a tight closure with the opening into the nasal cavity. This makes it possible for them to drink and breath at the same time because water (or food) can pass around the larynx into the esophagus without risk of getting into the airway. Adult humans cannot match this feat, though infants can.

In forming constrictions of the vocal tract various parts of the tongue touch or approach several important landmarks along the roof of the mouth. The most important of these landmarks for describing English consonants are the teeth, the alveolar ridge (a slight prominence that you can feel with your tongue, just behind your upper teeth), the hard palate (the bony part of the roof of your mouth), and the velum. These are used to make or shape the constrictions of the vocal tract that characterize many consonants. Different parts of the tongue are used for different consonants, the constriction being produced with the tip of the tongue, the tongue blade (the area just behind the tip), various points along the upper surface of the tongue, or the tongue root.

5. *Distinguishing consonants*: Consonants can be differentiated in any language by reference to three parametres; place of articulation, manner of articulation, and voicing. Other parametres will also be relevant in some languages. We will apply this principle here to the description and differentiation of English consonants.

   A. *Place of Articulation*: The place of articulation for a consonant is the point in the vocal tract where the constriction for that consonant is formed. For each of the places of articulation listed below, consider what other consonants there might be (other than those used as examples below) that use the same place of articulation.

      i. *Bilabial*: A bilabial place of articulation is used for the first sound in words like *pin* and *bin*. Notice that in saying these words you begin by bringing your lips together.

      ii. *Labiodental*: Words like *fin* begin with a labiodental articulation in which the upper teeth contact or approach the lower lip.

      iii. *Dental*: Dental articulations are those like the first consonant in *thin* that involve the tongue touching or approaching the back of the teeth.

      iv. *Alveolar*: The front of the tongue touches or approaches the alveolar ridge in forming consonants such at those at the beginning of *tin* and *den*.

v. *Palatal*: Notice that the first sounds in *chump* and *jump* also involve the front of the tongue touching the roof of the mouth, but a bit further back than with the alveolar examples above. This more back point of contact is the (hard) palate. Though most palatal sounds use the front of the tongue, there is one in English that uses the back of the tongue; this is the first sound in *yet*.

vi. *Velar*: In the first sounds in *cow* and *gout*, the back of the tongue rises high enough to touch the velum, making a closure there.

vii. *Glottal*: Sometimes the vocal folds are drawn close enough together to produce a slight hissing or whispering sound. This is called a glottal place of articulation and occurs in the first sound of words like *how* and *who* in English.

Other places of articulation that are not relevant to any English consonants are used in some other languages.

B. *Manner of Articulation*: Obviously, there must be some further way to differentiate consonants because in English there are two or more consonants that are produced at each of the places of articulation described above (except for glottals). The next basic distinction has to do with how much the flow of air is constricted in the vocal tract. *Tack* and *sack* both begin with alveolar sounds, but they are not identical. What distinguishes them is the extent to which a constriction is made at the alveolar ridge in these two cases.

i. *Stop*: *Tack* begins with what is known as a stop consonant. Stop consonants are those where there is a momentary complete closure of the vocal tract. Notice that while making the first sound in *tack* you cannot hum or breathe. If you were to start to say *tack* very slowly and a little loudly (as though you were trying very hard to be clear in a noisy environment), and you then were to freeze at the moment when the tongue touches the alveolar ridge, your vocal tract would be completely closed, with no air able to enter or leave through your mouth or nose. You canít hum through stop consonants because humming requires moving air through the vocal folds, which you canít do when the vocal tract is completely blocked higher up. Such a complete blockage is characteristic of consonants that have the stop manner of articulation. The constriction that characterizes the consonant is made by briefly completely stopping the flow of air. In normal fast speech, however, this interruption of the flow of air can be extremely brief, sometimes only a few milliseconds (thousandths of a second).

ii. *Fricative*: Another way to interrupt the flow of air out of the mouth occurs in the first sound in *sack*. Here the tongue approaches the alveolar ridge, but allows a small channel to form between the tongue and the roof of the mouth. Air rushing through this small channel becomes very turbulent and produces the hissing sound that is characteristic of this sort of consonant. Notice that the first sound in *sack* can be sustained. You can take a deep breath and make the *s* in *ssssssssack* last as long as your air holds out.

iii. *Affricate*: Affricates combine the stop and fricative manners of articulation into a single new type. In words like *chat* the first sound begins with a palatal stop, but then very quickly moves into a fricative at the same point of articulation.

iv. *Nasal*: The first sound in *Macintosh* is a nasal, a sound where the flow of air is blocked in the mouth but allowed to flow freely through the nasal cavity. Nasals involve an articulation inside the oral cavity that corresponds to some stop. Thus, the first sounds in *Mack* and *back* are both stop consonants in so far as the activity of the lips is concerned (closing off the airstream altogether). However, youíll notice that you can hum through the first sound in *Mack*, but not the first sound in *back*. The reason for this is that we produce nasals by lowering the velum to allow air to pass from the pharynx into the nasal cavity and out the nose.

v. *Liquid*: Liquids are somewhat vowel-like articulations that allow quite free passage of air around an obstruction. The air may flow freely around the sides of the tongue, as in the first sound in *lake*, or it may flow over a curled back tongue, as in the first sound in *rake*.

vi. *Glide*: The first sounds in *we* and *yes* are called glides, which are the most vowel-like of the consonants. In these sounds the air flow is quite free. Notice that the first sound in *we* is very similar to the first sound in *oops*, and the first sound in *yes* is quite similar to the first sound in *eat*.

C. *Voicing*: Overlaid on top of the two dimensions of place of articulation and manner of articulation there is a third dimension, that of voicing. As weíll see, there are pairs of consonants that have the same place and manner of articulation, but different voicing properties.

If you were to watch a slow motion video of someone saying *sap* and *zap* it would be difficult to impossible to tell which was which without the sound because the motions in the mouth for these two consonants are identical. Nevertheless, you can not only hear but also feel a difference between these two. To make the difference clear, place your fingers on your adamís apple and produce a long hissing sound that alternates between being an *s* or *z*sound, like this: You should feel a slight buzzing sensation in your fingers on the *z* sounds (but not on the *s*sounds). The source of this buzzing sensation is vibration of the vocal folds. During the *z* articulation, the vocal folds are drawn close together and air is forced between them, which causes them to vibrate. During the *s* articulations, the folds are held apart and air flows freely through the glottis (the opening between the vocal folds). Thus, we say that *zap* begins with a voiced consonant while *sap* begins with a voiceless consonant.

`This contrast is used widely in English. In each of the following pairs there are two consonants of the same place and manner of articulation that are distinguished in terms of voicing: *pat* and *bat, fat* and *vat, thin* and *then*, and *cot* and *got*.

6. *Distinguishing vowels*: Vowels are voiced and vowel articulations involve little constriction of the vocal tract. Thus, vowels are distinguished by way of different timbres or qualities in the sound that are produced by giving the inside of the mouth different shapes.

   You may have noticed that if you speak or sing into a large barrel or a length of large-diametre pipe, your voice suddenly sounds very different. In fact, it will sound noticeably different in different diametres and lengths of pipe. The vocal tract takes advantage of the same acoustical principles that produce these differences to produce the acoustical qualities of different vowels.

This is achieved largely by shifting the tongue into different postures. By raising the tongue high into the forward part of the mouth (and enlarging the spaces at the back of the mouth) we produce the vowel quality in words like *bee* and *key*. By pulling the tongue down and somewhat back toward the back wall of the pharynx we produce sounds like the vowels in *cot* and *pot*. The vowels in *loot* and *coot* are produced by raising the back of the tongue toward the velum, but not getting it close enough to produce any constriction or noise.

These differences in tongue posture can be described in terms of two parametres, those of tongue height and backness. Thus, the vowel in *key* is a high front vowel, the first one in *father* is a low back vowel and the one in *coot* is a high back vowel.

Another important factor in the differentiation of vowels is lip rounding. The vowels in *keep* and *coop* are different in two respects. The first is high front and the second high back, but you will notice that if you switch back and forth between these vowels, you will purse your lips somewhat on the vowel in *coop*, but not on the vowel in *keep*. This drawing together of the lips is called rounding and it plays a role in a number of back vowels in English.

7. *Consonant and vowel charts*: The various ways of distinguishing consonants and vowels that we have discussed above are used in the two charts shown below. These charts illustrate how the consonants and vowels of English can be distinguished by reference to the several parametres we have discussed above. An IPA symbol is given for each sound in each table, along with a common English word that uses the sound.

A. English Consonants

Manner of Articulation		Place of Articulation: Bilabial	Labio-dental	Dental	Alveolar	Palatal	Velar	Glottal
Stops	Voiceless	p (pat)			t (tack)		k (cat)	
	Voiced	b (bat)			d (dig)		g (get)	
Fricatives	Voiceless		f (fat)	θ (thin)	s (sat)	š (fish)		h (hat)
	Voiced		v (vat)	ð (then)	z (zap)	ž (azure)		
Affricates	Voiceless					č (church)		
	Voiced					ǰ (judge)		
Nasals		m (mat)			n (nat)		ŋ (sing)	
Liquids					l (late)	r (rate)		
Glides		w (win)				y (yet)		

B. English Vowels

	Front	Center	Back
	i (beet)		u (boot)
High			U (book)
	I (bit)		
			o (bode)
	e (baby)		
		ə (Sofa)	
Middle	ɛ (bet)		ɔ (bought)
	æ (bat)	ʌ (but)	
Low			
			a (palm)

USING PHONETICS

Phonetic Transliteration is a method of using English alphabet for writing in non-English languages. Below is a mapping table for Marathi, Hindi and Gujarati script characters (vowels, consonants) respectively to corresponding English alphabets, followed by some illustrative examples. To make it easy to remember, the corresponding English alphabets are as close as possible to how the script characters are pronounced.

VOWELS

अ अ અ a	आ आ આ A	इ इ ઇ i	ई ई ઈ I	उ उ ઉ u
ऊ ऊ ઊ u	ए ए એ e	ऐ ऐ ઐ AY	ओ ओ ઓ o	औ औ ઔ AW
ऋ ऋ ઋ HRI	अॅ अॅ -- AE	ऑ ऑ -- OE	अं अं અં aM	अः अः અઃ a:

CONSONANTS

क	क	ક	ka	ख	ख	ખ	kha	ग	ग	ગ	ga	घ	घ	ઘ	gha	ङ	ङ	ઙ	Nga
च	च	ચ	kha	छ	छ	છ	chha	ज	ज	જ	ja	झ	झ	ઝ	jha	ञ	ञ	ઞ	Nja
ट	ट	ટ	Ta	ठ	ठ	ઠ	Tha	ड	ड	ડ	Da	ढ	ढ	ઢ	Dha	ण	ण	ણ	Na
त	त	ત	ta	थ	थ	થ	tha	द	द	દ	da	ध	ध	ધ	dha	न	न	ન	na
प	प	પ	pa	फ	फ	ફ	pha	ब	ब	બ	ba	भ	भ	ભ	bha	म	म	મ	ma
य	य	ય	ya	र	र	ર	ra	ल	ल	લ	la	व	व	વ	va	श	श	શ	sha
ष	ष	ષ	Sha	स	स	સ	sa	ह	ह	હ	ha	ळ	ळ	ળ	La				

OTHER CHARACTERS

क्ष	क्ष	ક્ષ	kSha	श्र	श्र	શ્ર	Shra	ज्ञ	ज्ञ	જ્ઞ	dnya	कृ	कृ	---	kHRI	त्र	त्र	ત્ર	tra
त्त	त्त	ત્ત	tta	क्त	क्त	ક્ત	kta	ऱ्ह	---	---	.rh	ऽ	ऽ	ઽ	.S	ढ	ढ	ઢ	DHa

SAMPLE WORDS

भाग्य	भाग्य	ભાગ્ય	bhAgya	वळण	वळण	વળણ	vaLaNa
राज्य	राज्य	રાજ્ય	rAjya	निर्माण	निर्माण	નિર્માણ	nirmANa
विद्या	विद्या	વિદ્યા	vidyA	म्हैस	म्हैस	મ્હૈસ	mhAYsa
शिष्या	शिष्या	શિષ્યા	shiShyA	ऋषि	ऋषि	ઋષિ	HRIShi
त्याग	त्याग	ત્યાગ	tyAga	नोव्हेंबर	नोव्हेंबर	નોવ્હેંબર	novheMbara
ध्यान	ध्यान	ધ્યાન	dhyAna	चतुर्थी	चतुर्थी	ચતુર્થી	chaturthI
चांदण्या	चांदण्या	ચાંદણ્યા	chAMdaNyA	ज्ञानेश्वर	ज्ञानेश्वर	જ્ઞાનેશ્વર	dnyAneshvara
कल्याण	कल्याण	કલ્યાણ	kalyANa	महाराष्ट्र	महाराष्ट्र	મહારાષ્ટ્ર	mahArAShTra
सज्जन	सज्जन	સજ્જન	sajjana	फक्त	फक्त	ફક્ત	phakta
पत्ता	पत्ता	પત્તા	pattA	वाऱ्या	----	---- .	vA.ryA

PHONETIC CODE

Aspell is in fact the spell checker that comes up with the best suggestions if it finds an unknown word. One reason is that it does not just compare the word with other words in the dictionary (like Ispell does) but also uses phonetic comparisons with other words.

The new table driven phonetic code is very flexible and setting up phonetic transformation rules for other languages is not difficult but there can be a number of stumbling blocks — that's why I wrote this section.

The main phonetic code is free of any language specific code and should be powerful enough to allow setting up rules for any language. Anything which is language specific is kept in a plain text file and can easily be edited. So it's even possible to write phonetic transformation rules if you don't have any programming skills. All you need to know is how words of the language are written and how they are pronounced.

SYNTAX OF TRANSFORMATION ARRAY

In the translation array there are two strings on each line; the first one is the search string (or switch name) and the second one is the replacement string (or switch parametre).

```
version version
```

The line is also required to appear somewhere in the translation array. The version string can be anything but it should be changed whenever a new version of the translation array is released. This is important because it will keep Aspell from using a compiled dictionary with the wrong set of rules. For example, if when coming up with suggestion for hallo, Aspell will use the new rules to come up with the soundslike say H*L*, but if 'hello' is stored in the dictionary using the old rules as HLinstead of H*L* Aspell will never be able to come up with 'hello'. So to solve this problem Aspell checks if the version strings match and aborts with an error if they don't. Thus it is important to update it whenever a new version of the translation array is released. This is only a problem with the main word list as the personal word lists are now stored as simple word lists with a single header line (i.e. no soundslike data).

Each non switch line represents one replacement (transformation) rule. Words beginning with the same letter must be grouped together; the order inside this group does not depend on alphabetical issues but it gives priorities; the higher the rule the higher the priority. That's why the first rule that matches is applied. In the following example:

```
GH _
G K
```

'GH→ _' has higher priority than 'G → K'

'_' represents the empty string "". If 'GH →_' came after 'G→ K', the second rule would never match because the algorithm would stop searching for more rules after the first match. The above rules transform any 'GH' to an empty string (delete them) and transforms any other 'G' to 'K'.

At the end of the first string of a line (the search string) there may optionally stand a number of characters in brackets. One (only one!) of these characters must fit. It's comparable with the '[ ]' brackets in regular expressions. The rule 'DG(EIY) → J' for example would match any 'DGE', 'DGI' and 'DGY' and replace them with 'J'. This way you can reduce several rules to one.

Before the search string, one or more dashes '-' may be placed. Those search strings will be matched totally but only the beginning of the string will be replaced. Furthermore, for these rules no follow-up rule will be searched (what this is will be explained later). The rule 'TCH— '→ _ will match any word containing 'TCH' (like 'match') but will only replace the first character 'T' with an empty string. The number of dashes determines how many characters from the end will not be replaced. After the replacement, the search for transformation rules continues with the not replaced 'CH'!

If a '<' is appended to the search string, the search for replacement rules will continue with the replacement string and not with the next character of the word. The rule 'PH< -> F' for example would replace 'PH' with 'F' and then again start to search for a replacement rule for 'F...'. If there would also be rules like 'FO '→ 'O' and 'F → _' then words like 'PHOXYZ' would be transformed to 'OXYZ' and any occurrences of 'PH' that are not followed by an 'O' will be deleted like 'PHIXYZ -> IXYZ'. The second replacement however is not applied if the priority of this rule is lower than the priority of the first rule.

Priorities are added to a rule by putting a number between 0 and 9 at the end of the search string, for example 'ING6 → N'. The higher the number the higher is the priority.

Priorities are especially important for the previously

mentioned follow-up rules. Follow-up rules are searched beginning from the last string of the first search string. This is a bit complicated but I hope this example will make it clearer:

```
CHS X
CH     G
HAU—1 H
SCH SH
```

In this example 'CHS' in the word 'FUCHS' would be transformed to 'X'. If we take the word 'DURCHSCHNITT' then things look a bit different. Here 'CH' belongs together and 'SCH' belongs together and both are spoken separately. The algorithm however first finds the string 'CHS' which may not be transformed like in the previous word 'FUCHS'. At this point the algorithm can find a follow-up rule. It takes the last character of the first matching rule ('CHS') which is 'S' and looks for the next match, beginning from this character. What it finds is clear: It finds 'SCH → SH', which has the same priority (no priority means standard priority, which is 5). If the priority is the same or higher the follow-up rule will be applied. Let's take a look at the word 'SCHAUKEL'. In this word 'SCH' belongs together and may not be taken apart. After the algorithm has found 'SCH '-> 'SH' it searches for a follow-up rule for 'H+"AUKEL'. It finds 'HAU—1 -> H', but does not apply it because its priority is lower than the one of the first rule. You see that this is a very powerful feature but it also can easily lead to mistakes. If you really don't need this feature you can turn it off by putting the line:

```
followup   0
```

at the beginning of the phonetic table file. As mentioned, for rules containing a '-' no follow-up rules are searched but giving such rules a priority is not totally senseless because they can be follow-up rules and in that case the priority makes sense again. Follow-up rules of follow-up rules are not searched because this is in fact not needed very often.

The control character '^' says that the search string only matches at the beginning of words so that the rule 'RH → R' will only apply to words like 'RHESUS' but not 'PERHAPS'.

You can append another '^' to the search string. In that case the algorithm treats the rest of the word totally separately from the first matched string at the beginning. This is useful for prefixes whose pronunciation does not depend on the rest of the word and vice versa like 'OVER^^' in English for example.

The same way as '^' works does '$' only apply to words that end with the search string. 'GN$ → N' only matches on words like 'SIGN' but not 'SIGNUM'. If you use '^' and '$' together, both of them must fit 'ENOUGH^$ → NF' will only match the word 'ENOUGH' and nothing else.

Of course you can combine all of the mentioned control characters but they must occur in this order: '← priority ^ $'. All characters must be written in CAPITAL letters.

If absolutely no rule can be found — might happen if you use strange characters for which you don't have any replacement rule — the next character will simply be skipped and the search for replacement rules will continue with the rest of the word.

If you want double letters to be reduced to one you must set up a rule like 'LL- → L'. If double letters in the resulting phonetic word should be allowed, you must place the line:

```
collapse_result 0
```

at the beginning of your transformation table file; otherwise set the value to '1'. The English rules for example strip all vowels from words and so the word "GOGO" would be transformed to "K" and not to "KK" (as desired) if collapse_result is set to 1. That's why the English rules have collapse_result set to 0.

By default, all accents are removed from a word before it is matched to the soundslike rules. If you do not want this then add the line

```
remove_accents 0
```

at the beginning of your file. The exact definition of an accent is language dependent and is controlled via the character set file. If you set remove_accents to '0' then you should also set "store-as" to "lower" in the language data file (not the phonetic transformation file) otherwise Aspell will have problems when both the accented and the de-accented version of a word appearing in the dictionary; it will consider one of them as incorrectly spelled.

HOW DO I START FINALLY

Before you start to write an array of transformation rules, you should be aware that you have to do some work to make sure that things you do will result in correct transformation rules.

Things that Come in Handy

First of all, you need to have a large word list of the language you want to make phonetics for. It should contain about as many words as the dictionary of the spell checker. If you don't have such a list, you will probably find an Ispell dictionary at which will help you. You can then make affix expansion via ispell -e and then pipe it through tr " " "\n" to put one word on each line. After that you eventually have to convert special characters like `é' from Ispell's internal representation to latin1 encoding. sed s/e'/é/g for example would replace all `e'' with `é'.

The second is that you know how to use regular expressions and know how to use grep. You should for example know that:

```
grep ^[^aeiou]qu[io] wordlist | less
```

will show you all words that begin with any character but 'a', 'e', 'i', 'o' or 'u' and then continue with 'qui' or 'quo'. This stuff is important for example to find out if a phonetic replacement rule you want to set up is valid for all words which match the expression you want to replace. Taking a look at the regex(7) man page is a good idea.

What the Phonetic Code Should do

Normal text comparison works well as long as the typer misspells a word because he pressed one key he didn't really want to press. In these cases, mostly one character differs from the original word.

In cases where the writer didn't know about the correct

spelling of the word, the word may have several characters that differ from the original word but usually the word would still sound like the original. Someone might think that 'tough' is spelled 'taff'. No spell checker without phonetic code will come to the idea that this might be 'tough', but a spell checker who knows that 'taff' would be pronounced like 'tough' will make good suggestions to the user. Another example could be 'funetik' and 'phonetic'.

From these examples you can see that the phonetic transformation should not be too fussy and too precise. If you implement a whole phonetic dictionary as you can find it in books this will not be very useful because then there could still be many characters differing from the misspelled and the desired word. What you should do if you implement the phonetic transformation table is to reduce the number of used letters to the only really necessary ones.

Characters that sound similar should be reduced to one. In the English language for example 'Z' sounds like 'S' and that's why the transformation rule 'Z -> S' is present in the replacement table. "PH is spoken like "F and so we have a 'PH -> F' rule.

If you take a closer look you will even see that vowels sound very similar in the English language: 'contradiction', 'cuntradiction', 'cantradiction' or 'centradiction' in fact sound nearly the same, don't they? Therefore the English phonetic replacement rules not only reduce all vowels to one but even remove them all (removing is done by just setting up no rule for those letters). The phonetic code of "contradiction" is "KNTRTKXN" and if you try to read this letter-monster loud you will hear that it still sound a bit like 'contradiction'. You also see that "D" is transformed to "T" because they nearly sound the same.

If you think you have found a regularity you should always take your word list and grep for the corresponding regular expression you want to make a transformation rule for. An example: If you come to the idea that all English words ending on 'ough' sound like 'AF' at the end because you think of 'enough' and 'tough'. If you thengrep for the corresponding regular expression by grep -i ough$ wordlist you will see that the rule you wanted to set up is not correct because the rule doesn't fit to words like 'although' or 'bough'. So you have to define your rule more precisely or you have to set up exceptions if the number of words that differ from the desired rule is not too big.

Don't forget about follow-up rules which can help in many cases but which also can lead to confusion and unwanted side effects. It's also important to write exceptions in front of the more general rules ('GH' before 'G' etc.).

If you think you have set up a number of rules that may produce some good results try them out! If you run Aspell as aspell --lang=your_language pipe you get a prompt at which you can type in words. If you just type words Aspell checks them and eventually makes suggestions if they are misspelled. If you type in $$Swword you will see the phonetic transformation and you can test out if your work does what you want.

Another good way to check that changes you make to your rules don't have any bad side effects is to create another list from your word list which contains not only the word of the word list but also the corresponding phonetic version of this word on the same line. If you do this once before the change and once after the change you can make a diff (see man diff) to see what really changed. To do this use the command aspell --lang=your_language soundslike. In this mode Aspell will output the the original word and then its soundslike separated by a tab character for each word you give it. If you are interested in seeing how the algorithm works you can download a set of useful programmes from This includes a programme that produces a list as mentioned above and another programme which illustrates how the algorithm works. It uses the same transformation table as Aspell and so it helps a lot during the process of creating a phonetic transformation table for Aspell.

During your work you should write down your basic ideas so that other people are able to understand what you did (and you still know about it after a few weeks). The

English table has a huge documentation appended as an example.

Now you can start experimenting with all the things you just read and perhaps set up a nice phonetic transformation table for your language to help Aspell to come up with the best correction suggestions ever seen also for your language. Take a look at the Aspell homepage to see if there is already a transformation table for your language. If there is one you might also take a look at it to see if it could be improved.

Chapter 2

Phonology

THE BASIS OF PHONETICS AND PHONOLOGY

Greek word, *phone* meaning 'sound, voice') is the study of the sounds of human speech. It is concerned with the actual properties of speech sounds (phones), and their production, audition and perception, as opposed to phonology, which is the study of sound systems and abstract sound units (such as phonemes and distinctive features). Phonetics deals with the sounds themselves rather than the contexts in which they are used in languages. Discussions of meaning (semantics) do not enter at this level of linguistic analysis.

Phonetics has three main branches:

- Articulatory phonetics, concerned with the positions and movements of the lips, tongue, vocal tract and folds and other speech organs in producing speech;
- Acoustic phonetics, concerned with the properties of the sound waves and how they are received by the inner ear; and
- Auditory phonetics, concerned with speech perception, principally how the brain forms perceptual representations of the input it receives.

There are over a hundred different phones recognized as distinctive by the International Phonetic Association (IPA) and transcribed in their International Phonetic Alphabet.

Phonetics was studied as early as 2,500 years ago in ancient India, with PâGini's account of the place and manner of articulation of consonants in his 5th century BCE treatise on Sanskrit. The major Indic alphabets today, except Tamil script, order theii consonants according to PâGini's classification.

Success in mastering any language requires knowledge in speaking, reading, and writing the language. The speaking component requires the understanding and use of correct pronunciation, emphasis, and syntactic patterns. The written component requires mastery of the alphabet, spelling, and the ability to write, print, or type the pattern.

Very early in the learning process, English-language speakers become keenly aware of the language's lack of sound to symbol correspondence. Any young child studying the alphabet can point out that *cat* starts with the letter c that sounds like a/k/and the word *race* ends in the letters ce but sounds like an/s/.

In order to help speech/language pathologists, linguists, media personnel, individuals learning English as a second language (ESL) and others interested in correct pronunciation the International Phonetic Alphabet (IPA) was devised.

Phonetics is the study of the physical aspects of speech. It looks at human speech from three distinct but related and interdependent perspectives. Accordingly, the tree main branches of phonetics are: *articulatory phonetics, auditory phonetics* and *acoustic phonetics*. Articulatory phonetics studies the way in which speech sounds are produced, i.e. it is closely linked with speech production.

Understanding of how sounds are produced involves understanding of the anatomy of speech, i.e. of the organs involved in the production of speech sounds (the lungs, the larynx and the vocal tract), and understanding of the airstream mechanisms.

In English, all speech sounds are initiated by a *pulmonic* (= lung-based) *egressive* (= directed outwards) airstream which is then pushed through the *larynx* ("Adam's apple"), and then proceeds through the glottis into the *vocal tract*. The larynx is a box made of cartilage across which two strips of muscles lie: these are the *vocal cords* (or vocal folds). They produce audible *vibration* as the result of air being forced through a narrow opening between the vocal cords: the *glottis*. In the vocal tract the airstream is modified by means of several articulators: *active articulators* (e.g. the lips and the tongue) which can actively affect the airstream, and *passive articulators* (e.g. the teeth, the alveolar ridge, the palate, the velum) which serve as contact positions for the active articulators.

The production of speech sounds through these organs is referred to as *articulation*. Along the lines of articulatory criteria, two well-known types of speech sounds are differentiated: *consonants* and *vowels*. They are the *basic segments of speech*. The production of consonants involves some sort of obstruction to the airstream in the vocal tract.

Classification of consonants is along three criteria: the *place of articulation* (= where does the obstruction occur?), the *manner of articulation* (= what type of obstruction is involved), and the *state of the glottis/voicing* (= do the vocal cords vibrate or not?). (To give you an example: The sound/p/as in *pint* is referred to as a *voiceless bilabial plosive,* where *voiceless* refers to the state of the glottis (the vocal cords are apart, the airstream has a relatively free passage on its way up), *bilabial* refers to the place of articulation (both lips are involved in the articulation; they obstruct the airstream due to their closure), and *plosive* indicates the manner of articulation: after complete obstruction due to the closure of the lips and air compression, the air is released, resulting in a burst of sound.)

The production of vowels involves less obstruction than the production of consonants. Vowels are defined in terms of the *Cardinal Vowel Chart* which relates to the *position of the tongue* (high vs. low, front vs. back), *lip rounding, nasalisation* as articulatory parametres.

Since the orthography of the languages is only imperfectly phonetic and since the number of speech sounds exceeds the number of characters in the Roman alphabet, International Phonetic Alphabet has been invented by the International Phonetic Association (IPA) as a separate system to represent the actual sounds of the human language. This alphabet is applicable to all languages.

Consonants and vowels as the basic segments of speech form syllables, then larger units such as words, then complete utterances. Superimposed on these segments are a number of additional features known as suprasegmental features (also: *prosodic features*). These are: *stress, loudness, pitch, length.*

Acoustic phonetics studies the physical properties of speech sounds, i.e. the *properties of sound waves* and the *acoustic of speech.* Sound waves can be *simple* (e.g. the sound originating from a tunig fork) or *complex.* However, sound waves involved in human speech are complex due to the simultaneous use of different sound sources in the vocal tract. *Simple sound waves* are regular in motion – they are referred to as *periodic.*

Among the measurable properties of simple sound waves are the *frequency,* i.e. the number of cycles of a sound wave per second measured in Hertz (Hz), and the *amplitude,* which denotes the maximum of a sound wave in a cycle of movement. *Loudness* is a combination of frequency and amplitude.

The term *intensity,* measured in decibels (dB) is used to refer to the overall loudness of a sound. *Complex sound waves* are a conglomeration of a number of simple sound waves. *Vowels* are basically periodic complex sound waves, whereas *consonants* range from periodic to aperiodic complex sound waves.

The sound wave created by a sound source is referred to as *fundamental frequency* (F0). In speech, F0 is the result of the vibration of the vocal cords. F0 of vocal cord vibration varies between 50 and 500 Hz. The typical F0 range for females is 150-350 Hertz (Hz), for males 80-200 Hz. F0 is filtered (e.g. intensified) by numerous parts of the resonating body. The resulting bundles of resonance frequencies are multiples of the original sound wave produced by the vocal cords. They are called *formants.*

Among the techniques to visualise the speech signal is the *spectrogram,* which is a three-dimensional plot of a sound wave. The horizontal axis displays time, the vertical axis represents the fundamental frequency, and the third dimension is intensity. (Here is another link to a spectrogram.) Any acoustic analysis of speech is, however, complicated by other variables such as e.g. background noise (imaging a conversation in a crowded bar or a running train), missing segments, or inter-speaker variation.

However, as listeners, we rely on a number of distinguishing features of the speech signal (*acoustic cues*) that allow us to recognise speech despite all the acoustic variation. Among the *acoustic cues* is *voice onset time*, i.e. the point when vocal cord vibration starts relative to the release of a closure.

Auditory phoneticsis closely related to speech perception: it studies the way in which humans perceive sounds. Just as articulatory phonetics involves the understanding of the anatomy of speech, auditory phonetics involves the understanding of the human hearing system, i.e. the anatomy and physiology of the human ear and brain.

The human ear consists of three central components: *the outer ear, the middle ear* and *the inner ear*. The sound signal enters the hearing system through and is modified by the outer ear. It is carried to the eardrum through the auditory canal. Behind the eardrum is the middle ear whose function is to convert the sound vibration at the eardrum into mechanical movements by means of a system of three small bones, the ossicles, and then transfer the signal to the inner ear.

The inner ear converts the signal into nerve impulses which are passed to the hearing centre of the brain via the auditory nerve. Naturally, the human hearing system cannot react to all the features present in a sound wave. It is therefore essential to investigate exactly what we perceive and how we perceive it.

This is exactly what speech perception does: it is the study of the way speech sounds are identified and analysed – this is an area that is also of interest to experimental psychologists. The questions that have been dealt with in this area are: What are the specific *acoustic cues* in the speech signal that help to filter out which features/which pieces of information in the speech signal are important in order to recognise what is being said (cf. above). And: How can this process of speech perception be described by means of a model, starting from the input (a complex acoustic signal) and leading to the eventual output (a representation of the phonological features).

Phonology deals with the linguistic patterning of sounds in human languages. Linguists distinguish two areas of phonology: *segmental phonology* and *suprasegmental phonology*. Segmental phonology roughly refers to "what you say".

It is concerned with the fundamental building blocks of sound structure: *phonemes* and *distinctive features*. A phoneme is an abstract phonological unit. In English, phonemes are distinctive structural elements, i.e. two words that differ in only one phoneme have different meanings. Compare *sun* and *pun* which differ only in the initial phoneme (/s/vs./p/).

Word pairs of this kind are referred to as *minimal pairs*. "Abstract" in this context means that the pronunciation of the phoneme is not fully specified, i.e. a phoneme can be pronounced in different ways depending on its environment. The actual realisation of a phoneme in a given environment is called *phone*, a set of *phones* that realise the same *phoneme* is referred to as its *allophones*.

Compare e.g. the/p/-sounds in *pull* and *temper*. The/p/in *pull* is aspirated, meaning that the production of this sound is accompanied by a "puff of air" (the emission of air), whereas in the production of the/p/in *temper* there is no such aspiration. The aspirated and the non-aspirated/p/are thus *allophones* of the same *phoneme.*

Distinctive features refer to units that are smaller still than phonemes. Relevant features are e.g. [+/- consonant], which distinguishes formally between vowels ([-consonant]) and consonants ([+consonant]), and [+/- voice], distinguishing between voiced and voiceless sounds. Evidence for these features is both internal and external. Internal evidence relates e.g. to the adequacy with which phonological phenomena can be described.

External evidence is based on linguistic behaviour. Consider *speech errors*: *Speech errors* are unintentional departures from what the speaker meant to say. Some types of speech errors are sensitive to distinctive phonological features. Imagine a speech error such as "*glear plue sky*" when your intention was to say *"clear blue sky"*. This is an example of an exchange of features.

The initial sound of the first word was intended to be voiceless (/k/in clear), whereas the initial sound of the second word (/b/in *blue*) was to be voiced. In the errorneous utterance, these features are exchanged.

Suprasegmental phonology on the other hand roughly refers to "how you say what you say". It involves phenomena such as the *structure of syllables, stress,* and *tone.* A syllable is an important structural unit in phonology, with a word being organised in syllables. A syllable consists of an optional *onset* (the initial consonant) and an obligatory *rhyme.* The rhyme itself consists of a (obligatory) *nucleus* (also called *peak*), which is normally a vowel, and a (optional) *coda,* the final consonant in a syllable.

Stress is the phonological correlate of a combination of loudness, pitch, and vowel length. In each word, at least one syllable must be stressed, i.e. must be most prominent/more prominent than other syllables. In the English word *computer* for example, the syllable/-pu-/is the most prominent one.

Tone is the phonological correlate of *pitch.* Tone, i.e. pitch variation, can serve different purposes across languages. On the one hand, in a language such as English (or German, Dutch), pitch variation can be used to express the intention of the speaker. In general, the constituent carrying important information will be marked by a pitch accent, whereas known information is deaccented.

A pitch accent is a local feature of a pitch contour which signals that the relevant syllable is *prominent* in the utterance. This is related to the term *intonation*. In languages such as English, F0 is the strongest correlate of how the listener perceives the speaker's intonation. The term *intonation* refers to the occurrence of recurring pitch patterns, to the prominence (and non-prominence) of syllables, to how and to what extent the syllables are made prominent, and to phonological phrasing.

Intonation conveys sentence-level pragmatic meanings in a linguistically structured way. *Pitch* concerns the varying height of the pitch of the voice, i.e. it refers to what the listener hears as high or low tonal properties, to rising and falling voice patterns. It is the prosodic feature most centrally involved in intonation.

On the other hand, in so called tone-languages such as Mandarin Chinese, Vietnamese, or the African Bantu languages, tone patterns serve to express lexical distinctions, i.e. pitch variation effects the meaning of a word. This means that one sequence of sounds can have different meanings depending on the tone pattern with which it is produced, i.e. whether it is produced at a continuous high level, a rising or a falling level.

The major goal of phonological research in general is to establish a general framework for the phonological structure of language. Phonological research is based on (i) language specific observations, i.e. the phonological patterns of isolated languages, such as the phonology of English, the phonology of German, the phonology of Vietnamese, and on (ii) comparative phonological studies, dealing with questions such as *What are the sounds in the languages of the world?*, *Are there any sounds within the human sound inventory that occur in all known languages?* and *What are the differences between the languages?*.

A number of theoretical frameworks have been suggested in the literature on phonology, among them *generative phonology* and *Optimality Theory*. Generative phonology has been modelled by Noam Chomsky and Morris Halle as part of *generative grammar*. As input of the phonological component of the language faculty in this framework serve syntactic surface structures, where each terminal node (or each lexical item) has its specific phonological feature representation.

Optimality Theory (OT) is the most influential linguistic theory of the 1990s. It originated in research on phonology but has been extended to other areas in linguistic theory. OT suggests that Universal Grammar contains a set of constraints that are all violable and which represent universal properties of language. The ranking of these constraints is language specific, thus giving rise to variation between languages.

INTERNATIONAL PHONETIC ALPHABET

In 1886, a group of phoneticians from France, Germany, Britain, and Denmark met to discuss the adoption of a universal system of pronunciation. The IPA based on an alphabet written by British phonetician Henry Sweet, represented the first successful attempt to systemize the pronunciation of speech sounds across most languages.

The IPA provides the user with a universally accepted symbol for each of the speech sounds. The IPA is phonetic, not phonemic in design. In other words, a particular symbol is used to represent the pronunciation of a speech sound, not to delineate a change in meaning. Linguistically significant, the IPA symbols summarize present linguistic theory. The IPA has been revised several times over the past century, the most recent changes taking place in 1996.

The International Phonetic Association, the agency governing the IPA, has a system of detailed principles applied to the formation and variation of the alphabet. In its present form, the IPA provides detailed information on vowels, consonants, other additional symbols, diacritics and suprasegmentals.

Classical Phonetics

Phoneticians since those of the Sanskrit era (4000 years ago) developed Classical Phonetics as a solid basis for the study of all of linguistics (phonetics was the primary 'component'). They were aware of major applications, such as language teaching and learning, elocution (long since disappeared because of its prescriptive stance), speech pathology and therapy.

An important point in the development of Classical Phonetics was the establishment towards the end of the 19th century of an agreed alphabet (or set of symbols) to provide a means of symbolic representation of 'all of the sounds of the world's languages'. Known as the International Phonetic Alphabet and proposed by the International Phonetic Association. There had been many attempts to provide a means of representing on paper exactly how people pronounced languages - the IPA was the final and most successful attempt to do this.

The basic idea was to provide a 'one symbol, one sound' system of transcription which would enable not just the faithful transcription of the sounds of a particular language but also cross-language comparison (for several reasons the idea fails at this point - why?).

The IPA consists of a basic set of symbols derived mostly from the alphabets used in ordinary orthography in Western Europe (the major impetus for the development of the IPA was from Britain and France). These symbols are used to represent individual sounds, but, if necessary, subtleties or details of pronunciation can be expressed by the addition of diacritics.

The Classical School made little distinction between a particular sound and the articulation (the vocal tract configuration) needed to produce it. Thus in a sense the symbols of the IPA are ambiguous in that they represent a sound AND how it is made. If there is any theoretical claim here it is that there is a one-to-one correlation between articulation and sound.

The idea of 'one symbol, one sound' encapsulates and important theoretical tenet of Classical Phonetics: speech consists of individual, separable sounds. For early phoneticians speech consisted of a string of sounds, and articulations were concatenated to produce utterances.

Firth's approach is remarkably similar in concept to the approach of Articulatory Phonology, first put forward in 1985, but also occurring 'by accident' or rather 'force majeure' in the parallel parametric speech synthesis systems developed in the 60s.

Classical phonetics included phonology. The distinction between a phonological level and a phonetic level, or even between phonologists as scientists distinct from phoneticians did not arise until the late 50s, though there had been rumblings among the Prague School phonologists in the 30s.

Phonology was a dimension of phonetic studies. You were doing phonology if you were considering how sounds function in a language. For example it is one thing to note that [k] is a voiceless velar stop or that [t] is a voiceless alveolar stop (phonetics), and another to note that in English/ k/and/t/can function to distinguish between words or morphemes; for example, in the words 'cat' and 'tack' (phonology).

Although the Classical Phoneticians spoke of the phonetics and phonology of this or that language, you can see that in a sense phonetics can be thought of as about the universal properties of speech sounds and phonology as about more the language-specific functional properties of sounds.

Important Points of Classical Phonetic Theory

- Speech is segmental in nature. An utterance is a string of concatenated sounds.
- Speech sounds are permutable. That is, they can be substituted in strings to alter the meaning. So, for example, [kæt] ('cat') can be changed into [kæp] ('cap') by substitution of the final sounds.
- Speech sounds can be 'captured' in a symbolic representation using an alphabet system. This can be refined to enable all relevant detail to be put onto paper.
- Sounds can be classified and shown to form systems.
- Phonetics is about classifying and describing surface phenomena (using modern terminology).

Classification

Speech sounds were seen to be divisible into two major subsets - the consonants and vowels (how? why?). Once identified each subset could be presented within the framework of a system of classification showing how the sounds relate to each other on an articulatory basis.

Consonants are classified basically two-dimensionally:

- According to 'place'– Where in the vocal tract a constriction of some kind is made, and
- According to 'manner'– How 'tight' the constriction is.

Thus, [b] is a bilabial (place) stop or plosive (manner); [f] is a labio-dental (place) fricative (manner). In a graphical representation of this classification a matrix is set up with the rows corresponding to the different manners of articulation and the columns corresponding to the different place of articulation.

In each cell of the matrix is entered a symbol indicating the sound produced at this intersection of the two parametres. This reveals, however, that for each cell there are often two possibilities. Thus there are two bilabial plosives in English: [p] and [b]. They are distinguished by whether or not there is accompanying vocal cord vibration. 'Voicing' therefore constitutes a third parametre for the classification of consonants.

Vowels are classified according to the position in the oral cavity on a cross sectional plane of the 'highest part of the tongue' (later modified to 'the most significant part of the tongue' - and both are false). Thus a two dimensional graph can be set up with rows representing a high-low dimension and columns representing a forward-backward dimension.

Points are marked on this graph showing the relevant tongue 'position' corresponding to a particular vowel. Thus [i] is shown high and forward on the graph (it is a high-front vowel) and [u] might be shown as a high back vowel. Two other dimensions which cannot be shown on a two-dimensional graph are necessary to exhaustively classify vowels: lip-rounding (necessary, but not phonologically significant in English, though it is, for example, in French and German, etc.), and nasality (not significant in English, but distinctive in French, Portuguese and Polish, etc.). An often neglected 5th dimension or parametre is 'tone'.

Basic Terminology

Allophone: The individual variation of the phoneme caused by such factors as position in the word, anatomical structure, and surrounding allophones. Allophones are nondistinctive variations of a phoneme. The use of an allophone does not change the meaning of a word.

Bisyllabic word: A word having two syllables.

Broad transcription: A general type of transcription using phonemes that appear in the vowel and consonant sections of the IPA. This type of transcription is used at the introductory level.

Coarticulation: The influence of the target phoneme on the surrounding phonemes.

Cognate: A pair of consonants produced with the same place and manner of articulation but one is voiced and one is voiceless. Examples:/p-b/,/s-z/.

Distinctive features: Articulatory or acoustic attributes of a phoneme necessary for distinguishing the difference between phonemes. Features are binary in nature meaning the feature is either present (+) or absent (–). Examples: the/ n/is (+) nasal and the/1/is (+) lateral.

General American Phonetics (GAP): The use of the symbols and markings from the IPA that represent the physical and articulatory aspects of the General American dialect.

Homorganic: Phonemes produced in the same place of articulation that differ in one or more features. Examples:/t-s/or/p-b-m/.

Loanword: A word that has entered the English language from another language, such as the word ballet.

Minimal pairs: Two words that are the same except for the one phoneme. Examples: hit and hip or pat and bat.

Monosyllabic word: A word having one syllable.

Morpheme: The smallest unit of meaning in the language. The two common types of morphemes are the free morphemes and the bound morphemes. The free morpheme provides meaning and stands alone. An example of a free morpheme is the word boy. The bound morpheme affixes to a free morpheme to convey meaning such as the plural "s" in boys.

Multisyllabic word: A word having more than two syllables.

Narrow transcription: A more specialized version of transcription using actual allophonic variations and specialized marking. Narrow transcription requires the use of the information from the other symbols, diacritics, and suprasegmental sections of the IPA.

Orthography: The part of the language that uses written symbols to represent the words in our language.

Phone: A single speech sound. Each symbol in the IPA represents a phone.

Phoneme: A family or group of sounds with distinctive acoustic characteristics. The phoneme is used to represent the target or ideal sound. A symbol from the phonetic alphabet is used for each phoneme.

Phonetics: The study of speech sounds in terms of physical and articulatory aspects.

Phonological rules: Rules that dictate how phonemes and allophones are used in the language. In addition, these rules dictate how phonemes and allophones are patterned into allowable syllable structures.

Phonology: The study of the rules and organization of sound units in the language.

Syllable: Unit of the speech consisting of a vowel. Consonants may or may not be present on one or both sides of the vowel.

Vocal tract: The area of the upper body inward from the lips to the lungs that is used in the production of speech. The vocal tract can be open or closed (occluded).

Voicing: The state of the vocal folds during the production of a phoneme or allophone. If the vocal folds are vibrating during the production, the subsequent sound is voiced. If the vocal folds are open or not vibrating during the production, the subsequent sound is voiceless or unvoiced.

Word: A part of language consisting of one or more phonemes and one or more syllables. The meaning of a word is dependent on the entire sequence of phonemes.

Vowels

Vowels are defined by the IPA using the three dimensions of height, frontness, and rounding. A quadrilateral space is used to visualize the relationships between the vowels. The height of a vowel refers to the position of the mandible (open or close) and the tongue in vertical relationship to the top or bottom of the mouth (low or high). The four variations of height are open (or low), open-mid, close-mid, and close (or high).

Frontness refers to the horizontal position of the tongue in relation to the front or back of the mouth. The three variations of frontness are front, central, and back. Rounding pertains to the pucker or spread posture of the lips. The two lip positions are rounded and unrounded. It is important to note that all vowels are produced with an open vocal tract and are voiced.

Table: IPA-Vowels Summary Chart

Dimensions	**Delineations**
Height	Open, open-mid, close-mid, and close
Frontness	Front, central, back
Rounding	Rounded and unrounded

Consonants

Consonants are delineated by the IPA in terms of manner of articulation, place of articulation, and voicing. Manner of articulation refers to how the air stream from the lungs is directed to the mouth and modified by the various structures to produce a consonant phoneme. Place of articulation refers to the location and constriction of the structures used in the production of a given consonant phoneme. Voicing refers to the presence or absence of the vibration of the vocal folds during the production of a phoneme.

The manners of articulation in the IPA are plosive (the obstruction of the air stream from the lungs followed by a release of the air stream), nasal (the release of the sound through the nasal area), trill (the rapid fluttering of the lips, uvula, or tongue tip), tap or flap (a single tap of the tongue tip against the teeth), fricative (modification of a continued air stream from the lungs by the articulators), lateral fricative (frictionlike sound being emitted with a lateral airstream), approximant (proximity of two articulators without the presence of turbulence), lateral approximant (the air stream along the centre of the oral cavity is obstructed forcing the emission of air laterally), ejective stop (an abrupt production of a plosive sound followed by a puff of air), and implosive (a weakened production of a plosive sound without a puff of air). Using the consonant section, manner of articulation can be found on the vertical axis.

Table. IPA Manner of Articulation Summary Chart

Manner	Modification
Plosive	Obstruction of air stream from the lungs followed by a release of the air stream
Nasal	Release of sound through the nasal area
Trill	Rapid fluttering of the lips, uvula, or the tongue
Tap or flap	Single tap of the tongue tip against the teeth
Fricative	Modification of a continued air stream from the lungs by the articulators
Lateral fricative	Frictionlike sound being emitted with a lateral air stream
Approximant	Proximity of two articulators without turbulence
Lateral approximant	Air stream along the centre of the oral cavity is obstructed forcing lateral air emission
Ejective stop	Abrupt production of a plosive sound followed by a puff of air
Implosive	A plosive without a puff of air; a weakened version

The places of articulation in the IPA are bilabial (using both lips), labiodental (using the lower lip and the upper central and lateral incisors), dental (placing the tongue between the upper and lower central and lateral incisors), alveolar (placing the tongue tip on the alveolar ridge), postalveolar (placing the tongue tip in the area directly behind the alveolar ridge), retroflex (curling the tongue so that the tip points toward the velum), palatal (placing the tongue tip on the hard palate), velar (moving the muscles of the velum), uvular (movement of the uvula), pharyngeal (movement of the muscles in the pharyngeal area) and glottal (movement of air through the glottis).

Consonants are formed at each of the locations using the structures and functions outlined. Using the consonant section, place of articulation can be found on the horizontal axis.

Table. IPA Place of Articulation Summary Chart

Place	Structures
Bilabial	Both lips
Labiodental	The lower lip and the upper and lateral incisors
Dental	The tongue placed between the upper and lower central and lateral incisors
Alveolar	The tongue tip on the alveolar ridge
Postalveolar	The tongue tip placed in the area directly behind the alveolar ridge
Retroflex	The tongue curled so that the tip points toward the velum
Palatal	The tongue tip placed on the hard palate
Velar	The movement of the muscles of the velum
Uvular	Movement of the uvula
Pharyngeal	Movement of the muscles in the pharyngeal area
Glottal	Movement of air through the glottis

The aspects of voicing in the IPA are voiced consonants and voiceless or unvoiced consonants. Using the consonant section, consonants appear as both paired and single entries. By convention, the symbol in the right half of the square is voiced, whereas the symbol in the left half of the square is voiceless or unvoiced.

Table. IPA-Voicing Summary Chart

Voiceless Consonants	Voiced Consonants
p, t, k	b, d, g
	m, n,ŋ
f, è, s,ʃ , h	v, ð, z, 3
	ɹ, j
	l

Other Symbols, Diacritics, And Suprasegmentals

Other symbols, diacritics and suprasegmental are the

three subsections of the IPA used to enhance and further delineate production. The other symbols category allows for the transcription of additional sounds not fully represented in the consonant and vowels categories. Diacritics are symbols designed to be added to consonant, vowel or other symbols to further describe the phoneme.

Suprasegmentals provide information on stress, boundaries, timing and pitch. It is important to note that the IPA does not use capital letters for proper nouns, names, or to indicate the beginning of a sentence. Proper nouns and names receive no special delineation. Sentences are delineated through the use of suprasegmental double slash mark at the end.

Distinctive Features

In addition to classifying phonemes into consonant and vowel categories, they can be classified by distinctive features. The purpose of a distinctive feature classification is to combine the articulatory and acoustic information in order to describe both vowels and consonants. Features are binary in nature meaning the feature is either present (+) or absent (–). Chomsky and Halle proposed the use of 17 features to describe phonemes.

These features include: vocalic, consonantal, high, back, low, anterior, coronal, round, tense, voice, continuant, nasal, strident, sonorant, interrupted, distributed and lateral. Features are best thought of as theortical and are not entirely useful in speech production process. It is important to note; however, the relationship between the IPA and distinctive features.

Distinctive Feature Summary Chart:

- *Vocalic:* A voiced phoneme produced with an open vocal tract. The phonemes that are (+) vocalic are the vowels, the approximant/ɹ/, and the lateral approximant/1/.
- *Consonant:* Phonemes produced with a constriction of the vocal tract. All consonants with the exception of the/h/are consonantal.

- *High:* Phonemes made with an elevated tongue position./ɔ/and/i/are (+) high.
- *Back:* Phonemes made with a retracted tongue position./T/and/g/are (+) back.
- *Low:* Phonemes produced with a low tcngue position./æ/and/h/are (+) low.
- *Anterior:* Phonemes produced when the point of constriction is anterior to the point of constriction for the/ʃ/,/1/, and/z/are (+) anterior.
- Coronal: Phonemes produced with the tongue blade in a raised position./è/and/t/are (+) coronal.
- *Round:* Phonemes produced with the lips in a rounded position./o/and/w/are (+) round.
- *Tense:* Phonemes produced with tension in the muscles./i/and/u/are (+) tense.
- *Voice:* Phonemes produced with vibration of the vocal folds./z/and/v/are (+) voice.
- *Continuant:* Phonemes produced in a steady state./è/ and/s/are (+) continuant.
- *Nasal:* Phonemes produced when air is emitted directly through the nasal cavity./n/and/m/are (+) nasal.
- *Strident:* Phonemes produced when air is forced through a small opening causing friction./f/and/v/are (+) strident.
- *Sonorant:* Phonemes produced when the airstream is unimpeded by any structure in the nasal or oral cavity./m/and/1/are (+) sonorant.
- *Interrupted:* Phonemes produced when the airstream is completely occluded at some point during the production./p/and/b/are (+) interrupted.
- *Distributed:* Phonemes produced when the constriction is extended through the vocal tract./è/ and/ʃ/are (+) distributed.
- *Lateral:* A phoneme produced when the air stream is emitted laterally. /1/is (+) lateral.

Phonology

The phone is the basic unit of phonology. This single

speech sound can take the form of either a phoneme (the target) or the allophone (individual variations of the target). Phonological rules for a particular language dictate both the phonemes and allophones used by the language and the acceptable syllable structures (phoneme/allophone combinations).

Basic patterns used in monosyllabic words are consonant—vowel (CV) as in the word *tea* [ti], vowel—consonant (VC) as in the word *at* [æt], consonant—vowel—consonant (CVC) as in the word *sin* [sIn], consonant—consonant—vowel—consonant (CCVC) as in the word *stop* [stap] and consonant—vowel—consonant—consonant (CVCC) in word *sand* [sænd]. The CVCC pattern is also commonly used to form plurals as in the word *tons* [tʌnz] and past tense as in the word *hopped* [hapt].

Phonetics And Phonology

Phonetics and phonology are strongly interrelated. Phonetics provides the speaker with the sound differentiation necessary to imply linguistic meaning, whereas phonology helps the speaker understand sound patterns, sequences, and coarticulatory interrelationships. Both of these areas are presented in more detail in the subsequent chapters.

General American Phonetics

Because the IPA is universal in nature and includes symbols and markings for sounds in numerous languages, it is best for the beginning student to focus on a limited version of the alphabet. The primary focus of this text is to introduce the student to General American Phonetics (GAP).

Although dialectal variations and various standards of pronunciations are present within the United States, GAP represents the speech patterns used by the media, businesses, and for instruction purposes. The understanding of GAP will provide basic information that can be enhanced with additional study of the IPA.

Review Questions

1. What problem is faced by a speaker who uses the

alphabet or the spelling of a word for pronunciation?
2. When was the IPA first used?
3. Who actually wrote the IPA?
4. When was the IPA last revised?
5. What are the five main sections of the IPA?
6. Define each of the following terms briefly.

Phonetics, orthography, phone, phoneme, allophone, morpheme, minimal pairs, cognate, homorganic, distinctive features, broad transcription, narrow transcription, General American Phonetics, syllable, word, monosyllabic word, bisyllabic word, multisyllabic word, vocal tract, voicing, phonology, phonological rules, coarticulation, and loanword.

1. What three aspects are used to delineate consonants?
2. List and define briefly the places of articulation.
3. List and define briefly the manners of articulation.
4. What determines the presence or absence of voicing?
5. List and define briefly the three dimensions used to define vowels.
6. What is vowel height and what are the four variations used by the IPA?
7. What is frontness and what are the three variations used by the IPA?
8. What is rounding and what are the two variations used by the IPA?
9. When are the other symbols or diacritics categories in transcription used?
10. What are suprasegmentals?
11. How are proper nouns, names, and sentences delineated in the IPA?
12. Distinctive features are binary in nature. What does this mean?
13. List and describe briefly the 17 distinctive features according to Chomsky and Halle.
14. What do the phonological rules dictate to the language?
15. What are the five basic phonological patterns found in monosyllabic words in GAP?
16. Are phonetics and phonology interrelated?

17. What do the initials GAP represent?

Exercises

1. Using the IPA chart as a reference, write 10 symbols that you are not familiar with and try to pronounce them using manner and place of articulation information.
2. Considering pronunciation, which of these words do not have direct sound to symbol correspondence? Psalm, though, hat, ballet, scare, pea, wrist, gnome, tomb, knight
3. List 20 words (not including those listed in Exercise 2) that do not have a direct sound to symbol correspondence.
4. Can you identify the number of sounds and the phonological patterns in the following words? (Remember to say the word aloud and ignore the spelling!)

run	vase
feed	bee
me	key
if	wheat
it	knee
eight	zoo
up	loot

5. At the library, find a phonetics textbook written prior to 1996. Using this text, compare the IPA and GAP symbols. Note changes.

Chapter 3

Phonetic Law

LANGUAGE AS A HISTORICAL PRODUCT

I have preferred to take up in some detail the analysis of our hesitation in using a locution like "Whom did you see?" and to point to some of the English drifts, particular and general, that are implied by this hesitation than to discuss linguistic change in the abstract. What is true of the particular idiom that we started with is true of everything else in language.

Nothing is perfectly static. Every word, every grammatical element, every locution, every sound and accent is a slowly changing configuration, molded by the invisible and impersonal drift that is the life of language. Every one knows that language is variable. Two individuals of the same generation and locality, speaking precisely the same dialect and moving in the same social circles, are never absolutely at one in their speech habits.

A minute investigation of the speech of each individual would reveal countless differences of detail—in choice of words, in sentence structure, in the relative frequency with which particular forms or combinations of words are used, in the pronunciation of particular vowels and consonants and of combinations of vowels and consonants, in all those features, such as speed, stress, and tone, that give life to spoken language. In a sense they speak slightly divergent dialects of the same language rather than identically the same language. There is an important difference, however, between individual and dialectic variations.

If we take two closely related dialects, say English as spoken by the "middle classes" of London and English as spoken by the average New Yorker, we observe that, however much the individual speakers in each city differ from each other, the body of Londoners forms a compact, relatively unified group in contrast to the body of New Yorkers. The individual variations are swamped in or absorbed by certain major agreements—say of pronunciation and vocabulary—which stand out very strongly when the language of the group as a whole is contrasted with that of the other group.

This means that there is something like an ideal linguistic entity dominating the speech habits of the members of each group, that the sense of almost unlimited freedom which each individual feels in the use of his language is held in leash by a tacitly directing norm. One individual plays on the norm in a way peculiar to himself, the next individual is nearer the dead average in that particular respect in which the first speaker most characteristically departs from it but in turn diverges from the average in a way peculiar to himself, and so on.

What keeps the individual's variations from rising to dialectic importance is not merely the fact that they are in any event of small moment—there are well-marked dialectic variations that are of no greater magnitude than individual variations within a dialect—it is chiefly that they are silently "corrected" or canceled by the consensus of usage. If all the speakers of a given dialect were arranged in order in accordance with the degree of their conformity to average usage, there is little doubt that they would constitute a very finely intergrading series clustered about a well-defined centre or norm. The evidence is overwhelming that this drift has a certain consistent direction.

Its speed varies enormously according to circumstances that it is not always easy to define. We have already seen that Lithuanian is to-day nearer its IndoEuropean prototype than was the hypothetical Germanic mother-tongue five hundred or a thousand years before Christ. German has moved more slowly than English; in some respects it stands roughly midway between English and Anglo-Saxon, in others it has of course diverged from the Anglo-Saxon line. When I pointed out that dialects formed because a language broken up into local segments could not move along the same drift in all of these segments, I meant of course that it could not move along identically the same drift.

The general drift of a language has its depths. At the surface the current is relatively fast. In certain features dialects drift apart rapidly. By that very fact these features betray themselves as less fundamental to the genius of the language than the more slowly modifiable features in which the dialects keep together long after they have grown to be mutually alien forms of speech.

But this is not all. The momentum of the more fundamental, the pre-dialectic, drift is often such that languages long disconnected will pass through the same or strikingly similar phases. In many such cases it is perfectly clear that there could have been no dialectic interinfluencing. These parallelisms in drift may operate in the phonetic as well as in the morphological sphere, or they may affect both at the same time. Here is an interesting example.

The English type of plural represented by *foot: feet, mouse: mice* is strictly parallel to the German *Fuss: Füsse, Maus: Müuse*. One would be inclined to surmise that these dialectic forms go back to old Germanic or West-Germanic alternations of the same type. But the documentary evidence shows conclusively that there could have been no plurals of this type in primitive Germanic. There is no trace of such vocalio mutation ("*umlaut*") in Gothic, our most archaic Germanic language.

More significant still is the fact that it does not appear in our oldest Old High German texts and begins to develop only at the very end of the Old High German period (circa 1000 A.D.). In the Middle High German period the mutation was carried through in all dialects. The typical Old High German forms are singular *fuoss*, plural *fuossi*; singular *mus*, plural *musi*. The corresponding Middle High German forms are *fuoss, füesse; mus, müse*.

Modern German *Fuss: Füsse, Maus: Müuse* are the regular developments of these medieval forms. Turning to Anglo-Saxon, we find that our modern English forms correspond to *fot, fet; mus, mys*. These forms are already in use in the earliest English monuments that we possess, dating from the eighth century, and thus antedate the Middle High German forms by three hundred years or more. In other words, on this particular point it took German at least three hundred years to catch up with a phoneticmorphological drift that had long been under way in English.

The mere fact that the affected vowels of related words (Old High German *uo*, Anglo-Saxon *o*) are not always the same shows that the affection took place at different periods in German and English. There was evidently some general tendency or group of tendencies at work in early Germanic, long before English and German had developed as such, that eventually drove both of these dialects along closely parallel paths. How did such strikingly individual alternations as *fot: fet, fuoss: füesse* develop? We have now reached what is probably the most central problem in linguistic history, gradual phonetic change. "Phonetic laws" make up a large and fundamental share of the subjectmatter of linguistics. Their influence reaches far beyond the proper sphere of phonetics and invades that of morphology, as we shall see. A drift that begins as a slight phonetic readjustment or unsettlement may in the course of millennia bring about the most profound structural changes.

The mere fact, for instance, that there is a growing tendency to·throw the stress automatically on the first syllable of a word may eventually change the fundamental type of the language, reducing its final syllables to zero and driving it to the use of more and more analytical or symbolic methods. The English phonetic laws involved in the rise of the words *foot, feet, mouse* and *mice* from their early West-Germanic prototypes *fot, foti, mus, musi* may be briefly summarized as follows:

1. In *foti* "feet" the long o was coloured by the following i to long ö, that is, o kept its lip-rounded quality and

its middle height of tongue position but anticipated the front tongue position of the i; ö is the resulting compromise. This assimilatory change was regular, i.e., every accented long o followed by an i in the following syllable automatically developed to long ö; hence *tothi* "teeth" became *töthi, fodian* "to feed" became *födian*. At first there is no doubt the alternation between o and ö was not felt as intrinsically significant. It could only have been an unconscious mechanical adjustment such as may be observed in the speech of many today who modify the "oo" sound of words like *you* and *few* in the direction of German *ü* without, however, actually departing far enough from the "oo" vowel to prevent their acceptance of *who* and *you* as satisfactory rhyming words. Later on the quality of the ö vowel must have departed widely enough from that of o to enable ö to rise in consciousness as a neatly distinct vowel. As soon as this happened, the expression of plurality in *föti, töthi,* and analogous words became symbolic and fusional, not merely fusional.

2. In *musi* "mice" the long u was coloured by the following i to long *ü*. This change also was regular; *lusi* "lice" became *lüsi, kui* "cows" became *küi* (later simplified to *kü*; still preserved as *ki-* in *kine*), fulian "to make foul" became *fülian* (still preserved as *-file* in *defile*). The psychology of this phonetic law is entirely analogous to that of 1.
3. The old drift toward reducing final syllables, a rhythmic consequence of the strong Germanic stress on the first syllable, now manifested itself. The final -i, originally an important functional element, had long lost a great share of its value, transferred as that was to the symbolic vowel change (*o: ö*). It had little power of resistance, therefore, to the drift. It became dulled to a colourless *-e; föti* became *föte*.
4. The weak -e finally disappeared. Probably the forms *föte* and *föt* long coexisted as prosodic variants

according to the rhythmic requirements of the sentence, very much as *Füsse* and *Füss'* now coexist in German.

5. The ö of *föt* became "unrounded" to long e (our present a of *fade*). The alternation of fot: foti, transitionally *fot: föti, föte, föt*, now appears as *fot: fet*. Analogously, *töth* appears as *teth, födian* as *fedian*, later *fedan*. The new long e-vowel "fell together" with the older e-vowel already existent (e.g., *her* "here," *he* "he"). Henceforward the two are merged and their later history is in common. Thus our present *he* has the same vowel as *feet, teeth,* and *feed*. In other words, the old sound pattern *o, e,* after an interim of *o, ö, e,* reappeared as *o, e,* except that now the e had greater "weight" than before.
6. *Fot: fet, mus: müs* (written *mys*) are the typical forms of Anglo-Saxon literature. At the very end of the Anglo-Saxon period, say about 1050 to 1100 A.D., the *ü*, whether long or short, became unrounded to i. *Mys* was then pronounced *mis* with long i (rhyming with present niece). The change is analogous to 5, but takes place several centuries later.
7. In Chaucer's day (circa 1350-1400 A.D.) the forms were still *fot: fet* (written *foot, feet*) and *mus: mis* (written very variably, but *mous, myse* are typical). About 1500 all the long i-vowels, whether original (as in *write, ride, wine*) or unrounded from Anglo-Saxon *ü* (as in *hide, bride, mice, defile*), became diphthongized to ei (i.e., e of *met* + short i). Shakespeare pronounced *mice* as *meis* (almost the same as the present Cockney pronunciation of *mace*).
8. About the same time the long u- vowels were diphthongized to *ou* (i.e., o of present Scotch *not* + u of *full*). The Chaucerian *mus: mis* now appears as the Shakespearean *mous: meis*. This change may have manifested itself somewhat later than 7; all English dialects have diphthongized old Germanic long i, but the long undiphthongized u is still preserved in

Lowland Scotch, in which *house* and *mouse* rhyme with our *loose*. 7 and 8 are analogous developments, as were 5 and 6; 8 apparently lags behind 7 as 6, centuries earlier, lagged behind 7.

9. Some time before 1550 the long *e* of *fet* (written feet) took the position that had been vacated by the old long *i*, now diphthongized, i.e., *e* took the higher tongue position of *i*. Our (and Shakespeare's) "long *e*" is, then, phonetically the same as the old long *i*. *Feet* now rhymed with the old write and the present *beat*.
10. About the same time the long *o* of *fot* (written *foot*) took the position that had been vacated by the old long *u*, now diphthongized (see 8), i.e., *o* took the higher tongue position of *u*. Our (and Shakespeare's) "long *oo*" is phonetically the same as the old long *u*. *Foot* now rhymed with the old *out* and the present *boot*. To summarize 7 to 10, Shakespeare pronounced *meis, mous, fit, fut,* of which *meis* and *mous* would affect our ears as a rather "mincing" rendering of our present *mice* and *mouse*, *fit* would sound practically identical with (but probably a bit more "drawled" than) our present *feet*, while *foot*, rhyming with *boot*, would now be set down as "broad Scotch."
11. Gradually the first vowel of the diphthong in mice (see 7) was retracted and lowered in position The resulting diphthong now varies in different English dialects, but *ai* (i.e., *a* of *father*, but shorter, + short *i*) may be taken as a fairly accurate rendering of its average quality. What we now call the "long *i*" (of words like *ride, bite, mice*) is, of course, an *ai*-diphthong. *Mice* is now pronounced *mais*.
12. Analogously to 11, the first vowel of the diphthong in *mouse* (see 8) was unrounded and lowered in position. The resulting diphthong may be phonetically rendered *au*, though it too varies considerably according to dialect. *Mouse*, then, is now pronounced *maus*.

13. The vowel of *foot* (see 10) became "open" in quality and shorter in quantity, i.e., it fell together with the old short *u*-vowel of words like *full, wolf, wool*. This change has taken place in a number of words with an originally long *u* (Chaucerian long close *o*), such as *forsook, hook, book, look, rook, shook*, all of which formerly had the vowel of *boot*. The older vowel, however, is still preserved in most words of this class, such as *fool, moon, spool, stoop*. It is highly significant of the nature of the slow spread of a "phonetic law" that there is local vacillation at present in several words. One hears *roof, soot, and hoop*, for instance, both with the "long" vowel of *boot* and the "short" of *foot*. It is impossible now, in other words, to state in a definitive manner what is the "phonetic law" that regulated the change of the older *foot* (rhyming with *boot*) to the present *foot*.

We know that there is a strong drift towards the short, open vowel of *foot*, but whether or not all the old "long *oo*" words will eventually be affected we cannot presume to say. If they all, or practically all, are taken by the drift, phonetic law 13 will be as "regular," as sweeping, as most of the twelve that have preceded it.

If not, it may eventually be possible, if past experience is a safe guide, to show that the modified words form a natural phonetic group, that is, that the "law" will have operated under certain definable limiting conditions, e.g., that all words ending in a voiceless consonant (such as *p, t, k, f*) were affected (e.g., *hoof, foot, look, roof*), but that all words ending in the *oo*-vowel or in a voiced consonant remained unaffected (e.g., *do, food, move, fool*).

Whatever the upshot, we may be reasonably certain that when the "phonetic law" has run its course, the distribution of "long" and "short" vowels in the old *oo*-words will not seem quite as erratic as at the present transitional moment. We learn, incidentally, the fundamental fact that phonetic laws do not work with spontaneous automatism, that they are simply a formula for a consummated drift that sets in at a psychologically exposed point and gradually worms its way through a gamut of phonetically analogous forms.

It will be instructive to set down a table of form sequences, a kind of gross history of the words *foot, feet, mouse, mice* for the last 1500 years:

- *Fot: foti; mus*: musi (West Germanic),
- *Fot: föti; mus*: müsi
- *Fot: föte; mus*: müse
- *Fot: föt; mus*: müs
- *Fot: fet; mus*: müs (Anglo-Saxon)
- *Fot: fet; mus*: mis (Chaucer)
- *Fot: fet; mous*: meis
- *Fut (rhymes with boot): fit; mous*: meis (Shakespeare)
- *Fut*: fit; maus: mais
- *Fut (rhymes with put)*: fit; maus: mais (English of 1900)

It will not be necessary to list the phonetic laws that gradually differentiated the modern German equivalents of the original West Germanic forms from their English cognates.

The following table gives a rough idea of the form sequences in German:

- *Fot*: foti; mus: musi (West Germanic)
- *Foss*: fossi; mus: musi
- *Fuoss*: fuossi; mus: musi (Old High German)
- *Fuoss*: füessi; mus: müsi
- *Fuoss*: füesse; mus: müse (Middle High German)
- *Fuos*: füesse; mus: müze
- *Fuos*: füesse; mus: müze
- *Fuos*: füesse; mous: möüze
- *Fus*: füse; mous: möüze (Luther)
- *Fus*: füse; mous: moize (German of 1900)

We cannot even begin to ferret out and discuss all the psychologocal problems that ar concealed behind these bland tables. Their general parallelism is obvious. Indeed we might say that to-day the English and German forms resemble aech other more than does either set the West Germanic prototypes from which each is independently derived.

Each point illustrates the tendency to reduction of unaccented syllables, the vocalic modification of the radical element under the influence of the following vowel, the rise in tongue position of the long middle vowels (English *o* to *u*, *e* to *i*; German *o* to *uo* to *u*, *üe* to*ü*), the diphthongizing of the old high vowels (English *i* to *ei* to *ai*; English and German *u* to *ou* to *au*; German*ü* to *öü* to *oi*). These dialectic parallels cannot be accidental. They are rooted in a common, pre-dialectic drift.

Phonetic changes are "regular." All but one, and that as yet uncompleted, of the particular phonetic laws represented in our tables affect all examples of the sound in question or, if the phonetic change is conditional, all examples of the same sound that are analogously circumstanced. An example of the first type of change is the passage in English of all old long *i*-vowels to diphthongal *ai via ei*. The passage could hardly have been sudden or automatic, but it was rapid enough to prevent an irregularity of development due to cross drifts.

The second type of change is illustrated in the development of Anglo-Saxon long *o* to long *e*, via *ö*, under the influence of a following *i*. In the first case we may say that *au* mechanically replaced long *u*, in the second that the old long *o* "split" into two sounds—long *o*, eventually *u*, and long *e*, eventually *i*. The former type of change did no violence to the old phonetic pattern, the formal distribution of sounds into groups; the latter type rearranged the pattern somewhat.

If neither of the two sounds into which an old one "splits" is a new sound, it means that there has been a phonetic leveling, that two groups of words, each with a distinct sound or sound combination, have fallen together into one group. This kind of leveling is quite frequent in the history of language. In English, for instance, we have seen that all the old long *ü*-vowels, after they had become unrounded, were indistinguishable from the mass of long *i*-vowels. This meant that the long *i*-vowel became a more heavily weighted point of the phonetic pattern than before.

It is curious to observe how often languages have striven to drive originally distinct sounds into certain favourite positions, regardless of resulting confusions. In Modern Greek, for instance, the vowel *i* is the historical resultant of no less than ten etymologically distinct vowels (long and short) and diphthongs of the classical speech of Athens. There is, then, good evidence to show that there are general phonetic drifts toward particular sounds.

More often the phonetic drift is of a more general character. It is not so much a movement toward a particular set of sounds as toward particular types of articulation. The vowels tend to become higher or lower, the diphthongs tend to coalesce into monophthongs, the voiceless consonants tend to become voiced, stops tend to become spirants. As a matter of fact, practically all the phonetic laws enumerated in the two tables are but specific instances of such far-reaching phonetic drifts.

The raising of English long *o* to *u* and of long *e* to *i*, for instance, was part of a general tendency to raise the position of the long vowels, just as the change of *t* to *ss* in Old High German was part of a general tendency to make voiceless spirants of the old voiceless stopped consonants. A single sound change, even if there is no phonetic leveling, generally threatens to upset the old phonetic pattern because it brings about a disharmony in the grouping of sounds. To reestablish the old pattern without going back on the drift the only possible method is to have the other sounds of the series shift in analogous fashion.

If, for some reason or other, *p* becomes shifted to its voiced correspondent *b*, the old series *p, t, k* appears in the unsymmetrical form *b, t, k*. Such a series is, in phonetic effect, not the equivalent of the old series, however it may answer to it in etymology. The general phonetic pattern is impaired to that extent. But if *t* and *k* are also shifted to their voiced correspondents *d* and *g*, the old series is reestablished in a new form: *b, d, g*. The pattern as such is preserved, or restored. Provided that the new series *b, d, g* does not become confused with an old series *b, d, g* of distinct historical antecedents. If there is no such older series, the creation of a *b, d, g* series causes no difficulties. If there is, the old patterning of sounds can be kept intact only by shifting the old *b, d, g* sounds in some way.

They may become aspirated to *bh, dh, gh* or spirantized or nasalized or they may develop any other peculiarity that keeps them intact as a series and serves to differentiate them from other series. And this sort of shifting about without loss of pattern, or with a minimum loss of it, is probably the most important tendency in the history of speech sounds. Phonetic leveling and "splitting" counteract it to some extent but, on the whole, it remains the central unconscious regulator of the course and speed of sound changes.

The desire to hold on to a pattern, the tendency to "correct" a disturbance by an elaborate chain of supplementary changes, often spread over centuries or even millennia—these psychic undercurrents of language are exceedingly difficult to understand in terms of individual psychology, though there can be no denial of their historical reality.

What is the primary cause of the unsettling of a phonetic pattern and what is the cumulative force that selects these or those particular variations of the individual on which to float the pattern readjustments we hardly know. Many linguistic students have made the fatal error of thinking of sound change as a quasi-physiological instead of as a strictly psychological phenomenon, or they have tried to dispose of the problem by bandying such catchwords as "the tendency to increased ease of articulation" or "the cumulative result of faulty perception" (on the part of children, say, in learning to speak). These easy explanations will not do.

"Ease of articulation" may enter in as a factor, but it is a rather subjective concept at best. Indians find hopelessly difficult sounds and sound combinations that are simple to us; one language encourages a phonetic drift that another does everything to fight. "Faulty perception" does not explain that impressive drift in speech sounds which I have insisted upon. It is much better to admit that we do not yet understand the primary cause or causes of the slow drift in phonetics, though we can frequently point to contributing factors.

It is likely that we shall not advance seriously until we study the intuitional bases of speech. How can we understand the nature of the drift that frays and reforms phonetic patterns when we have never thought of studying sound patterning as such and the "weights" and psychic relations of the single elements (the individual sounds) in these patterns?

Every linguist knows that phonetic change is frequently followed by morphological rearrangements, but he is apt to assume that morphology exercises little or no influence on the course of phonetic history. I am inclined to believe that our present tendency to isolate phonetics and grammar as mutually irrelevant linguistic provinces is unfortunate.

There are likely to be fundamental relations between them and their respective histories that we do not yet fully grasp. After all, if speech sounds exist merely because they are the symbolic carriers of significant concepts and groupings of concepts, why may not a strong drift or a permanent feature in the conceptual sphere exercise a furthering or retarding influence on the phonetic drift? I believe that such influences may be demonstrated and that they deserve far more careful study than they have received.

This brings us back to our unanswered question: How is it that both English and German developed the curious alternation of unmodified vowel in the singular (*foot, Fuss*) and modified vowel in the plural (*feet, Fusse*)? Was the pre-Anglo-Saxon alternation of *fot* and *foti* an absolutely mechanical matter, without other than incidental morphological interest? It is always so represented, and, indeed, all the external facts support such a view. The change from *o* to *ö,* later *e,* is by no means peculiar to the plural. It is found also in the dative singular (*fet*), for it too goes back to an older *foti.* Moreover, *fet* of the plural applies only to the nominative and accusative; the genitive has *fota,* the dative fotum. Only centuries later was the alternation of *o* and *e* reinterpreted as a means of distinguishing number; *o* was generalized for the singular, *e* for the plural. Only when this reassortment of forms took place was the modern symbolic value of the *foot: feet* alternation clearly established. Again, we must not forget that *o* was modified to *ö (e)* in all manner of other grammatical and derivative formations.

Thus, a preAnglo-Saxon *hohan* (later *hon*) "to hang" corresponded to a *höhith, hehith* (later *hehth*) "hangs"; to *dom* "doom," *blod* "blood," and *fod* "food" corresponded the verbal derivatives *dömian* (later *deman*) "to deem," *blödian* (later *bledan*) "to bleed," and *födian* (later *fedan*) "to feed." All this seems to point to the purely mechanical nature of the modification of *o* to *ö* to *e*. So many unrelated functions were ultimately served by the vocalic change that we cannot believe that it was motivated by any one of them.

The German facts are entirely analogous. Only later in the history of the language was the vocalic alternation made significant for number. And yet consider the following facts. The change of *foti* to *föti* antedated that of *föti* to *föte, föt*. This may be looked upon as a "lucky accident," for if *foti* had become *fote, fot* before the *-i* had had the chance to exert a retroactive influence on the o, there would have been no difference between the singular and the plural. This would have been anomalous in Anglo-Saxon for a masculine noun.

But was the sequence of phonetic changes an "accident"? Consider two further facts. All the Germanic languages were familiar with vocalic change as possessed of functional significance. Alternations like *sing, sang, sung* (Anglo-Saxon *singan, sang, sungen*) were ingrained in the linguistic consciousness.

Further, the tendency toward the weakening of final syllables was very strong even then and had been manifesting itself in one way and another for centuries. I believe that these further facts help us to understand the actual sequence of phonetic changes. We may go so far as to say that the *o* (and *u*) could afford to stay the change to *ö* (and*ü*) until the destructive drift had advanced to the point where failure to modify the vowel would soon result in morphological embarrassment.

At a certain moment the -i ending of the plural (and analogous endings with i in other formations) was felt to be too weak to quite bear its functional burden. The unconscious Anglo-Saxon mind, if I may be allowed a somewhat summary way of putting the complex facts, was glad of the opportunity afforded by certain individual variations, until then automatically canceled out, to have some share of the burden thrown on them. These particular variations won through because they so beautifully allowed the general phonetic drift to take its course without unsettling the morphological contours of the language. And the presence of symbolic variation (*sing, sang, sung*) acted as an attracting force on the rise of a new variation of similar character. All these factors were equally true of the German vocalic shift.

Owing to the fact that the destructive phonetic drift was proceeding at a slower rate in German than in English, the preservative change of *uo* to *üe* (u to*ü*) did not need to set in until 300 years or more after the analogous English change. Nor did it. And this is to my mind a highly significant fact.

Phonetic changes may sometimes be unconsciously encouraged in order to keep intact the psychological spaces between words and word forms. The general drift seizes upon those individual sound variations that help to preserve the morphological balance or to lead to the new balance that the language is striving for.

I would suggest, then, that phonetic change is compacted of at least three basic strands:

1. A general drift in one direction, concerning the nature of which we know almost nothing but which may be suspected to be of prevailingly dynamic character (tendencies, e.g., to greater or less stress, greater or less voicing of elements);
2. A readjusting tendency which aims to preserve or restore the fundamental phonetic pattern of the language;
3. A preservative tendency which sets in when a too serious morphological unsettlement is threatened by the main drift. I do not imagine for a moment that it is always possible to separate these strands or that this purely schematic statement does justice to the complex forces that guide the phonetic drift.

The phonetic pattern of a language is not invariable, but it changes far less readily than the sounds that compose it.

Every phonetic element that it possesses may change radically and yet the pattern remain unaffected. It would be absurd to claim that our present English pattern is identical with the old Indo-European one, yet it is impressive to note that even at this late day the English series of initial consonants:

p t k
b d g
f th h

Corresponds point for point to the Sanskrit series:

b d g
bh dh gh
p t k

The relation between phonetic pattern and individual sound is roughly parallel to that which obtains between the morphologic type of a language and one of its specific morphological features. Both phonetic pattern and fundamental type are exceedingly conservative, all superficial appearances to the contrary notwithstanding. Which is more so we cannot say? I suspect that they hang together in a way that we cannot at present quite understand.

If all the phonetic changes brought about by the phonetic drift were allowed to stand, it is probable that most languages would present such irregularities of morphological contour as to lose touch with their formal ground-plan. Sound changes work mechanically. Hence they are likely to affect a whole morphological group here—this does not matter—, only part of a morphological group there—and this may be disturbing. Thus, the old Anglo-Saxon paradigm:

	Sing.	Plur.
N. Ac.	fot	fet (older foti)
G.	fotes	fota
D.	fet (older foti)	fotum

The o—e alternation was welcome in so far as it roughly distinguished the singular from the plural. The dative singular *fet,* however, though justified historically, was soon felt to be an intrusive feature. The analogy of simpler and more numerously represented paradigms created the form *fote* (compare, e.g., *fisc* "fish," dative singular *fisce*). *Fet* as a dative becomes obsolete. The singular now had o throughout.

But this very fact made the genitive and dative o-forms of the plural seem out of place. The nominative and accusative *fet* was naturally far more frequently in use than were the corresponding forms of the genitive and dative. These, in the end, could not but follow the analogy of *fet*. At the very beginning of the Middle English period, therefore, we find that the old paradigm has yielded to a more regular one:

	Sing.	**Plur.**
N. Ac.	*fot	*fet
G.	*fotes	fete
D.	fote	feten

The starred forms are the old nucleus around which the new paradigm is built. The unstarred forms are not genealogical kin of their formal prototypes. They are analogical replacements.

The history of the English language teems with such levelings or extensions. *Elder* and *eldest* were at one time the only possible comparative and superlative forms of *old* (compare German *alt, älter, der älteste*; the vowel following the *old-, alt-* was originally an i, which modified the quality of the stem vowel).

The general analogy of the vast majority of English adjectives, however, has caused the replacement of the forms *elder* and *eldest* by the forms with unmodified vowel, *older* and *oldest*. *Elder* and *eldest* survive only as somewhat archaic terms for the older and oldest brother or sister.

This illustrates the tendency for words that are psychologically disconnected from their etymological or formal group to preserve traces of phonetic laws that have otherwise left no recognizable trace or to preserve a vestige of a morphological process that has long lost its vitality. A careful study of these survivals or atrophied forms is not without value for the reconstruction of the earlier history of a language or for suggestive hints as to its remoter affiliations.

Analogy may not only refashion forms within the

confines of a related cluster of forms (a "paradigm") but may extend its influence far beyond. Of a number of functionally equivalent elements, for instance, only one may survive, the rest yielding to its constantly widening influence. This is what happened with the English -s plural. Originally confined to a particular class of masculines, though an important class, the -s plural was gradually generalized for all nouns but a mere handful that still illustrate plural types now all but extinct (*foot: feet, goose: geese, tooth: teeth, mouse: mice, louse: lice; ox: oxen; child: children; sheep: sheep, deer; deer*).

Thus analogy not only regularizes irregularities that have come in the wake of phonetic processes but introduces disturbances, generally in favour of greater simplicity or regularity, in a long established system of forms. These analogical adjustments are practically always symptoms of the general morphological drift of the language.

A morphological feature that appears as the incidental consequence of a phonetic process, like the English plural with modified vowel, may spread by analogy no less readily than old features that owe their origin to other than phonetic causes. Once the e-vowel of Middle English *fet* had become confined to the plural, there was no theoretical reason why alternations of the type *fot: fet* and *mus: mis* might not have become established as a productive type of number distinction in the noun. As a matter of fact, it did not so become established. The *for: fet* type of plural secured but a momentary foothold.

It was swept into being by one of the surface drifts of the language, to be swept aside in the Middle English period by the more powerful drift toward the use of simple distinctive forms. It was too late in the day for our language to be seriously interested in such pretty symbolisms as *foot: feet*. What examples of the type arose legitimately, in other words *via* purely phonetic processes, were tolerated for a time, but the type as such never had a serious future.

It was different in German. The whole series of phonetic changes comprised under the term "umlaut," of which *u:ü* and *au: oi* (written *äu*) are but specific examples, struck the

German language at a time when the general drift to morphological simplification was not so strong but that the resulting formal types (e.g., *Fuss: Füsse; fallen* "to fall": *fällen* "to fell"; *Horn* "horn":

Gehörne "group of horns"; *Haus* "house": *Häuslein* "little house") could keep themselves intact and even extend to forms that did not legitimately come within their sphere of influence. "*Umlaut*" is still a very live symbolic process in German, possibly more alive to-day than in medieval times.

Such analogical plurals as *Baum* "tree": *Bäume* (contrast Middle High German *boum*: *boume*) and derivatives as *lachen* "to laugh": *Gelächter* "laughter" (contrast Middle High German *gelach*) show that vocalic mutation has won through to the status of a productive morphologic process.

Some of the dialects have even gone further than standard German, at least in certain respects. In Yiddish, for instance, "umlaut" plurals have been formed where there are no Middle High German prototypes or modern literary parallels, e.g., *tog* "day": *teg* "days" (but German *Tag*: *Tage*) on the analogy of *gast* "guest": *gest* "guests" (German *Gast: Gäste*), *shuch* "shoe": *shich* "shoes" (but German *Schuh: Schuhe*) on the analogy of *fus* "foot": *fis* "feet." It is possible that "umlaut" will run its course and cease to operate as a live functional process in German, but that time is still distant.

Meanwhile all consciousness of the merely phonetic nature of "*umlaut*" vanished centuries ago. It is now a strictly morphological process, not in the least a mechanical phonetic adjustment. We have in it a splendid example of how a simple phonetic law, meaningless in itself, may eventually colour or transform large reaches of the morphology of a language.

The differences between any two neighbouring speakers of the series would be negligible for any but the most microscopic linguistic research. The differences between the outermost members of the series are sure to be considerable, in all likelihood considerable enough to measure up to a true dialectic variation.

What prevents us from saying that these untypical individuals speak distinct dialects is that their peculiarities, as a unified whole, aren't referable to another norm than the norm of their own series. If the speech of any member of the series could actually be made to fit into another dialect series, we should have no true barriers between dialects (and languages) at all.

We should merely have a continuous series of individual variations extending over the whole range of a historically unified linguistic area, and the cutting up of this large area (in some cases embracing parts of several continents) into distinct dialects and languages would be an essentially arbitrary proceeding with no warrant save that of practical convenience. But such a conception of the nature of dialectic variation does not correspond to the facts as we know them.

Isolated individuals may be found who speak a compromise between two dialects of a language, and if their number and importance increases they may even end by creating a new dialectic norm of their own, a dialect in which the extreme peculiarities of the parent dialects are ironed out. In course of time the compromise dialect may absorb the parents, though more frequently these will tend to linger indefinitely as marginal forms of the enlarged dialect area.

Chapter 4

Sounds of Language

INNER FACT OF LANGUAGE

We have seen that the mere phonetic framework of speech does not constitute the inner fact of language and that the single sound of articulated speech is not, as such, a linguistic element at all. For all that, speech is so inevitably bound up with sounds and their articulation that we can hardly avoid giving the subject of phonetics some general consideration. Experience has shown that neither the purely formal aspects of a language nor the course of its history can be fully understood without reference to the sounds in which this form and this history are embodied.

A detailed survey of phonetics would be both too technical for the general reader and too loosely related to our main theme to warrant the needed space, but we can well afford to consider a few outstanding facts and ideas connected with the sounds of language.

The feeling that the average speaker has of his language is that it is built up, acoustically speaking, of a comparatively small number of distinct sounds, each of which is rather accurately provided for in the current alphabet by one letter or, in a few cases, by two or more alternative letters.

As for the languages of foreigners, he generally feels that, aside from a few striking differences that cannot escape even the uncritical ear, the sounds they use are the same as those he is familiar with but that there is a mysterious "accent" to these foreign languages, a certain unanalysed phonetic character, apart from the sounds as such, that gives them their air of strangeness. This naive feeling is largely illusory on both scores. Phonetic analysis convinces one that the number of clearly distinguishable sounds and nuances of sounds that are habitually employed by the speakers of a language is far greater than they themselves recognize. Probably not one English speaker out of a hundred has the remotest idea that the t of a word like *sting* is not at all the same sound as the *t* of *teem*, the latter *t* having a fullness of "breath release" that is inhibited in the former case by the preceding s; that the *ea* of *meat* is of perceptibly shorter duration than the *ea* of *mead*; or that the final s of a word like *heads* is not the full, buzzing z sound of the s in such a word as *please*.

It is the frequent failure of foreigners, who have acquired a practical mastery of English and who have eliminated all the cruder phonetic shortcomings of their less careful brethren, to observe such minor distinctions that helps to give their English pronunciation the curiously elusive "accent" that we all vaguely feel. We do not diagnose the "accent" as the total acoustic effect produced by a series of slight but specific phonetic errors for the very good reason that we have never made clear to ourselves our own phonetic stock in trade.

If two languages taken at random, say English and Russian, are compared as to their phonetic systems, we are more apt than not to find that very few of the phonetic elements of the one find an exact analogue in the other. Thus, the t of a Russian word like *tam* "there" is neither the English *t* of *sting* nor the English *t* of *teem*.

It differs from both in its "dental" articulation, in other words, in being produced by contact of the tip of the tongue with the upper teeth, not, as in English, by contact of the tongue back of the tip with the gum ridge above the teeth; moreover, it differs from the *t* of *teem* also in the absence of a marked "breath release" before the following vowel is attached, so that its acoustic effect is of a more precise, "metallic" nature than in English.

Again, the English *l* is unknown in Russian, which possesses, on the other hand, two distinct *l*-sounds that the normal English speaker would find it difficult exactly to reproduce a "hollow," guttural-like *l* and a "soft," palatalized *l*-sound that is only very approximately rendered, in English terms, as *ly*. Even so simple and, one would imagine, so invariable a sound as *m* differs in the two languages. In a Russian word like *most* "bridge" the *m* is not the same as the *m* of the English word *most*; the lips are more fully rounded during its articulation, so that it makes a heavier, more resonant impression on the ear.

The vowels, needless to say, differ completely in English and Russian, hardly any two of them being quite the same. I have gone into these illustrative details, which are of little or no specific interest for us, merely in order to provide something of an experimental basis to convince ourselves of the tremendous variability of speech sounds. Yet a complete inventory of the acoustic resources of all the European languages, the languages nearer home, while unexpectedly large, would still fall far short of conveying a just idea of the true range of human articulation.

In many of the languages of Asia, Africa, and aboriginal America there are whole classes of sounds that most of us have no knowledge of. They are not necessarily more difficult of enunciation than sounds more familiar to our ears; they merely involve such muscular adjustments of the organs of speech as we have never habituated ourselves to. It may be safely said that the total number of possible sounds is greatly in excess of those actually in use.

Indeed, an experienced phonetician should have no difficulty in inventing sounds that are unknown to objective investigation. One reason why we find it difficult to believe that the range of possible speech sounds is indefinitely large is our habit of conceiving the sound as a simple, unanalyzable impression instead of as the resultant of a number of distinct muscular adjustments that take place simultaneously.

A slight change in any one of these adjustments gives us a new sound which is akin to the old one, because of the continuance of the other adjustments, but which is acoustically distinct from it, so sensitive has the human ear become to the nuanced play of the vocal mechanism. Another reason for our lack of phonetic imagination is the fact that, while our ear is delicately responsive to the sounds of speech, the muscles of our speech organs have early in life become exclusively accustomed to the particular adjustments and systems of adjustment that are required to produce the traditional sounds of the language.

All or nearly all other adjustments have become permanently inhibited, whether through inexperience or through gradual elimination. Of course the power to produce these inhibited adjustments is not entirely lost, but the extreme difficulty we experience in learning the new sounds of foreign languages is sufficient evidence of the strange rigidity that has set in for most people in the voluntary control of the speech organs.

The point may be brought home by contrasting the comparative lack of freedom of voluntary speech movements with the all but perfect freedom of voluntary gesture. Our rigidity in articulation is the price we have had to pay for easy mastery of a highly necessary symbolism. One cannot be both splendidly free in the random choice of movements and selective with deadly certainty.

There are, then, an indefinitely large number of articulated sounds available for the mechanics of speech; any given language makes use of an explicit, rigidly economieal selection of these rich resources; and each of the many possible sounds of speech is conditioned by a number of independent muscular adjustments that work together simultaneously towards its production.

A full account of the activity of each of the organs of speech—in so far as its activity has a bearing on language—is impossible here, nor can we concern ourselves in a systematic way with the elassification of sounds on the basis of their mechanics.

A few bold outlines are all that we can attempt. The organs of speech are the lungs and bronchial tubes; the throat, particularly that part of it which is known as the larynx or, in popular parlance, the "Adam's apple"; the nose; the uvula, which is the soft, pointed, and easily movable organ that depends from the rear of the palate; the palate, which is divided into a posterior, movable "soft palate" or velum and a "hard palate"; the tongue; the teeth; and the lips.

The palate, lower palate, tongue, teeth, and lips may be looked upon as a combined resonance chamber, whose constantly varying shape, chiefly due to the extreme mobility of the tongue, is the main factor in giving the outgoing breath its precise quality of sound. The lungs and bronchial tubes are organs of speech only in so far as they supply and conduct the current of outgoing air without which audible articulation is impossible.

They are not responsible for any specific sound or acoustic feature of sounds except, possibly, accent or stress. It may be that differences of stress are due to slight differences in the contracting force of the lung muscles, but even this influence of the lungs is denied by some students, who explain the fluctuations of stress that do so much to colour speech by reference to the more delicate activity of the glottal cords.

These glottal cords are two small, nearly horizontal, and highly sensitive membranes within the larynx, which consists, for the most part, of two large and several smaller cartilages and of a number of small muscles that control the action of the cords. The cords, which are attached to the cartilages, are to the human speech organs what the two vibrating reeds are to a clarinet or the strings to a violin.

They are capable of at least three distinct types of movement, each of which is of the greatest importance for speech. They may be drawn towards or away from each other, they may vibrate like reeds or strings, and they may become lax or tense in the direction of their length. The last class of these movements allows the cords to vibrate at different "lengths" or degrees of tenseness and is responsible for the variations in pitch which are present not only in song but in the more elusive modulations of ordinary speech.

The two other types of glottal action determine the nature of the voice, "voice" being a convenient term for breath as utilized in speech. If the cords are well apart, allowing the breath to escape in unmodified form, we have the condition technically known as "voicelessness." All sounds produced under these circumstances are "voiceless" sounds.

Such are the simple, unmodified breath as it passes into the mouth, which is, at least approximately, the same as the sound that we write *h*, also a large number of special articulations in the mouth chamber, like *p* and *s*. On the other hand, the glottal cords may be brought tight together, without vibrating. When this happens, the current of breath is checked for the time being. The slight choke or "arrested cough" that is thus made audible is not recognized in English as a definite sound but occurs nevertheless not infrequently.

This momentary check, technically known as a "glottal stop," is an integral element of speech in many languages, as Danish, Lettish, certain Chinese dialects, and nearly all American Indian languages. Between the two extremes of voicelessness, that of completely open breath and that of checked breath, lies the position of true voice. In this position the cords are close together, but not so tightly as to prevent the air from streaming through; the cords are set vibrating and a musical tone of varying pitch results.

A tone so produced is known as a "voiced sound." It may have an indefinite number of qualities according to the precise position of the upper organs of speech. Our vowels, nasals (such as *m* and *n*), and such sounds as *b*, *z*, and l are all voiced sounds. The most convenient test of a voiced sound is the possibility of pronouncing it on any given pitch, in other words, of singing on it. The voiced sounds are the most clearly audible elements of speech.

As such they are the carriers of practically all significant differences in stress, pitch, and syllabification. The voiceless sounds are articulated noises that break up the stream of voice with fleeting moments of silence. Acoustically intermediate between the freely unvoiced and the voiced sounds are a number of other characteristic types of voicing, such as murmuring and whisper. These and still other types of voice are relatively unimportant in English and most other European languages, but there are languages in which they rise to some prominence in the normal flow of speech.

The nose is not an active organ of speech, but it is highly important as a resonance chamber. It may be disconnected from the mouth, which is the other great resonance chamber, by the lifting of the movable part of the soft palate so as to shut off the passage of the breath into the nasal cavity; or, if the soft palate is allowed to hang down freely and unobstructively, so that the breath passes into both the nose and the mouth, these make a combined resonance chamber. Such sounds as *b* and *a* (as in *father*) are voiced "oral" sounds, that is, the voiced breath does not receive a nasal resonance.

As soon as the soft palate is lowered, however, and the nose added as a participating resonance chamber, the sounds *b* and *a* take on a peculiar "nasal" quality and become, respectively, *m* and the nasalized vowel written *an* in French (e.g., *sang, tant*). The only English sounds that normally receive a nasal resonance are *m, n,* and the *ng* sound of *sing*. Practically all sounds, however, may be nasalized, not only the vowels—nasalized vowels are common in all parts of the world—but such sounds as l or z. Voiceless nasals are perfectly possible.

They occur, for instance, in Welsh and in quite a number of American Indian languages. The organs that make up the oral resonance chamber may articulate in two ways. The breath, voiced or unvoiced, nasalized or unnasalized, may be allowed to pass through the mouth without being checked or impeded at any point; or it may be either momentarily checked or allowed to stream through a greatly narrowed passage with resulting air friction. There are also transitions between the two latter types of articulation.

The unimpeded breath takes on a particular colour or quality in accordance with the varying shape of the oral resonance chamber.

This shape is chiefly determined by the position of the movable parts—the tongue and the lips. As the tongue is raised or lowered, retracted or brought forward, held tense or lax, and as the lips are pursed ("rounded") in varying degree or allowed to keep their position of rest, a large number of distinct qualities result.

These oral qualities are the vowels. In theory their number is infinite, in practice the ear can differentiate only a limited, yet a surprisingly large, number of resonance positions. Vowels, whether nasalized or not, are normally voiced sounds; in not a few languages, however, "voiceless vowels" also occur. The remaining oral sounds are generally grouped together as "consonants." In them the stream of breath is interfered with in some way, so that a lesser resonance results, and a sharper, more incisive quality of tone. There are four main types of articulation generally recognized within the consonantal group of sounds. The breath may be completely stopped for a moment at some definite point in the oral cavity. Sounds so produced, like *t* or *d* or *p*, are known as "stops" or "explosives." Or the breath may be continuously obstructed through a narrow passage, not entirely checked. Examples of such "spirants" or "fricatives," as they are called, are s and z and *y*.

The third class of consonants, the "laterals," are semi-stopped. There is a true stoppage at the central point of articulation, but the breath is allowed to escape through the two side passages or through one of them. Our English d, for instance, may be readily transformed into *l*, which has the voicing and the position of *d*, merely by depressing the sides of the tongue on either side of the point of contact sufficiently to allow the breath to come through. Laterals are possible in many distinct positions.

They may be unvoiced (the Welsh *ll* is an example) as well as voiced. Finally, the stoppage of the breath may be rapidly intermittent; in other words, the active organ of contact—generally the point of the tongue, less often the uvula —may be made to vibrate against or near the point of contact. These sounds are the "trills" or "rolled consonants," of which the normal English r is a none too typical example.

They are well developed in many languages, however, generally in voiced form, sometimes, as in Welsh and Paiute, in unvoiced form as well. The oral manner of articulation is naturally not sufficient to define a consonant. The place of articulation must also be considered. Contacts may be formed at a large number of points, from the root of the tongue to the lips. It is not necessary here to go at length into this somewhat complicated matter.

The contact is either between the root of the tongue and the throat, some part of the tongue and a point on the palate (as in *k* or *ch* or *l*), some part of the tongue and the teeth (as in the English *th* of *thick* and *thęn*), the teeth and one of the lips (practically always the upper teeth and lower lip, as in *f*), or the two lips (as in *p* or English *w*). The tongue articulations are the most complicated of all, as the mobility of the tongue allows various points on its surface, say the tip, to articulate against a number of opposed points of contact.

Hence arise many positions of articulation that we are not familiar with, such as the typical "dental" position of Russian or Italian *t* and *d*; or the "cerebral" position of Sanskrit and other languages of India, in which the tip of the tongue articulates against the hard palate. As there is no break at any point between the rims of the teeth back to the uvula nor from the tip of the tongue back to its root, it is evident that all the articulations that involve the tongue form a continuous organic (and acoustic) series.

The positions grade into each other, but each language selects a limited number of clearly defined positions as characteristic of its consonantal system, ignoring transitional or extreme positions. Frequently a language allows a certain latitude in the fixing of the required position. This is true, for instance, of the English k-sound, which is articulated much further to the front in a word like kin than in *cool*. We ignore this difference, psychologically, as a non-essential, mechanical one.

Another language might well recognize the difference, or only a slightly greater one, as significant, as paralleling the distinction in position between the *k* of *kin* and the *t* of *tin*. The organic classification of speech sounds is a simple matter after what we have learned of their production. Any such sound may be put into its proper place by the appropriate answer to four main questions:—What is the position of the glottal cords during its articulation? Does the breath pass into the mouth alone or is it also allowed to stream into the nose?

Does the breath pass freely through the mouth or is it impeded at some point and, if so, in what manner? What are the precise points of articulation in the mouth? This four- fold classification of sounds, worked out in all its detailed ramifications, is sufficient to account for all, or practically all, the sounds of language. The phonetic habits of a given language are not exhaustively defined by stating that it makes use of such and such particular sounds out of the all but endless gamut that we have briefly surveyed.

There remains the important question of the dynamics of these phonetic elements. Two languages may, theoretically, be built up of precisely the same series of consonants and vowels and yet produce utterly different acoustic effects. One of them may not recognize striking variations in the lengths or "quantities" of the phonetic elements, the other may note such variations most punctiliously (in probably the majority of languages long and short vowels are distinguished; in many, as in Italian or Swedish or Ojibwa, long consonants are recognized as distinct from short ones).

Or the one, say English, may be very sensitive to relative stresses, while in the other, say French, stress is a very minor consideration. Or, again, the pitch differences which are inseparable from the actual practice of language may not affect the word as such, but, as in English, may be a more or less random or, at best, but a rhetorical phenomenon, while in other languages, as in Swedish, Lithuanian, Chinese, Siamese, and the majority of African languages, they may be more finely graduated and felt as integral characteristics of the words themselves. Varying methods of syllabifying are also responsible for noteworthy acoustic differences.

Most important of all, perhaps, are the very different possibilities of combining the phonetic elements. Each language has its peculiarities. The ts combination, for instance, is found in both English and German, but in English it can only occur at the end of a word (as in *hats*), while it occurs freely in German as the psychological equivalent of a single sound (as in *Zeit, Katze*). Some languages allow of great heapings of consonants or of vocalic groups (diphthongs), in others no two consonants or no two vowels may ever come together.

Frequently a sound occurs only in a special position or under special phonetic circumstances. In English, for instance, the z-sound of *azure* cannot occur initially, while the peculiar quality of the *t* of *sting* is dependent on its being preceded by the s. These dynamic factors, in their totality, are as important for the proper understanding of the phonetic genius of a language as the sound system itself, often far more so.

We have already seen, in an incidental way, that phonetic elements or such dynamic features as quantity and stress have varying psychological "values." The English *ts* of *hats* is merely a t followed by a functionally independent s, the ts of the German word *Zeit has* an integral value equivalent, say, to the t of the English word tide. Again, the *t* of *time* is indeed noticeably distinct from that of *sting,* but the difference, to the consciousness of an English-speaking person, is quite irrelevant.

It has no "value." If we compare the *t*-sounds of Haida, the Indian language spoken in the Queen Charlotte Islands, we find that precisely the same difference of articulation has a real value. In such a word as *sting* "two," the t is pronounced precisely as in English, but in *sta* "from" the t is clearly "aspirated," like that of *time*. In other words, an objective difference that is irrelevant in English is of functional value in Haida; from its own psychological standpoint the *t* of *sting* is as different from that of *sta* as, from our standpoint, is the *t* of *time* from the *d* of *divine.*

Further investigation would yield the interesting result that the Haida ear finds the difference between the English t of sting and the *d* of *divine* as irrelevant as the naïve English ear finds that of the *t*-sounds of *sting* and *time*. The objective comparison of sounds in two or more languages is, then, of no psychological or historical significance unless these sounds are first "weighted," unless their phonetic "values" are determined. These values, in turn, flow from the general behaviour and functioning of the sounds in actual speech.

These considerations as to phonetic value lead to an important conception. Back of the purely objective system of sounds that is peculiar to a language and which can be arrived at only by a painstaking phonetic analysis, there is a more restricted "inner" or "ideal" system which, while perhaps equally unconscious as a system to the naïve speaker, can far more readily than the other be brought to his consciousness as a finished pattern, a psychological mechanism.

The inner sound-system, overlaid though it may be by the mechanical or the irrelevant, is a real and an immensely important principle in the life of a language. It may persist as a pattern, involving number, relation, and functioning of phonetic elements, long after its phonetic content is changed. Two historically related languages or dialects may not have a sound in common, but their ideal sound-systems may be identical patterns. I would not for a moment wish to imply that this pattern may not change.

It may shrink or expand or change its functional complexion, but its rate of change is infinitely less rapid than that of the sounds as such. Every language, then, is characterized as much by its ideal system of sounds and by the underlying phonetic pattern (system, one might term it, of symbolic atoms) as by a definite grammatical structure. Both the phonetic and conceptual structures show the instinctive feeling of language for form.

But such phenemena—and they are common enough in the history of language—are evidently quite secondary. They are closely linked with such social developments as the rise of nationality, the formation of literatures that aim to have more than a local appeal, the movement of rural populations into the cities, and all those other tendencies that break up the intense localism that unsophisticated man has always found natural.

The explanation of primary dialectic differences is still to seek. It is evidently not enough to say that if a dialect or language is spoken in two distinct localities or by two distinct social strata it naturally takes on distinctive forms, which in time come to be divergent enough to deserve the name of dialects. This is certainly true as far as it goes.

Dialects do belong, in the first instance, to very definitely circumscribed social groups, homogeneous enough to secure the common feeling and purpose needed to create a norm. But the embarrassing question immediately arises, if all the individual variations within a dialect are being constantly leveled out to the dialectic norm, if there is no appreciable tendency for the individual's peculiarities to initiate a dialectic schism, why should we have dialectic variations at all?

Ought not the norm, wherever and whenever threatened, automatically to reassert itself? Ought not the individual variations of each locality, even in the absence of intercourse between them, to cancel out to the same accepted speech average?

If individual variations "on a flat" were the only kind of variability in language, I believe we should be at a loss to explain why and how dialects arise, why it is that a linguistic prototype gradually breaks up into a number of mutually unintelligible languages. But language is not merely something that is spread out in space, as it were—a series of reflections in individual minds of one and the same timeless picture.

Language moves down time in a current of its own making. It has a drift. If there were no breaking up of a language into dialects, if each language continued as a firm, self-contained unity, it would still be constantly moving away from any assignable norm, developing new features unceasingly and gradually transforming itself into a language so different from its starting point as to be in effect a new language. Now dialects arise not because of the mere fact of individual variation but because two or more groups of individuals have become sufficiently disconnected to drift apart, or independently, instead of together.

So long as they keep strictly together, no amount of individual variation would lead to the formation of dialects. In practice, of course, no language can be spread over a vast territory or even over a considerable area without showing dialectic variations, for it is impossible to keep a large population from segregating itself into local groups, the language of each of which tends to drift independently. Under cultural conditions such as apparently prevail to-day, conditions that fight localism at every turn, the tendency to dialectic cleavage is being constantly counteracted and in part "corrected" by the uniformizing factors already referred to.

Yet even in so young a country as America the dialectic differences are not inconsiderable. Under primitive conditions the political groups are small, the tendency to localism exceedingly strong. It is natural, therefore, that the languages of primitive folk or of non-urban populations in general are differentiated into a great number of dialects. There are parts of the globe where almost every village has its own dialect.

The life of the geographically limited community is narrow and intense; its speech is correspondingly peculiar to itself. It is exceedingly doubtful if a language will ever be spoken over a wide area without multiplying itself dialectically.

No sooner are the old dialects ironed out by compromises or ousted by the spread and influence of the one dialect which is culturally predominant when a new crop of dialects arises to undo the leveling work of the past. This is precisely what happened in Greece, for instance. In classical antiquity there were spoken a large number of local dialects, several of which are represented in the literature.

As the cultural supremacy of Athens grew, its dialect, the Attic, spread at the expense of the rest, until, in the so-called Hellenistic period following the Macedonian conquest, the Attic dialect, in the vulgarized form known as the "Koine," became the standard speech of all Greece.

But this linguistic uniformity did not long continue. During the two millennia that separate the Greek of to-day from its classical prototype the Koine gradually split up into a number of dialects. Now Greece is as richly diversified in speech as in the time of Homer, though the present local dialects, aside from those of Attica itself, are not the lineal descendants of the old dialects of pre-Alexandrian days. The experience of Greece is not exceptional.

Old dialects are being continually wiped out only to make room for new ones. Languages can change at so many points of phonetics, morphology, and vocabulary that it is not surprising that once the linguistic community is broken it should slip off in different directions. It would be too much to expect a locally diversified language to develop along strictly parallel lines. If once the speech of a locality has begun to drift on its own account, it is practically certain to move further and further away from its linguistic fellows.

Failing the retarding effect of dialectic inter influences, which I have already touched upon, a group of dialects is bound to diverge on the whole, each from all of the others. In course of time each dialect itself splits up into sub-dialects, which gradually take on the dignity of dialects proper while the primary dialects develop into mutually unintelligible languages.

And so the budding process continues, until the divergences become so great that none but a linguistic student, armed with his documentary evidence and with his comparative or reconstructive method, would infer that the languages in question were genealogically related, represented independent lines of development, in other words, from a remote and common starting point. Yet it is as certain as any historical fact can be that languages so little resembling each other as Modern Irish, English, Italian, Greek, Russian, Armenian, Persian, and Bengali are but end-points in the present of drifts that converge to a meeting-point in the dim past.

There is naturally no reason to believe that this earliest "Indo-European" (or "Aryan") prototype which we can in part reconstruct, in part but dimly guess at, is itself other than a single "dialect" of a group that has either become largely extinct or is now further represented by languages too divergent for us, with our limited means, to recognize as clear kin. All languages that are known to be genetically related, i.e., to be divergent forms of a single prototype, may be considered as constituting a "linguistic stock." There is nothing final about a linguistic stock.

When we set it up, we merely say, in effect, that thus far we can go and no farther. At any point in the progress of our researches an unexpected ray of light may reveal the "stock" as but a "dialect" of a larger group. The terms dialect, language, branch, stock—it goes without saying—are purely relative terms. They are convertible as our perspective widens or contracts. It would be vain to speculate as to whether or not we shall ever be able to demonstrate that all languages stem from a common source. Of late years linguists have been able to make larger historical syntheses than were at one time deemed feasible, just as students of culture have been able to show historical connections between culture areas or institutions that were at one time believed to be totally isolated from each other.

The human world is contracting not only prospectively but to the backward-probing eye of culture-history. Nevertheless we are as yet far from able to reduce the riot of spoken languages to a small number of "stocks." We must still operate with a quite considerable number of these stocks. Some of them, like Indo-European or Indo-Chinese, are spoken over tremendous reaches; others, like Basque, have a curiously restricted range and are in all likelihood but dwindling remnants of groups that were at one time more widely distributed.

As for the single or multiple origin of speech, it is likely enough that language as a human institution (or, if one prefers, as a human "faculty") developed but once in the history of the race, that all the complex history of language is a unique cultural event. Such a theory constructed "on general principles" is of no real interest, however, to linguistic science. What lies beyond the demonstrable must be left to the philosopher or the romancer.

We must return to the conception of "drift" in language. If the historical changes that take place in a language, if the vast accumulation of minute modifications which in time results in the complete remodeling of the language, are not in essence identical with the individual variations that we note on every hand about us, if these variations are born only to die without a trace, while the equally minute, or even minuter, changes that make up the drift are forever imprinted on the history of the language, are we not imputing to this history a certain mystical quality? Are we not giving language a power to change of its own accord over and above the involuntary tendency of individuals to vary the norm? And if this drift of language is not merely the familiar set of individual variations seen in vertical perspective, that is historically, instead of horizontally, that is in daily experience, what is it? Language exists only in so far as it is actually used—spoken and heard, written and read.

What significant changes take place in it must exist, to begin with, as individual variations. This is perfectly true, and yet it by no means follows that the general drift of language can be understood from an exhaustive descriptive study of these variations alone. They themselves are random phenomena, like the waves of the sea, moving backward and forward in purposeless flux.

The linguistic drift has direction. In other words, only those individual variations embody it or carry it which move in a certain direction, just as only certain wave movements in the bay outline the tide. The drift of a language is constituted by the unconscious selection on the part of its speakers of those individual variations that are cumulative in some special direction. This direction may be inferred, in the main, from the past history of the language.

In the long run any new feature of the drift becomes part and parcel of the common, accepted speech, but for a long time it may exist as a mere tendency in the speech of a few, perhaps of a despised few. As we look about us and observe current usage, it is not likely to occur to us that our language has a "slope," that the changes of the next few centuries are in a sense prefigured in certain obscure tendencies of the present and that these changes, when consummated, will be seen to be but continuations of changes that have been already effected. We feel rather that our language is practically a fixed system and that what slight changes are destined to take place in it are as likely to move in one direction as another. The feeling is fallacious. Our very uncertainty as to the impending details of change makes the eventual consistency of their direction all the more impressive. Sometimes we can feel where the drift is taking us even while we struggle against it.

Probably the majority of those who read these words feel that it is quite "incorrect" to say "Who did you see?" We readers of many books are still very careful to say "Whom did you see?" but we feel a little uncomfortable (uncomfortably proud, it may be) in the process. We are likely to avoid the locution altogether and to say "Who was it you saw?" conserving literary tradition (the "whom") with the dignity of silence. The folk makes no apology. "Whom did you see?" might do for an epitaph, but "Who did you see?" is the natural form for an eager inquiry. It is of course the uncontrolled speech of the folk to which we must look for advance information as to the general linguistic movement.

It is safe to prophesy that within a couple of hundred years from to-day not even the most learned jurist will be saying "Whom did you see?" By that time the "whom" will be as delightfully archaic as the Elizabethan "his" for "its."

No logical or historical argument will avail to save this hapless "whom." The demonstration "I:me=he:him=who :whom" will be convincing in theory and will go unheeded in practice. Even now we may go so far as to say that the majority of us are secretly wishing they could say "Who did you see?"

It would be a weight off their unconscious minds if some divine authority, overruling the lifted finger of the pedagogue, gave them *carte blanche.* But we cannot too frankly anticipate the drift and maintain caste. We must affect ignorance of whither we are going and rest content with our mental conflict—uncomfortable conscious acceptance of the "whom," unconscious desire for the "who."

Meanwhile we indulge our sneaking desire for the forbidden locution by the use of the "who" in certain twilight cases in which we can cover up our fault by a bit of unconscious special pleading. Imagine that some one drops the remark when you are not listening attentively, "John Smith is coming to-night." You have not caught the name and ask, not "Whom did you say?" but "Who did you say?"

There is likely to be a little hesitation in the choice of the form, but the precedent of usages like "Whom did you see?" will probably not seem quite strong enough to induce a "Whom did you say?" Not quite relevant enough, the grammarian may remark, for a sentence like "Who did you say?" is not strictly analogous to "Whom did you see?" or "Whom did you mean?" It is rather an abbreviated form of some such sentence as "Who, did you say, is coming to-night?" This is the special pleading that I have referred to, and it has a certain logic on its side.

Yet the case is more hollow than the grammarian thinks it to be, for in reply to such a query as "You're a good hand at bridge, John, aren't you?" John, a little taken aback, might mutter "Did you say me?" hardly "Did you say I?" Yet the logic for the latter ("Did you say I was a good hand at bridge?") is evident. The real point is that there is not enough vitality in the "whom" to carry it over such little difficulties as a "me" can compass without a thought.

The proportion "I:me=he:him=who:whom" is logically and historically sound, but psychologically shaky. "Whom did you see?" is correct, but there is something false about its correctness. It is worth looking into the reason for our curious reluctance to use locutions involving the word "whom," particularly in its interrogative sense.

The only distinctively objective forms which we still possess in English are *me, him, her* (a little blurred because of its identity with the possessive *her*), *us, them,* and *whom.* In all other cases the objective has come to be identical with the subjective—that is, in outer form, for we are not now taking account of position in the sentence. We observe immediately in looking through the list of objective forms that *whom* is psychologically isolated. *Me, him, her, us,* and *them* form a solid, well-integrated group of objective personal pronouns parallel to the subjective series *I, he, she, we, they.*

Chapter 5

Phoneme and Phonological Development

PHONEME DEVELOPMENT

Infants begin making sounds at birth. These early sounds are cries that can be differentiated by a familiar ear. As the infant continues to mature, cooing and babbling noises develop into consonant and vowel sounds. These early preconsonant and prevowel sounds gradually become shaped into words. Although research indicates that some phonemes are present in neonates, phoneme development for purposes of speech generally begins between the first and second birthdays.

Phoneme development is influenced by the child's environment; his or her physical, motor, and intellectual capabilities; and the child's need for communication. The forms *who* and *whom* are technically "pronouns" but they are not felt to be in the same box as the personal pronouns. *Whom* has clearly a weak position, an exposed flank, for words of a feather tend to flock together, and if one strays behind, it is likely to incur danger of life.

Now the other interrogative and relative pronouns (*which, what, that*), with which *whom* should properly flock, do not distinguish the subjective and objective forms. It is psychologically unsound to draw the line of form cleavage between *whom* and the personal pronouns on the one side, the remaining interrogative and relative pronouns on the other. The form groups should be symmetrically related to, if not identical with, the function groups. Had *which, what,* and *that* objective forms parallel to *whom,* the position of this last would be more secure.

As it is, there is something unesthetic about the word. It suggests a form pattern which is not filled out by its fellows. The only way to remedy the irregularity of form distribution is to abandon the *whom* altogether, for we have lost the power to create new objective forms and cannot remodel our *which-what-that* group so as to make it parallel with the smaller group *who-whom.*

Once this is done, *who* joins its flock and our unconscious desire for form symmetry is satisfied. We do not secretly chafe at "Whom did you see?" without reason. But the drift away from *whom* has still other determinants. The words *who* and *whom* in their interrogative sense are psychologically related not merely to the pronouns *which* and *what,* but to a group of interrogative adverbs—*where, when, how*—all of which are invariable and generally emphatic. I believe it is safe to infer that there is a rather strong feeling in English that the interrogative pronoun or adverb, typically an emphatic element in the sentence, should be invariable.

The inflective *-m of whom* is felt as a drag upon the rhetorical effectiveness of the word. It needs to be eliminated if the interrogative pronoun is to receive all its latent power. There is still a third, and a very powerful, reason for the avoidance of *whom.* The contrast between the subjective and objective series of personal pronouns (*I, he, she, we, they: me, him, her, us, them*) is in English associated with a difference of position. We say *I see the man* but *the man sees me; he told him,* never *him he told* or *him told he.* Such usages as the last two are distinctly poetic and archaic; they are opposed to the present drift of the language.

Even in the interrogative one does not say *Him did you see?* It is only in sentences of the type *Whom did you see?* that an inflected objective before the verb is now used at all. On the other hand, the order in *Whom did you see?* is imperative because of its interrogative form; the interrogative pronoun or adverb normally comes first in the sentence (*What are you doing? When did he go? Where are you from?*). In the "whom" of *Whom did you see?* there is concealed, therefore, a conflict between the order proper to a sentence containing an inflected objective and the order natural to a sentence with an interrogative pronoun or adverb. The solution *Did you see whom?* or *You saw whom?* is too contrary to the idiomatic drift of our language to receive acceptance. The more radical solution *Who did you see?* is the one the language is gradually making for.

THE DEVELOPMENT OF VOWELS

Vowels begin to develop from random sounds produced by infants its young as 2 months. At 2 months, the/ɛ/,/I/, and/ʌ/vowels are frequently identified in cooing patterns. These vowels fade after several months and are not consistently used again until after 30 months of age.

At the same time that the/ɛ/,/I/, and/ʌ/are fading, the front vowels/i/,/e/, and/æ/are appearing. These three front vowels, along with the back vowels/a/,/ɔ/,/o/,/ʊ/, and/u/, are consistently used and mastered over the next 2 years. As the first words appear between the first and second birthdays, CV patterns consisting of/a/,/æ, and/o/dominate speech patterns.

The Development of Consonants

Although numerous researchers have studied the concept of phoneme acquisition, the two most significant recent studies have been completed by Smit, Hand, Frelinger, Bernthal, and Bird and Sander. Although completed more than 20 years ago, Sander's information provides the most clinically applicable data. Sander included in his information a range of ages associated with the development of various consonant phonemes.

According to Sander, the first consonant phonemes to develop are the/p/,/m/,/h/,/n/,/w/, and/b/. These phonemes begin to develop before the age of 2, and all but the/b/are mastered by age 3. The/b/is not mastered! until age 4. These phonemes consist of two highly visible plosives—the/p/and the/b/—two nasal sounds—the/n/and the/m/—and the fricative/h/. These phonemes require little adjustment of the vocal tract, and the approximant/w/is highly visible and similar to the bilabial plosives.

The next group of consonant phonemes to develop includes the/k/,/g/,/d/,/t/, and/b/. Each of these phonemes begins to develop at age 2. The plosives/k/,/g/, and/d/are mastered at age 4, whereas the plosive/t/and the nasal/ŋ/are not mastered until age 6. Considering the first two groups of phonemes, it is obvious that plosives and nasals are common in a child's early vocabulary.

Although it is possible for a child to have difficulty with the pronunciation of any phoneme, most of these early phonemes, except perhaps/k/, are not problematic. Young children's frequent substitution of the/t/for the/k/is called velar fronting. This substitution is possibly due to either the lack of visibility of the/k/or poor musculature control of the velum. The delayed mastery of the/t/is also associated with the syntactic use of the/t/as a past tense marker.

The later mastery of the/ŋ/is associated with its syntactic role forming the present progressive and the fact that the phonological rules of American-English do not allow for the production of the/ŋ/in the initial position of words. Because children generally master the target phoneme in the initial position of words first, the/ŋ/would necessarily be mastered later in the developmental sequence.

The/f/and/j/phonemes begin to develop before the age of 3 and are mastered by the age of 4. The/f/is the first fricative phoneme to be mastered, probably because of its visible place of articulation. Some children substitute the/p/for the/f/at an early age. This error represents a manner of articulation error that is common only in children less than age 4. The/j/is the first approximant phoneme to be mastered and it requires a neutral position of the articulators. Because this phoneme is easy to produce, it is often used as a substitute for more difficult phonemes.

The/ɹ/,/l/and/s/begin to develop at age 3, but require a lengthy period of time before mastery is accomplished. The/

ɹ/and the/l/are mastered at age 6, whereas the/s/is not fully mastered age 8. These three phonemes are often considered the most difficult to learn and thus are usually the most frequently mispronounced. The consonantal/y/, which appears only in the initial position of words or syllables in GAP, is often replaced by the/w/or the/j/. Both of these phonemes are easier to produce.

In addition, the/a/and the/l/are very complex phonemes and the various allophonic variations make their mastery difficult. The/s/phoneme requires well-coordinated use of the intrinsic and extrinsic muscles of the tongue. This sophisticated phoneme also uses a higher frequency (about 4000 Hz.) than any other phoneme. The phonemes/a/,/l/, and/s/are also found in initial position CC contexts more often than any other consonant phoneme.

The/tʃ/,/ʃ/, and/z/are the next phonemes to develop. A 3½-year-old child can produce these phonemes in selected situations, but mastery is not achieved until age 7 for the/tʃ/ and/ʃ/and age 8 for the/z/. The affricate/tʃ/requires the mastery of two phonemes before it can be produced.

Thus, the/ʃ/and/tʃ/are often used interchangeably by children developing speech. Although the/z/is used in some vocabulary words, its primary role in the English language is as a plural marker. This syntactic mastery is not achieved until a later age. The/dʒ/and the/v/are the next group phonemes to develop. These phonemes begin to develop at age 4 and are mastered by ages 6 and 7, respectively. The/dʒ/ is an affricate that requires mastery of two phonemes. Because the/ʒ/is not yet mastered by many children, the production of/dʒ/is often difficult. Substitution of/b/for/v/is common in children up to the age of 5 or 6 because the/v/is not commonly used.

The/è/begins to develop before age 4 and is mastered by age 7, whereas the/ð/begins to develop at age 5 and is mastered by age 8. The/è/is a weak phoneme, but its visibility and interdental tongue positions make it a common substitution for the more difficult but frequently appearing/s/phoneme.

The substitution of the/è/for the/s/is often called an interdental lisp. The/ð/is used primarily in function words such as *the, them,* and *these*. Because the use of function words is directly related to the development of the noun and verb phrases, the use of/ð/increases as the complexity of the phrase increases. The last two phonemes to develop are the/ʒ/and the/ʍ/. The/ʒ/begins to develop at age 6 and is mastered after age 8. The/ʍ/begins to develop at age 6 and is not mastered until after age 9. The/ʒ/is one of the last phonemes to be mastered because of its lack of frequency in early vocabulary words and its presence in only the medial and final position of words. The/ʍ/is often replaced by the/w/in conversational speech.

Development of Single Phonemes

Not all children develop the consonants with ease at the target age. Some children experience a slower than normal development of the phonemes, whereas others exhibit common developmental patterns of substitution, omission, and distortion. Substitution is the replacing of one phomene for another, such as/b/for the/v/resulting in *ban* [bæn] for van [væn].

Omission is when a sound is omitted from the word. The endings are omitted from the word, such as lef [ɛ]] for left [lɛft]. Distortion occurs when the phoneme is produced using an incorrect allophonic variation such as [s+˜un] for [sun]. Children substitute, omit, or distort phonemes for a variety of reasons including developmental, hearing, physical, or dental limitations; imitation; or problems learning the language's rule system. Developmental limitation is one of the most common causes of phoneme errors. The following are common developmental substitutions:/p/f/,/t/k/,/b/v/,/f/v/ ,/f/è/,/w/a/,/w/l/,/j/l/,/l/j/,/è/s/,/n/ŋ/, and/w/ʍ/. These are probably used by children because one phoneme is easier to produce than another.

PHONOLOGICAL DEVELOPMENT

In addition to learning the phonemes of the language,

distinct syllable patterns begin to develop shortly before the end of a child's first year or as soon as two phonemes are produced consecutively. The earliest patterns consist of CV *hi* [haI] or VC *up*[+p] patterns. These early patterns develop into CVCV *mama* ['mΛmY] reduplication patterns or CVCV *cookie* ['kuk+]. During this developmental time frame, a few CVC cat [kæt] patterns also develop, but in most cases the final consonant is omitted during the production. Phonological processes are a series of patterns used by children to simplify adult speech. These patterns are used because the child does not yet have the capacity to produce adult speech. These patterns seem to be innate in all children but do not always develop at the same rate. Phonological patterns consist of syllable combinations, cluster combinations, and CV combinations. These processes account for patterns of substitutions, omissions, and additions present in developing speech between the ages of 2 and 5.

Basic Terminology

Some of the terms used in phonology differ from terms used by the IPA. To avoid confusion, the following definitiohs are provided.

Assimilation: The effect of one phoneme on another in a sequence of phonemes.

Backing: The production of consonants near the velar or glottal area.

Cluster: Two or more consonant phonemes in a sequence without being separated by a vowel.

Final consonants: The last consonant in the word or syllable.

Fronting: The production of consonants near the lips or the central and lateral incisors.

Initial consonant: The first consonant in the syllable or word.

Liquid: Term referring to the/l/or/y/phonemes or allophones.

Medial consonant: The consonant in the medial position of the word.

Palatal: The area on the roof of the mouth that covers the maxillary bone.

Reduplication: The repetition of a CV syllable.

Stop: Another term for a plosive.

Stridency: A term used to apply to the consonants/s, z, f, v, ', tʃ, d'/.

PHONOLOGICAL PROCESSES

There are numerous systems of phonological processes available for consideration. According to Khan and Lewis, there are 15 key phonological processes (12 occur as a part of normal development and 3 are not developmental in nature) and 15 less common phonological processes.

It is important to note that considerable interaction occurs among the processes. Those listed here are the pure forms. The processes according to Khan and Lewis are as follow here.

Processes Associated With Normal Phonological Development

Deletion of final consonants: The final consonant in a word or syllable is deleted changing the syllable shape from CVC *bag* [bæg] to CV ([bæ]), CCVC *stop* [stap] to CCV [sta], or CVCC *box* [baks] to CV [ba]. The syllable changes from a closed to an open syllable.

Initial voicing: The use of the voiced consonant in place of a voiceless consonant in the initial position of the word or syllable. In the purest form, the child substitutes the cognate, for example, *dog* [dɔg] becomes [tog]. It is also considered initial consonant voicing when other processes are added and the child substitutes a voice consonant with a different place or manner of articulation, such as when *dog* [dɔg] becomes [gɔg].

Syllable reduction: One or more syllables in the word are deleted, such as when *library* ['laɪ, bɹɛɹ ɨ] becomes ['lI, bɛɹ ɨ]. Palatal fronting: The place of articulation is changed from the postalveolar area to the alveolar area, such as when *ship* [ʃp] becomes [sɪp].

Deaffrication: The stop part of the affricate is deleted. The word *cheek* [tʃk] becomes [ʃk].

Velar fronting: The place of articulation of the velar phonemes is shifted to the alveolar area. The word *cap* [kæp] becomes [tæp].

Consonant harmony: If the word has two or more consonants, the consonants are produced with the same place of articulation, such as when *cup* [kʌP] becomes [pʌp].

Stridency deletion: The stridency consonant is either deleted, as when *sun* [sʌn] becomes [ʌn], or is replaced with a glottal, as when *chip* [tʃjp] becomes [ʔIp].

Stopping of fricatives and affricates: This is when a stop consonant is substituted for a fricative. For example, the word *thank* [èæŋk] becomes [pæŋk]. When an affricate is stopped, only the plosive component of the affricate is produced, such as when [ʃjn] becomes [tin].

Cluster simplification: One or more of the consonants in a CC or CCC context in any position of the word is deleted or a schwa is inserted, for example, *lamp* [lImp] becomes [læm].

Final devoicing: The voicing is deleted on the final consonant in the word or syllable. The result is usually the production of the voiceless cognate, such as when *bud* [bæd] becomes [bʌt].

Liquid simplification—gliding of liquids: The liquid phonemes/l/and/a/are produced as/w/and/j/, for example, *light* [lIt] becomes [waIt].

Gliding of fricatives: Any fricative phoneme is produced as a/j/or/w/, for example five [fIv] becomes [jIv]. (This process is not very common.).

Vocalization of liquids: A vowel is produced instead of the final/l/in an unstressed syllable or the/ɚ/, which is found only in unstressed syllables, for example, *flower* ['flʊ wɚ] becomes ['flʊ wə].

Processes That Are Non-developmental

These processes are not developmental and represent a phonological error at all ages.

Deletion of initial consonants: The first consonant in the word or syllable is deleted, such as when *top* [tap] becomes [ap].

Glottal replacement: A glottal is used to replace a consonant or a consonant cluster usually in the medial position of the word, for example, *sleeping* ['slIp Iŋ] becomes ['slʔ Iŋ].

Backing to velars: This is when any consonant is produced as a velar phoneme or an/h/, such as when *up* [ʌp] becomes [ʌk].

Ingram divided the phonological processes into three general categories: syllable structure processes such as final consonant deletion, assimilatory processes such as final consonant devoicing, and substitution processes such as stopping of fricatives and affricates. Grunwell listed nine processes that are common in the speech of children between ages 2 and 5. These processes are weak syllable deletion, final consonant deletion, reduplication, consonant harmony, cluster reduction, stopping, fronting, gliding, and context sensitive voicing.

Although phonological processes are used primarily by children learning the language and diminish over the first 5 years, they can also be identified in the speech patterns of adults. In using these various processes individual variations become part of a speech pattern. These processes are not rules but are often used consistently in conversational speech.

Phonological Rules/Phonotactics

Phonotactics are the rules that govern the combinations and ordering of phonemes in a syllable or a word. There are 16 phonological syllable patterns used in GAP. Note the V can also appear as a word in GAP making the number of patterns 17. Following is a list of the syllables and an example for each.

One phoneme pattern	V	I [I], oh [o]
Two phoneme patterns	VC	on [ɑn], it [It]
	CV	be [bi], see [sæ]
Three phoneme patterns	CVC	dog [dèg], cat [kæt]
	CCV	tree [tɹ], ski [ski]
	VCC	its [Its], eats [its]
Four phoneme patterns	CCVC	slab [slæb]

		bread [bɹɛd]
	CCCV	stray [stɹ]
		spree [spɹi]
	VCCC	asked [æskt]
	CVCC	desk [dɛsk]
		fist [fIst]
Five phoneme patterns	CCVCC	brown [bɹaʊn]
		spunk [spʌŋk]
	CCCVC	street [stɹæt]
		strap [stɹæp]
	CVCCC	selves [sɛlvz]
		folds [foldz]
Six phoneme patterns	CCCVCC	strand [stɹænd]
		sprint [spɹInt]
	CCVCCC	stamps [stæmps]
		trenched [tɹɛnt ʃd]
	CVCCCC	sixths [sèksès]
Seven phoneme pattern	CCCVCCC	scrimped [skɹImpt]

Table given indicates order and frequency of occurrence of 14 of the 17 patterns in American-English. Specific phoneme combinations are also governed by phonological rules.

For example, the/ɹ/is combined with the/b, f, g, k, p/in the initial position but not with the/h, l, m, n, s, v, z/. Rules applying to/ɹ/,/l/,/ô/, and other factors that will influence articulation are discussed.

Table. Order and Frequency of Occurrence of Phonologic Syllables in American English

Syllable	Per cent%	Total
CV	32.40	
CVC	30.22	
VC	16.34	
V	8.11	
		87.07
CVCC	5.55	
CCVC	2.84	
CCV	2.64	
VCC	.72	
CCVCC	.60	

CCCVC	.24	
CCCVCC	.19	
CVCCC	.12	
CCVCCC	.02	
CCCV	.01	
		12.93
All syllables		100

These three conflicts—on the score of form grouping, of rhetorical emphasis, and of order—are supplemented by a fourth difficulty. The emphatic *whom,* with its heavy build (half-long vowel followed by labial consonant), should contrast with a lightly tripping syllable immediately following. In *whom did,* however, we have an involuntary retardation that makes the locution sound "clumsy."

This clumsiness is a phonetic verdict, quite apart from the dissatisfaction due to the grammatical factors which we have analysed. The same prosodic objection does not apply to such parallel locutions as *what did* and *when did.* The vowels of *what* and *when* are shorter and their final consonants melt easily into the following *d,* which is pronounced in the same tongue position as *t* and *n.* Our instinct for appropriate rhythms makes it as difficult for us to feel content with *whom did* as for a poet to use words like *dreamed* and *hummed* in a rapid line.

Neither common feeling nor the poet's choice need be at all conscious. It may be that not all are equally sensitive to the rhythmic flow of speech, but it is probable that rhythm is an unconscious linguistic determinant even with those who set little store by its artistic use. In any event the poet's rhythms can only be a more sensitive and stylicized application of rhythmic tendencies that are characteristic of the daily speech of his people.

e have discovered no less than four factors which enter into our subtle disinclination to say "Whom did you see?" The uneducated folk that says "Who did you see?" with no twinge of conscience has a more acute flair for the genuine drift of the language than its students. Naturally the four restraining factors do not operate independently. Their separate energies, if we may make bold to use a mechanical concept, are "canalized" into a single force. This force or minute embodiment of the general drift of the language is psychologically registered as a slight hesitation in using the word *whom*. The hesitation is likely to be quite unconscious, though it may be readily acknowledged when attention is called to it.

The analysis is certain to be unconscious, or rather unknown, to the normal speaker. How, then, can we be certain in such an analysis as we have undertaken that all of the assigned determinants are really operative and not merely some one of them? Certainly they are not equally powerful in all cases. Their values are variable, rising and falling according to the individual and the locution. But that they really exist, each in its own right, may sometimes be tested by the method of elimination.

If one or other of the factors is missing and we observe a slight diminution in the corresponding psychological reaction ("hesitation" in our case), we may conclude that the factor is in other uses genuinely positive. The second of our four factors applies only to the interrogative use of *whom*, the fourth factor applies with more force to the interrogative than to the relative.

We can therefore understand why a sentence like *Is he the man whom you referred to?* though not as idiomatic as *Is he the man (that) you referred to?* (remember that it sins against counts one and three), is still not as difficult to reconcile with our innate feeling for English expression as *Whom did you see?*

If we eliminate the fourth factor from the interrogative usage, say in *Whom are you looking at?* where the vowel following *whom* relieves this word of its phonetic weight, we can observe, if I am not mistaken, a lesser reluctance to use the *whom*. *Who are you looking at?* might even sound slightly offensive to ears that welcome *Who did you see?*

We may venture to surmise that while *whom* will ultimately disappear from English speech, locutions of the type *Whom did you see?* will be obsolete when phrases like *The man whom I referred to* are still in lingering use. It is impossible to be certain, however, for we can never tell if we have isolated all the determinants of a drift. In our particular case we have ignored what may well prove to be a controlling factor in the history of *who* and *whom* in the relative sense.

This is the unconscious desire to leave these words to their interrogative function and to concentrate on *that* or mere word order as expressions of the relative (e. g., *The man that I referred to* or *The man I referred to*). This drift, which does not directly concern the use of *whom* as such (merely of *whom* as a form of *who*), may have made the relative *who* obsolete before the other factors affecting relative *whom* have run their course.

A consideration like this is instructive because it indicates that knowledge of the general drift of a language is insufficient to enable us to see clearly what the drift is heading for. We need to know something of the relative potencies and speeds of the components of the drift. It is hardly necessary to say that the particular drifts involved in the use of *who* are of interest to us not for their own sake but as symptoms of larger tendencies at work in the language.

Chapter 6

Models of Speech

PRODUCTION

What is a model? It is difficult to give an answer that fits everything that has been called a model in the literature on speech production. One source of difficulty is that the words *model* and *theory* are not used consistently, so that one person's theory may be another person's model. However, there are reasons to distinguish between theory and model. A model is a simplified description of a complex system or process. The ultimate challenge for speech recognition is to make it indistinguishable from humans speech perception system. At present, when users interact with any existing speech recognition system, they have to be fully aware of the fact that their conversation partner is a machine.

The machine would easily break if the users were to speak in a casual and natural style as if they were talking with a friend. In order to enable mainstream use of speech recognition, naturalness or free style of speaking on the users part should not incur so many recognition errors that make the recognition systems unusable as it is the case today.

In fact, after the problem of free-style speech recognition or transcription becomes solved, many kinds of killer applications will be possible that are currently unimaginable. By that time, pervasive adaptation of speech recognition will become natural.

It has been broadly hypothesized that new computational paradigms beyond the conventional are needed to reach the goal of all-purpose recognition technology for unconstrained, natural human-human and human-machine speech, and that statistical models capitalizing on essential properties of the structures of natural speech and language are beneficial in establishing such paradigms. The thrust of the research described in this proposal is to pursue an approach based on the above hypothesis using advanced learning techniques, and to integrate the results of this investigation into state-of-the-art speech recognition systems that may be used for effective, high-performance speech to text.

The common thread tying the various aspects of research described in this proposal is the powerful statistical modeling techniques that are capable of effectively and parsimoniously characterizing long-span dependency properties in natural human speech.

A model is always an abstraction or simplification. Modeling helps the scientist to identify the important parametres or elements of a system or process that is too complicated to be comprehended in its complete, natural form. A model may be related to a theory, as in the case of implementing a theory, and may be used to test a theory directly or indirectly.

A theory is an overall conception that encompasses the known facts in a (preferably) parsimonious way and typically includes a set of assumptions and a number of principles from which predictions (hypotheses) can be derived. Another way of viewing the distinction between theory and model is that a model often is used as an analogy to the theory, especially as a way of visualizing the theory. Schmidt gives an example from atomic theory. When this theory was developed in the 1930s, electrons and protons were imaginary constructs.

A common model used to describe these constructs was a system of little balls, with neutrons and protons clustered in a central nucleus and with electrons orbiting the nucleus. Most of the ideas to be discussed in this chapter are better described as models than theories. They help us to visualize the processes and structures thought to be involved in speech production.

Because speech is a complex phenomenon, it can be modeled in various ways for different purposes. The variability in content and purpose of these models can make it difficult to compare or evaluate them because they are not necessarily intended to do exactly the same thing.

For example, a neural model of speech production is an account of the nervous system processes that control speaking. Such a model typically is couched in terms of neural regulatory loops, brain centres, or some other conception of neural organization. An articulatory model is concerned primarily with articulation, or the movements of the speech structures (e.g., the tongue, jaw, lips, and velum). This kind of model usually describes articulatory positions, movements, and configurations.

It may neglect neural processes altogether or treat them only indirectly. It also may neglect the muscles that make up the articulators and refer only to gross structural movements, such as a closing movement of the jaw or an alveolar closure of the tongue tip. Another kind of model, the vocal tract model, focuses on the shaping of the vocal tract (the pharyngeal, oral, and nasal cavities).

The vocal tract may be considered as an acoustic tube or combination of tubes that is adjusted in its cross-sectional dimensions and length for different speech sounds. Although human speech accomplishes these adjustments by means of articulatory actions that give shape to the vocal tract, a vocal tract model can neglect the underlying articulations and refer to the vocal tract only as an acoustic tube that undergoes changes in its overall length and its cross sectional area as a function of length.

A vocal tract model might refer to a constriction in the palatal region without explaining how such a constriction comes about. Other models of speech production are functional. For example, an information-processing model attempts to account for the ways various types of information regulate speaking.

An example is a servosystem model, in which feedback control is a major feature. An error signal derived from the feedback is used to generate the desired movement. Still other models are developed at the level of motor control.

These motor control models are concerned with the activation patterns of muscles or muscle groups and therefore may be explicitly defined in terms of motoric processes. It would be a very ambitious undertaking to develop a comprehensive model that incorporated all of these models. Most scientists work on a narrower set of issues, so it is important to recognize the type of model under discussion. All of these are models of speech production.

They all represent important knowledge about the act of speaking and guide research on speech production. Given the diversity among these theories and models and the limited space available to discuss them, this chapter summarizes major directions of theorizing and modeling rather than exhaustively reviewing individual proposals.

Table. Some General Types of Models of Speech Production

Model Type	Purpose
Neural	Accounts for nervous system processes that control speaking; may specify neural structures, control circuits, information flow, other neural variables.
Articulatory	Describes articulatory positions, movements, or configurations; typically specifies individual articulators, such as tongue, lips, jaw, velum.
Vocal tract	Focuses on the shaping of the vocal tract for the production of speech; does not necessarily specify actions of individual articulators; may be concerned with overall descriptions of vocal tract configuration.
Functional	Accounts for the ways in which various types of information regulate speech production; variables may be linguistic (syllables, phonemes, etc.), control signals (feedforward or feedback signals) or generally defined in terms of movement sequence.
Motor control	Describes the motor processes of the activation of muscles for the production of speech; usually expressed in motoric terms, such as specification of muscle synergies or kinematic descriptions of movement.

The various theories and models of speech production can be put into relief by asking of each: What is being modeled? What is the purpose of the theory or model? These two questions are important not only to understand the proposals themselves but also to identify the kinds of evidence against which they can be tested.

The following definitions will apply in this chapter: *A theory of speech production accounts for the conversion of a linguistic representation of a message to the actions of the speech production system. A model of speech production is a simplified representation of speech production or some aspect of speech production.* The linguistic representation typically is viewed as a symbolic string, for example, a string of phonemes.

The speech production system includes the respiratory subsystem, the laryngeal subsystem, and the supraglottal subsystem (the latter corresponding to the vocal tract). This definition can accommodate several types of theories. It also announces the fundamental problem that all such theories face: how to relate the output of language formulation to the working of a speech production model.

Although some proposals ignore this problem, it must be faced if the theories and models are to account for speech as a language modality. Carre and Mrayati proposed some general criteria by which models of vocal tract function (particularly articulatory-acoustic phonetic relations) can be evaluated. The same criteria, given here in slightly modified form, are useful in evaluating the models to be discussed in this chapter:

1. The model should closely describe natural phenomena, such as coarticulation, vowel and consonant production, declination of fundamental frequency, speech breathing, and adjustment to speaking rate. Naturally, the more of these phenomena the model addresses, the better.
2. The parametres of the model should be based on observations of the system to be modeled. Ideally, the parametres should be orthogonal (independent of one another, so as to be maximally efficient) and

capable of producing all possible states or functions of the modeled system.

3. The number of model parametres should be as small as possible (*parsimony*), and the command strategies should be simple yet significant (*economy with power*).
4. The model should enable simple interpretations across domains (e.g., neural to articulatory, articulatory to acoustic, acoustic to phonetic).
5. The model should exhibit nonlinear phenomena characteristic of speech production. That is, some aspects of speech cannot be described as linear operations. A purely linear model would not account for these aspects.
6. The model should account for relevant scientific facts.

CONCEPTUALIZING SPEECH QUA LANGUAGE

Theorizing about speech production is complicated by several factors. One is the relationship between speech and language. Because speech is a modality of language, it cannot be separated from its role as language expression. Speech is derived from intent to communicate and formulation of a linguistic message. If some articulatory or acoustic pattern is to be called speech, then the implicit assumption is that the pattern expresses an underlying linguistic message known to the speaker.

There are a few exceptions to this general assumption, including speaking in tongues as practiced in some churches, deliberate attempts of a talker to produce gibberish, and neologistic jargon produced by some individuals with aphasia. Knowing where to draw the line between language and speech helps in constructing and evaluating theories of speech production. Consider sequencing errors in speech, such as when a speaker says "food the peech" instead of "feed the pooch". If these errors are thought to arise in speech production processes, they become a source of information about speech production.

On the other hand, if they are thought to arise in processes that precede speech (such as a system for phonological assembly), they need not be accounted for in a speech production model and in fact may be irrelevant to such a model. Recent evidence indicates that speech errors are pertinent to speech production models and may have to be considered at the motoric level.

This is the fundamental question about the relationship of speech to language: What is the input to the model of speech production? In other words, what output of the language system drives the production of speech? A brief description of each component follows:

Cognition: Prelinguistic formulation; ideas not yet cast as language; may take the form of schema, notions, general plans.

*Affect: E*motional accompaniments of cognition and language.

Syntax: The rules governing the arrangements of words in an utterance; pertains to the linear order of words in sentences, the categorization of words into parts of speech, and the grouping of words into structural constituents.

Semantics: The meaning of words and of groups of words.

Phonology: The principles and patterns by which sounds are used in a language.

Lexicon: The vocabulary of a language user; may specify morphologic, phonologic, orthographic, syntactic, semantic, and pragmatic information for words and the morphemes of which words are composed.

Phonetics: The specification of ways phonologic units are produced; output is presumably the input to the motor processes of speech production. The more elaborate the output of the phonetic component, the fewer are the problems to be resolved at the level of motor control.

An output that specifies allophonic variations (detailed considerations of sound pattern) provides more information than a phonemic output. For example, a phonetic output of the form [s p=u n] is more detailed than the phonemic representation/s p u n/. The former specifies certain features, such as lack of aspiration for/p/following/s/and nasalization of the vowel/u/preceding the nasal consonant.

Motor control system: The structures and processes that regulate the muscular actions of the speech production system; composed of muscles and other tissues within the head, neck, thorax and abdomen.

An important feature of this diagram is that the processes of language formulation must relate to the processes of speech production. Exactly how this relation takes place is a matter of much speculation. To say that the phonological component of language accomplishes the relation is not satisfactory unless this component is clearly defined with respect to language processes on the one hand and to the motoric events in speech production on the other hand. Modern phonological theory may hold some interesting answers, and those who would understand speech should be aware of developments in phonology.

These developments can have important implications for the study of the production and perception of speech. Meyer and Gordon observed that conceptualizations of speech organization generally recognize three levels. Basically, this table is an elaboration of the motor control component. The first level in the box is a multiunit representation based on networks or sequences of some kind, typically extending over several segments or syllables.

For example, Kozhevnikov and Chistovich proposed the syntagma, a rhythmic grouping of syllables tending toward seven constituent syllables. Another perspective, after Chomsky, is that surface-structure sequences of words are the highest level of organization. The second level is the basic unit of phonetic or articulatory representation. Candidates at this level include the syllable, phoneme, allophone, and feature.

Possibly more than one unit is involved, as would be the case if units were nested into a hierarchical structure, such as features within phonemes and phonemes within syllables. The third level is motor control, or the direct regulation of the musculature. Here possibilities include an abstract articulatory target or goal (e.g., a kind of snapshot of the intended vocal tract configuration), a motor command (a specific neural instruction to a muscle or set of muscles), an acoustic template (an acoustic goal to be achieved by articulation), and a coordinative structure (a synergy or linkage among a group of muscles to accomplish a particular task).

These terms will be considered in more detail later in this chapter. The central point of this discussion is that speech organization can be modeled with different units selected from different levels of control or representation.

Indeed, models of speech production often reflect different levels of organization, and furthermore, different units or constructs have been proposed for each level. The possible permutations are impressive. But this feature also complicates the empirical test of these models. For example, if a multilevel model misses the mark in accounting for a phenomenon or predicting an experimental outcome, which stage should be revised?

Hypothesized levels of speech organization with candidate units at each level

Several models of speech production propose a multilevel organization, often reflecting the levels and units shown here.

The usual strategy is to select one or more units from each level to formulate a hierarchical control system of the form: sequence of units — pre-articulatory representation — motor realization.

- Sequence or Network of Units(Multi-Unit Assembly or Pattern)
  - Conceptual dependency networks
  - Surface structure word sequences
  - Syntagma
  - Breath group
  - Articulatory phrase
- Prearticulatory Representation
  - Syllables
  - Demisyllables
  - Phonemes

   - Allophones
   - Phonetic features
   - Gesture bundles
- Motor Realization (Vocal Tract Control)
   - Spatial targets
   - Motor commands
   - Acoustic templates
   - Coordinative structures
   - Vocal tract and articulatory model variables
   - Motor or gestural score

The principal reason that different levels have been proposed for speech organization is the belief that different phenomena seem to be explained more effectively at different levels. However, it is difficult to test a multilayered theory because processes or events at one level usually depend on processes or events at other levels. Therefore, a conceptual error at one level can affect the rest of the model.

A proper study of speech production models rests on a careful reading of this entire book. A useful theory draws from several sources of knowledge and accounts for a large number of facts with reasonable parsimony (simplicity). Beginning students may find it difficult to appreciate the parsimony of a theory until they have digested a volume of facts about speech production.

But a theory can also help to guide and integrate the facts on speech production. Always remember, any given theory may very well be wrong, if not in its major concepts, at least in its details. But an incorrect theory is not a bad theory if it clearly directs research efforts to disprove it.

CRITICAL ISSUES FACING SPEECH PRODUCTION MODELS

Why has it been difficult to model speech production? After all, if speech is regulated by a string of linguistic units, such as phonemes, then should it not be possible simply to define for each phoneme a set of muscle commands (or vocal tract adjustments) and execute them in the order specified by the linguistic string, much as one might type the consecutive letters that make up a word?

By this reasoning, a word like soon would be produced by sequentially executing the stored motor instructions for the phonemes [s], [u] and [n]. This has appealing simplicity: The language production system generates a string of phonemes (or segments of some kind), and the speech production system then gives physical realization to each phoneme in turn.

However, this simple idea does not survive empirical tests. The actual articulations in speech are not easily reconciled with a linear string of control units. Beyond the general issue of how linguistic units relate to the control of the speech production system, there are three major problems from a motor control perspective.

The Serial Order Problem

The problem of serial order in behaviour, classically formulated by Lashley, remains a challenge to contemporary speech research. Speech is a string or sequence that evolves in time. A fundamental issue in its regulation is the determination of how its elements are strung together. What are the elements of control? Several units have been proposed, including the extrinsic allophone, the phoneme, the syllable, the demisyllable, and so on. And even when two scientists agree on the choice of the element, they may differ on how serial ordering is accomplished.

For example, one might maintain that the elements cohere in a larger structure, such as a stress grouping. The other might argue that peripheral feedback mechanisms are sufficient to control the temporal ordering of speech events, so that feedback that verifies the completion of one event is sufficient to trigger the next. The simple word *soon* can be conceptualized in several ways; for example, as a string of phonemes, a string of allophones, a consonant vowel-consonant (CVC) syllable structure, or a syllable combination of consonant-vowel (CV), ([s] + [u]) followed by CV ([n] + null element).

The Degrees of Freedom Problem

The speech production system has potential for a large number of degrees of freedom. Gracco cites (but does not necessarily concur with) the frequent observation that there are more than 70 different muscular degrees of freedom in the production of speech. The tongue, lips, jaw, velum, larynx, and respiratory system all possess several possible types of movement with respect to range, direction, speed, and temporal combinations with one another.

Moreover, they can combine in various ways; for example, the lower lip and jaw can move in phase and in the same direction, out of phase but in the same direction, or in phase but in opposite directions. The degrees of freedom problem is general to action and not unique to speech. On the one hand, excessive degrees of freedom allow a great degree of behavioural flexibility. But on the other hand, many degrees of freedom also present a challenge: How does the control system contend with so many degrees of freedom to achieve a desired action?

The system must either expend a great deal of computational effort to manage a large number of degrees of freedom or somehow reduce the degrees of freedom. Production of even the simple word *soon* involves the respiratory system (which itself is multistructural, containing the abdominal muscles, the diaphragm, and the rib cage), the larynx (also a multistructural assembly of cartilage, muscles, and other tissues), the velopharynx, the tongue body, the tongue tip, and the lips.

The magnitude of the problem can be appreciated by attempting to list the sequence of articulations and other actions needed to utter this single monosyllabic word. The challenge grows considerably if we attempt such a listing for a longer utterance, such as "Soon the snow began to melt and the grass began to grow." How does the speech production system manage the movements of so many structures?

The Context-Sensitivity Problem

Another problem is that the production of a given sound

varies with the context in which it is produced. Just as the degrees of freedom problem is not unique to speech, neither is the context-sensitive aspect of action unique to speech; it is true of motor behaviour in general. In fact, any given sound of speech has a large number of physical instantiations. If speech were produced by a simple library of motor commands retrieved as needed for individual phonemes, how would the control system regulate action in the face of a tremendous number of degrees of freedom, and how would it permit extensive adjustments to context?

Many of these effects are subsumed under the term coarticulation, which means that at any one time the speech system shows adjustments for more than one segment. Some examples of coarticulatory patterns show how the tongue position for the velar consonants/k/and/g/varies with the tongue carriage for the following vowel. When the vowel is produced with a relatively front position of the tongue (as in *key*), the constriction for the velar consonant is also relatively front.

But when the vowel has a relatively back tongue position, the constriction for the velar consonant also is made with a back articulation. Careful observations of the lips during production of word pairs such as *soup* and *seep* show that the [s] in *soup* is produced with rounding of the lips, whereas the [s] in *seep* is not produced with such rounding and may even be associated with lip retraction. The labial articulation for the [s] sound apparently is affected by an upcoming sound in the string. The [s] in *soup* is rounded in anticipation of the rounded vowel [u].

However, the [s] in *seep* is not rounded because [i] is not a rounded vowel. Finally, the velum may be raised or lowered during a vowel, depending on whether the following segment is a nasal or oral sound. Vowels in English are typically nasalized when they occur before nasal consonants.

For the sample word *soon*, coarticulation is manifest in several ways, including these:

(1) During the production of the initial [s], the body of the tongue, to some degree, anticipates the retracted

and elevated position needed for the upcoming high-back vowel [u];

(2) The lips are rounded during the production of the initial [s] as preparation for the following rounded vowel [u];

(3) The velopharynx opens during production of the vowel [u] because of the influence of the following nasal consonant [n].

Coarticulation has come to subsume a number of phenomena, not all of which necessarily involve the same level of explanation. Some coarticulatory effects may result from anticipation of forthcoming phonetic requirements in a string of segments; other effects may be determined by biomechanical constraints; and still others may be determined by variations in the timing of articulatory movements within different sequences. These explanations can have profound implications for linguistic theory as well as speech production. Fujimura noted that some contextual variations traditionally classified as allophones may be interpreted as the expressions of variably timed characteristic gestures of different articulators. Browman and Goldstein (in press) described how variations in interarticulator timing could account for phenomena such as deletions, insertions, and feature alterations. Similar ideas have been used by Saltzman and Munhall and Lofqvist to explain the motor patterns of speech.

The articulatory movements can be variably timed during the production of a phonetic sequence. One way of understanding these complex patterns is to recognize that control of the vocal tract is determined by the strength or dominance of a given articular at a given time. At point a, the jaw and tongue have the greatest influence on shaping the vocal tract. Lofqvist viewed the segment as a bundle of gestures characterized by an internal stability of patterns of muscle activation, movement, or both.

The gestural coherence, or togetherness, can be defined at three levels:

(1) Spatial, meaning activation of the same set of muscles,

(2) Temporal, meaning that the gestures should be related by synchronicity, fixed temporal order, or fixed phase,

(3) Scaling, meaning that a scaling or parametre change is distributed over all activated gestures.

An example of scaling is the effect of placing stress on a syllable. When a syllable is given increased stress, several different articulations in the syllable tend to have a greater range of movement and greater movement velocities.

These issues speak directly to the question of input to a speech production model. One model might take allophones as the input segment, thereby referring the assignment of allophonic variations to a phonological stage that precedes speech production per se.

Another model might assume that phonemes (or a similar unit) are the input and that the so-called allophonic variations are a result of variably timed relationships among the articulators. However, *the form of a speech production model depends critically on the assumptions of its formation; one such assumption is the nature of the input to the model.*

Many models implicitly or explicitly assume that the phoneme or a similar segment is a major form of input to the speech production system. The phoneme is a convenient unit for the conversion from a phonological domain to an articulatory system, although the phoneme itself does not necessarily explain all of the details in this conversion. However, some interpretations of *segment* are highly restrictive.

The eminent phonetician Kenneth L. Pike spoke of language in terms of particles, waves, and fields, much as modern physics views light as having both a particle and wave nature.

Meyer emphasized that Pike's idea extends to the phoneme as well as to language more generally. That is, he argued that the phoneme has some properties of the particle, other properties of the wave, and still other properties of the field.

The phoneme has a unitary property insofar as listeners

can hear segments, that is, identify successive units in the speech stream. But the identification of phonemes also is subject to contextual influences, such that a given acoustic segment may be identified quite differently depending on the sound stream that surrounds it. Although this formulation makes it difficult to define the phoneme, it is an alternative to the more traditional conceptualizations, which tend to emphasize the phoneme as unit.

Schools Of Thought in the Modeling of Speech

Theories proposed to account for these problems fall into several general notions of the control of speech production. Some license has been taken in placing individual models within the following categories. A given model may in fact fall under more than one heading, depending on the emphasis given to its properties.

The first set of solutions consists of feedback and feed forward models. The strategy is to use characteristics of the output of the system to modify the controlling process. The reference signal is the *actuating signal,* which causes the system to act or respond in some way. For example, if we take the tongue as a speech structure to be controlled, the reference signal is a motor command (a neural instruction to the tongue muscles), and the output signal is a movement of the tongue. Information about the movement is sent to the brain via the feedback loop, which contains a feedback controller.

The loop for the tongue might include feedback from sensory receptors for touch, position, or movement. The controller has various purposes, typically to generate an error signal from the feedback. For example, if the tongue fails to move far enough to reach a specified target, the error signal is used to correct the deficiency. The error and reference signals are summed in the feedback operation.

The feedback system can work very well if the feedback loop is fast enough to regulate the movement. However, for many human movements, the response to feedback is too slow to keep up with precise movements. Hence, a limiting condition for a feedback model is the latency of the feedback signal. If the latency is too great for the time within which control must be exercised, the feedback model loses credibility.

A particular type of feedback model applied to speech is a servo system model. In control theory a servomechanism is a power-amplifying control system in which the controlled variable is a mechanical position or one of its time derivatives (velocity or acceleration). A familiar servomechanism is the power-steering system of an automobile. When the driver turns the steering wheel, the small rotational torque that the driver applies is amplified hydraulically so that the front wheels of the car move as desired. When the intended angular position of the front wheels is reached, negative feedback is used to decrease the torque from the hydraulic amplifier to zero.

The essential feature of the control system is the use of a feedback path that allows the output (the angular position of the front wheels) to affect the actuating signal (the signal that drives the hydraulic apparatus). To understand how this idea is applied to speech, consider the angular movements of the jaw around the temporomandibular joint. Just as the servo system ensures that the wheels of the car reach the desired position, it can ensure that the jaw reaches the intended amount of opening.

One of the early theories of speech production was the servosystem theory of Fairbanks, who proposed that speech relied on feedback to generate an error signal, which was the means by which the desired output could be achieved. Feedback control is one way to reduce the degrees of freedom in a system. The feedback loop allows for the correction of errors during the operation of the system. This kind of approach is still used today, often for subsystems of speech production.

The general application of feedback for the regulation of speech movements was discussed by MacNeilage, who considered how various receptors, particularly the muscle spindle, could participate in a feedback (closed loop) control system. The term *closed loop* implies that once the command to move has been issued, no further action of the command centre is needed because feedback loops control the outcome.

As noted earlier, the application of the feedback model to speech regulation is limited by the slowness of many important feedback signals. There is another important issue to consider. If speech is under feedback control, disruption of feedback channels should greatly disturb the production of speech. A number of experiments have tested this prediction.

Although the results are mixed, the most persistent conclusion is that attempts to eliminate or distort sensory feedback usually have, at most, slight effects on speech production. Kent, Martin, and Sufit concluded that speech regulation, at least in the mature speaker, does not appear to require *continuous* feedback information. Speakers often seem to compensate quite well for a variety of disruptions, including trigeminal nerve block, topical anesthesia, and noise masking. Although delayed auditory feedback can produce disruptive effects on speech, some speakers learn to speak fluently despite the delayed feedback.

In view of the difficulties with feedback models, several writers have proposed feedforward systems (possibly combined with feedback mechanisms) as a more appropriate model. Feedforward signals make adjustments at the periphery so that the system can respond efficiently to forthcoming instructions. Sometimes the signals bias the operational status of the system, giving it a status suited to the movement about to be performed. Feedforward is particularly useful for systems for planning or prediction.

This capability lets the system adjust for rapid movements and various disturbances or restrictions on motor performance and its sensory feedback. Gracco summarizes research indicating that sensory information plays two major roles in speech motor control.

They are:

(1) To allow comparison of feedback from the periphery with the intended speech goal,

(2) To set parametres or adjust predictively for forthcoming control actions.

One example of contemporary use of feedback control is the adaptive model theory which uses feedback adaptively to control speech. This theory does not assume that a highly practiced motor skill like speech requires continuous sensory feedback. Instead, movements are monitored to determine *whether* the regulatory process needs to be modified. Afference, or feedback, is the means by which errors are corrected if they are detected.

The essence of adaptive model theory is an adaptable store of information based on sensory feedback. This substrate, accomplished over time as feedback derived from motor sequences, generates new actions. A planned sensory trajectory (which prescribes the intended action) is transformed into a corresponding set of motor commands. Feedback is used to monitor the relationship between the motor commands and their multimodal sensory consequences. Iſ necessary, the relationship is modified. In this way the system performs intended movements and gains expertise in planning movements. This model allows for the capability for continual updating of the strategies that relate movement to its sensory outcomes. According to this model, continuous feedback is not essential to speech regulation, but feedback signals can be incorporated into speech production on a provisional and discontinuous basis.

Motor Programme Models

The second set of solutions is a motor programme perspective. A motor programme is a plan or prescription of movement. The word *preplanning* is sometimes used, apparently to emphasize that the movement plan is prepared in advance of its execution and therefore can be said to reside somewhere in the control system even before movements are performed. The ready-made plan is executed by the speech system, much as a computer executes a computer programme.

Different conceptualizations of motor programmes have been described. The extreme version makes no use of peripheral feedback; the commands contained in the programme are sufficient.

Other versions of motor programme theory make allowances for feedback participation in some aspects of regulation. Various terms have been introduced to convey the concept of motor programme, including *motor score, motor goal score, motor plan,* and *movement sequence*. At the heart of these concepts is the idea that speech movements are available in a preassembled form that directs the actual muscular regulation of the production system.

The concept of motor programming for speech has been criticized on several grounds, including its excessive rigidity, failure to account for corrections in the ongoing movement, and inability to assess the status of the periphery and take proper advantage of these initial conditions. These and other criticisms of motor programme theory are discussed at length in Reed. Some critics find it untenable to assume that the action sequences of speech are contained in the brain before the actions of speech are evident.

The concept of a programme has not been abandoned by all speech scientists. Its proponents believe that it accounts for some types of data that are not easily explained by other models. As one example, motor programmes can address latency data in the production of utterances of varying length.

When subjects read aloud words or digits, the voice-onset latency, or the interval from the onset of the stimulus (a visual display) to the beginning of voicing for the response, increases with the number of syllables to be uttered. In other words, the more complex the utterance, the longer it takes to produce it. However, if the speaker is given time to prepare the response before a signal to speak is given, the syllable latency effect disappears.

Therefore, the latency is not simply an initiation effect in which more time is needed to initiate long utterances than short ones. One interpretation is that the utterance to be produced is represented in a motor programme. The execution of this programme depends on its content, especially the number of syllables it contains. Latency effects occur even for simple tasks such as rapid repetition of the same utterance. It appears that latency depends on the motoric complexity of the utterance, not just on the length of the utterance in segments. For example, monosyllables containing the same number of phonetic segments are associated with different latencies.

A sequence composed of CV (consonant + vowel) syllables has shorter syllable durations *and* shorter intersyllable pauses than a sequence composed of VC (vowel + consonant) syllables. One interpretation of this observation is that the intersyllable pause reflects programming time. Using latency data from behavioural responses, Sternberg et al. proposed a three-stage process in the control of motor sequences such as those required for typing and speech:

1. *Retrieval stage*: A search is made for a unit in a preplanned buffer. The search continues until the unit is found, but the unit remains in the buffer after the search is complete.
2. *Unpacking stage*: The constituents of a retrieved unit are separated to make them available for motor execution.
3. *Execution stage*: The motor commands are sent for production of the utterance.

Each stage might contribute to latencies in a speech response. Levelt suggested that retrieval delay varies with the number of units in the buffer, that unpacking delay varies with the complexity of a motor unit, and that during actual production, a speaker can lengthen syllables to absorb latencies in retrieval.

More recently, Sternberg et al. described a two-process model for the control of rapid action sequences in speech production. The first process is subprogramme selection, the duration of which varies directly with sequence length. The second process is command, whose duration depends on the type of unit. Sternberg et al. also proposed that the stress group or metrical foot is the fundamental action unit of speech production. The model can be summarized as a series of two-process connections as follows:

[Unit 1 Selection + Unit 1 Command] + [Unit
2 Selection + Unit 2 Command] +...

Mulder has commented on certain limitations of the additive-factor method inherent to the motor programme model of Sternberg et al. First, this method does not directly show the duration or order of the various stages. Second, it does not yield a substantive interpretation of the proposed stages. Third, if an experimental variable affects both the duration and output of a stage, then the effect of one stage is carried over to subsequent stages.

These limitations complicate the experimental test of additive-factor stage models. The newer model is conceptually simpler than its predecessor and is therefore not so seriously challenged by Mulder's objections. An appealing simplicity is the distinction between the two processes of subprogramme selection and command and the way each relates to measurable properties of response timing.

An approach that may avoid some of the objections to the concept of motor programmes is a *generalized motor programme* (or schema theory), in which motor programmes are composed of *schemata*. Schemata are learned relationships among movement outcomes, control signals, and boundary conditions. For example, a schema may be based on the relationships among initial conditions (e.g., the momentary positions of the articulators), the intended outcome (desired goal of movement), expected sensory consequences (the predicted sensory feedback), and the actual sensory consequences (the actual feedback resulting from movement).

These relationships allow execution of responses, including ones not previously performed, based on a variety of experiences. An important feature of schema theory is that it can account for the learning of novel responses (ones not previously encountered). The schema represents learned relationships and the use of these learned patterns to prepare motor programmes for a response that has not been performed before.

The schemata are enhanced and strengthened by experience; therefore, practice with variable motoric requirements is a route to the development of effective schemata. The inputs are the desired outcome (e.g., a spatial target for a phonetic unit) and the initial conditions (the current state of the speech system, including the positions of the articulators). These inputs are needed for response recognition as a motor response schema.

Past outcomes (earlier speech) and their response specifications determine the response specifications for any desired outcome, even if it has never been produced before. This strategy applies to any motor skill, including athletic skills such as golf, tennis, and archery. In each case it is often necessary to perform a movement slightly different from earlier movements. Performance is based on experience represented in the motor schema, and motor programme is executed from this information. The expected sensory consequences are also generated. For the sake of simplicity, but a plurimodal feedback system is more likely. The expected feedback is compared with the actual feedback to derive error information (e1 and e2), which is used to adjust the motor response schema. A motivating feature of the schema approach is that it tries to account for motor learning. Kent discusses the possible relevance of this model to the learning of speech by children.

Models That Combine Motor Programmes and Feedback Control

Another way of viewing the regulation of speech movements is in terms of combined processes of programming and feedback control. One model that uses such an approach is Perkell's conceptual model of the physiology of speech production. This example of a functional model attempts to identify general processes and types of information used in speech production. It is "physiological" in the sense that it refers to classes of physiological information, such as sensory or motor goals.

It is also an example of a common approach to model building in speech production, to endow the model with various levels of regulation and allow selective feedback to operate across the levels. Perkell's model has three major components. The input is a matrix in which sensory goals are specified for phonetic segments. The sensory goals are regarded as correlates of phonetic features and may refer to patterns of articulatory contact, levels of intraoral air pressure, or articulatory configurations.

Accompanying suprasegmental information also is represented in the input matrix. Situated under the input matrix are three blocks arranged in descending order.

These blocks determine the following:

Block 1. Timing, reorganization, and coarticulation

Block 2. Motor commands

Block 3. Peripheral (vocal tract) events

Block 1 timing is thought to fulfill its role by assigning temporal specifications for sensory goals, such as a specified duration for an articulatory contact. Block 1 reorganization works by reconciling and integrating the sensory goals for different features and suprasegmental factors. The result is a temporal sequence of motor goal specifications, or a motor goal score. This can be thought of as a set of assigned times for individual articulatory actions.

Finally, block 1 look-ahead accounts for anticipatory coarticulation by scanning the input motor goal score (with a window size of about six segments). As it does so, it assigns urgency to each motor goal to reflect the immediacy of the need for achievement. The components of block 1 incorporate aspects of motor programming, including assignment of timing, preparation of a motor score, and forward scan of the score to make adjustments for coarticulation.

Perkell's model separates the biomechanical properties of the speech system from the major components of control. The input matrix and the three functions of block 1 are not immediately constrained by the physical characteristics of the periphery. For example, the timing specifications for the sensory and motor goals are set at early levels in the process. Furthermore, it is not clear that these need to take into account the articulatory biomechanics.

Dynamic Systems Models

Another set of solutions to speech production fall in the

category of dynamic systems (also known as *task dynamics* or *action theory*), in which motor behaviour is viewed in terms of the interactions between biomechanical and environmental variables. Concepts from dynamic systems theory have been applied to many fields of science, including speech and virtually all other human motor activities.

A fundamental idea is to emphasize the interactions of living systems (which are considered nonlinear) with the physical world on which these living systems operate. These interactions define a nonlinear dynamic model that has several stable operational regions with relatively simple control features. That is, the interactions give rise to conditions that afford a comparatively simple and powerful description. Identification of these regions of stability is an important step toward understanding the control of behaviour.

The interactions between any living system and the physical world occur in a number of regions of stable performance, each having relatively few degrees of freedom. These stable regions can be controlled quite easily because there are few degrees of freedom in their regulation. In this way, a system that appears highly complex when its individual components are described can be considered much simpler when the components are functionally linked. In dynamic systems theory (and in related theories known by other names), the degrees of freedom problem is resolved by recognizing functional groupings, or synergies, among the muscles that comprise a system.

This view avoids the implication that each degree of freedom in a system is controlled individually and continuously. Rather, muscles are grouped together to act as a unit in accord with shared afferent and efferent signals. An analogy sometimes used to explain this notion is the control of an airplane. Suppose that an airplane has five movable parts: the two ailerons on the trailing edge of the wings, the two elevators on the horizontal piece of the tail section, and the rudder on the vertical tail fin.

The student pilot initially contends with a control system having five degrees of freedom. (Of course, the degrees of freedom increase as other factors, such as speed of flight, is added.) The pilot soon learns that banking and turning are accomplished with a combination of aileron and rudder movements. This combined action can be defined by an equation of constraint, or a mathematical expression that defines their relative motions for the purpose of banking and turning. Similarly, the elevators have a combined action to change the elevation of the plane.

Smooth and effective control of the plane can be described by appropriate combinations of control actions. These combinations are analogies of coordinative systems in motor control. The essential point is that combined or coordinated control of a system can achieve the intended action of that system. *Coordination* and *intended action* are the key words. In the study of motor control, functional groupings have been called *linkages, synergies, collectives,* and *coordinative structures*. These terms may be regarded as essentially synonymous. The term *synergies* will be used in this chapter. Movements come about when synergies are selected for a given action. The synergies are by their nature task specific, context sensitive, and adaptive.

The synergies possess both essential and nonessential parametres, and these two types of parametres are important for their description. *Essential parametres* are qualitative aspects of a movement's structure (e.g., lip closure for the bilabial stop [b]). *Nonessential parametres* are quantitative, scalar variations (e.g., differing displacements of the lower lip in reaching bilabial closure when variations are introduced in phonetic context, stress, or speaking rate).

The combination can be economically powerful in accounting for speech movements because essential parametres can account for the phonetically distinctive (characteristic) aspects of movement, and the nonessential ones can account for the effects of stress, rate, and other scalar variables that operate within the phonetic requirements of the movements.

The following account describes how the fundamental ideas of task dynamics may be used to produce the syllable *bat* ([b æ t]). The phonological prescription for the syllable does not contain detailed production instructions but only a general form of the intended action. That is, there is no motor programme to direct the details of performance. The details of the motor events are determined by the coordinate grouping, or synergies, among the many possible active elements.

The relationships between the components of a synergetic group and the motor consequence of that synergy are determined by *equations of constraint* that specify how the members of the group can interact within the limits of a particular action and its environmental circumstances. The equations allow a principled variation in the actions of the group members. A given member may vary somewhat in its participation, depending on the actions of other members in the group.

For example, the consonant [b] can be instantiated (a term often used by action theorists to denote a particular motor action) by various combinations of jaw, lower lip, and upper lip movements. But the relative contributions of the mandibular and labial musculature to the final articulation are constrained by the equations that define their performance within the motor objective or goal. The goal is bilabial closure, so the jaw and lip are controlled to reach that goal.

The equation of constraint specifies the ways jaw and lower lip may covary while accomplishing the closure of the two lips. An important concept in dynamic systems is the *emergent property,* a function or action created through preexisting functions. The idea is not to create something out of nothing but rather to create a new thing out of things that already exist.

This possibility often rests on the combination of the preexisting functions into coalitions, or cooperative sets. As synergies combine within a nested or coalitional organization, particular combinations of synergies can bring about properties that were not fully defined in any one synergy acting alone. An emergent property arises naturally through the dynamics of the system. Whereas a motor programme account may specify in detail how components are arranged to accomplish a certain pattern of movement, action theory proposes that the pattern of movement is a natural and predictable consequence of the system's dynamics.

It has been proposed that coordination of movements is an emergent property in the sense that coordination is enabled by the dynamics of cooperating synergies. In this view, coordination is not preassigned, as by a motor programme, but rather follows directly from the system dynamics. How can this be? One possibility is that the dynamics of the different synergies are formed into a superordinate organization that is defined by the interactions of the various participating synergies.

Consider the simple motor act of reaching to grasp a pencil that someone has handed to you. A smooth and successful accomplishment of this act requires that the muscles of the shoulder, arm, wrist, and fingers be properly timed. Obviously, it will not suffice to close the fingers in a grasp before the arm is fully extended to bring the fingers close to the pencil. The dynamics of the grasping motions performed by the fingers must be properly timed with respect to the extension of the arm. Coordination therefore is a blending of the dynamics of the participating synergies.

Von Holst and Haken describe general principles by which the degrees of freedom problem can be solved in a number of physical and biological systems. The central idea is to compress system complexity to a small number of degrees of freedom, sometimes called *order parametres*. These parametres have equations of motion (dynamics) that are low dimensional and nonlinear. A first step in reducing the number of degrees of freedom in a system is to define the task or pattern of action. Take again the bilabial closure for a [b]. The task, closure of the lips, can be accomplished through various movement combinations of the jaw, upper lip, and lower lip.

The degrees of freedom can be precisely determined by examining this behaviour for phase transitions, or circumstances that introduce a qualitative change in the system's behaviour. For example, a horse demonstrates phase transitions as it changes from a trot to a gallop. Phase transitions are studied to determine the order parametre that characterizes the pattern and the control parametres within which patterns occur.

One way to search for phase transitions in speech is to study articulatory movements under changing conditions, such as rate of speech or stress pattern. The equations of motion can be used to identify attractors, or stable solutions. Attractors are a very interesting feature of dynamic systems theory. An especially important aspect of an attractor is that it represents a point of convergence for a system that may have had different initial conditions, or starting points.

That is, regardless of where the system might have been at the start, it can settle into certain regions of stability in its field of dynamic potential. Several types of attractors may define stable motor solutions. These include the *point attractor,* the *limit cycle,* and the *strange attractor*. A point attractor can be illustrated with a pan of water. Shake the pan vigourously so that the water is set into motion.

Place the pan on a table and observe the water. Eventually the water ceases its motion until it seems placid. This settled state is a point attractor. No matter how you shook the pan (clockwise rotation, up and down movements, rocking from side to side), the water will return to this stable state given time for the motions to dissipate. Finger-pointing tasks often are described as having a point attractor. The final goal of pointing is the attractor. An example in speech production is the contact of the tip of the tongue against the alveolar ridge. The tongue may have had very different initial conditions (different positions), but eventually it must reach the desired point of contact.

The limit cycle is a stable state of oscillatory systems such as the pendulum of a large clock. The pendulum settles into a highly repeatable movement. That is, it reaches a stable state defined by a cycle of limiting action. Do our bodies have limit cycles? Observe a person walking briskly. What happens to the person's arms? Are they held rigidly against the body?

No, they usually swing like the pendulum. Swinging is a stable oscillatory state. Limit cycles in speech conceivably could take the form of syllable sequences, stress groupings, or some other rhythmic pattern.

The strange attractor is so named because it is not easily explained. The system under examination has certain stable states, including some that occur only infrequently. Stability can be demonstrated by showing that if the right initial conditions are replicated, the system reaches the same condition. Flowing water is an interesting example because many people think that the detailed motions of falling water have no predictable pattern; that is, the motion seems random.

A person sitting close to a small waterfall may sit safely by the churning water for some time without feeling anything more than a weak spray or mist, but suddenly the action of the water changes and a cold splash arouses our complacent observer. Why did this abrupt change occur? Explanation by strange attractor holds that under certain conditions the overall pattern of the water flow changes and assumes a new form. The event is not random because this occasional form recurs *if the right conditions are repeated*. The person may have to sit by the waterfall for several hours before such patience is rewarded with another splash.

Much literature has accumulated on dynamic systems applied to speech. A special issue of the *Journal of Phonetics* was devoted to the theory of dynamic systems applied to speech production. Nolan and Wilson and Morton evaluated action theory as it relates to normal linguistic behaviour and pathologies of linguistic behaviour.

A primary argument used to support dynamic-system or action-theory approaches to speech production is that they overcome the inherent limitations of translation theories. Translation theory is based on the idea that information is passed through various levels of control of speech production. One problem with translation theories is that the degrees of freedom can quickly become very large, necessitating a complex control operation. Moreover, many studies of movement, both of speech and other systems, have shown that the control and coordination of motor actions are not necessarily determined in a rigid top-down process in which the topmost level has all of the information needed to control the motor events. To the contrary, lower-level systems may account for various aspects of control and coordination that are not specifically addressed at some higher level.

Proponents of dynamic systems also have asserted several advantages in the temporal features of motor regulation. Kelso, Saltzman, and Tuller described a model of movement control in which timing is not an absolute, independent property but rather a feature intrinsic to a more basic description in terms of stable phase relationships between events in various task-coupled articulators. In *phase stability* two or more movements have an invariant phase relationship.

Task-coupled articulators cooperate in the performance of a specific task. Consider the lower lip and jaw (coupled articulators) participating in the formation of bilabial closure (the task). Movement regulation based on absolute time may take a form such as this: The lower lip begins to close 14 ms after the jaw begins to elevate. This approach specifies the interarticulator patterns not in clock time but in phase relationships.

Kelso, Saltzman, and Tuller interpreted their data to support their hypothesis of stable phase relationships between lip and jaw articulations in a speaking task. However, this conclusion has been criticized on several grounds, including failure of replication, possible statistical artifacts, and dependence of the data on speech rates, which may fully explain the apparent phase stability. Moreover, Gentner, in a review of literature on rate variations in movement, concluded that the movements performed at different rates are quite variable and that relative timing measures do not describe the data well.

Another timing advantage was ascribed to dynamic systems theory by Fowler, who contrasts the dynamic systems approach with what she calls extrinsic timing models. She describes dynamic systems as having features of intrinsic timing to explain movement patterns. The extrinsic timing models must in some way impose time on a movement plan. Fowler sees particular advantage in proposing coproduction of consonants and vowels, that is, production in parallel, coordinated systems.

Coproduction is a possible explanation for coarticulation in that vowel and consonant movements can be performed in parallel to yield combined effects in articulation at a given time. (Coarticulation of consonants is not explained by this formulation.) Fowler also uses coproduction to account for the fact that variations in stress and speaking rate affect the relative timing of vowel and consonant movements.

However, Shaffer argues that the explanation does not work because it predicts one of two outcomes, both wrong:

(1) Only one stream of segments (vowels or consonants) should change because they are parallel,
(2) Both streams of segments should change proportionately because they are coordinated.

Whether temporal features are determined intrinsically, extrinsically, or both remains a fundamental question in the regulation of speech.

Interestingly, Gracco argues that coordinative structures (synergies) are *synonymous* with motor programmes. He writes, "Coordinative structures may be more rigidly specified than previously thought and the distinction between a flexible coordinative structure and a hard-wired motor programme algorithm may be more rhetorical than real."

Gracco proposes that speech relies on sensorimotor specifications that determine the relative contribution of the articulators to the overall configuration of the vocal tract. These fixed neuromuscular specifications are compatible with either a motor programme or coordinative structure hypothesis. As evidence of the rigidity of these specifications, Gracco points to studies showing that when the mandible is fixed with a block clenched between the teeth, the jaw closing muscles are nonetheless active.

In addition, experiments involving jaw perturbation demonstrated both functionally specific responses and nonfunctional responses. Some of the key ideas in task dynamics have been incorporated in other models of speech production that are discussed in the following section.

Models of Gestural Patterning

One recent development is the gestural patterning model. The term *gesture* in these models refers to a family of functionally equivalent movement patterns that are actively regulated to achieve a goal relevant to speech. Again, bilabial closure for [b] may include various combinations of jaw, lower lip, and upper lip movements. A gesture includes many aspects of speech production that have been discussed under categories such as context sensitivity and motor equivalence.

Saltzman and Munhall assumed that the invariant units of speech are gestures that relate to context-independent sets of parametres in a dynamical system. The spatiotemporal patterns of speech are considered to be the product of a dynamical system that has two interacting levels:

(a) An *intergestural level,* defined by a set of activation coordinates,

(b) An *interarticulator level,* defined by both model articulator and tract-variable coordinates.

The activation coordinate associated with a particular gestural unit gauges the strength of that gesture in effecting the vocal tract movements at a particular instant. Gestures may compete in terms of their activation coordinates.

Each gestural unit is associated with model articulator variables that specify articulatory movements and tract variables, hence vocal tract configurations. The tract variable coordinates pertain to *context-independent* gestural goals (e.g., bilabial closure). The model articulator coordinates pertain to *context-dependent* performances of a gesture. Therefore, a given vocal tract configuration can have various articulatory implementations, depending on the tractarticulator relationships that apply.

Activation of gestural units at the intergestural level accounts for patterns of relative timing and cohesion for a particular utterance. This level defines an active set of gestures that in turn are related to events at the interarticulator level, where the coordination among articulators is determined. Each gesture is related to a tract-variable dynamical system. In the computer implementation of the model, the dynamical systems are defined as tract-variable point attractors (or stable equilibrium points).

The attractors are modeled as damped second-order linear differential equations that permit the model to generate articulatory motions in an articulatory synthesizer. Early results are promising; the articulatory patterns are consistent with certain effects in natural speech, including articulatory compensation (motor equivalence) and coarticulation.

Saltzman and Munhall succinctly state the essence of their model: "It defines, in effect, a selective pattern of coupling among the articulators that is specific to the set of currently active gestures." In so doing, it gives an intrinsically dynamical account of multiarticulator coordination for gestural activation intervals. However, it does not provide a comparable intrinsically dynamical account of the *intergestural* timing patterns. That is, it lacks serial dynamics. Saltzman and Munhall point to connectionist approaches as a solution, and this recommendation brings us to the next class of models.

Table. Relationships Between Tract Variables and Model Articulatory Variables

Tract Variable	Model Articulator Variables
LP, lip protrusion	(Horizontal lip movement)
LA, lip aperture	(Jaw angle) (Upper lip vertical position) (Lower lip vertical position)
TDCL, tongue dorsum constriction location	(Jaw angle) (Tongue body radial position) (Tongue body angular position)
TDCD, tongue dorsum constriction degree	(Jaw angle) (Tongue body radial position) (Tongue body angular position)
LTH, lower tooth height	(Jaw angle)

TTCL, tongue tip constriction location	(Jaw angle) (Tongue body radial position) (Tongue body angular position) (Tongue tip radial position) (Tongue tip angular position)
TTCD, tongue tip constriction	(Jaw angle) (Tongue body radial position) (Tongue body angular position) (Tongue tip radial position) (Tongue tip angular position)
VEL, velic constriction	(Velar position)
GLO, glottic constriction	(Glottal configuration)

CONNECTIONIST AND SPREADING ACTIVATION MODELS

Connectionist models, also called paralleldistributed processing (PDP), have recently had great influence in a number of disciplines. Not surprisingly, these models have been applied to both speech production and speech perception. The common property of connectionist models, which differ in several particulars, is that they have networks of densely interconnected units. Depending on the particular connectionist model, the units can be arranged in various configurations, or layers.

The input lines to any given unit carry excitatory or inhibitory signals, often called activity, which in most models are simply summed by the unit to determine its state. The state usually is evaluated with respect to a threshold. The activity carried by a given connection can be modulated by a property called weight. The weights assigned to individual connections constitute a kind of memory and can be modified by experience. The overall behaviour of the network depends on the initial state of activation of its units and on the weights of the connections between units. The network can "learn" by using feedback to change the weights of its connections or its threshold values. The network as a whole is a computing device whose configuration of connections is an analog to a computer programme.

PDP is the use of cooperative and parallel processing elements, as opposed to the use of strictly serial steps. Parallel processing allows a great increase in the speed of operation, particularly when individual units have significant processing times.

Massively parallel systems can work much faster than serial systems, in which delays (serial bottlenecks) build up with the sequence of computations. As a crude analogy, imagine five statistics students, each of whom has a statistical calculation to solve. Only one calculator is available to the group of five. If each waits for his or her turn, some time will pass before the solutions to all five problems are in hand. But if five calculators are available, they can work in parallel and arrive at the full set of solutions in short order. The network includes input units, hidden units, and output units. The input units are the information given to the system. The output units are the product of the model.

The input units are connected to the output units by hidden units. The hidden units allow the network to create an internal representation as it works to generate an output. Without hidden units, the network simply links input to output units and may not be appropriate for complex tasks. Hidden units are a powerful addition to the network, particularly since they enable the network to construct an internal representation.

Connectionist models have been implemented on computers and have been used to recognize patterns (such as those of speech), to demonstrate rulelike behaviours (such as the rules of language), and to map the relationships between patterns of input and patterns of output. These models are considered by some to have another attractive feature — they are thought to work much as the brain works. Substitute "neuron" for "unit" and "synaptic connectivity" for "weighted connection," and the analogy comes clear.

The term *neural networks* sometimes is used to refer to connectionist systems. However, the analogy to the brain is not universally accepted. Dell developed a connectionist model for speech production errors, or slips of the tongue.

He defined these errors as unintended, nonhabitual deviations from a speech plan.

His goal was to determine whether a connectionist network could produce errors like those reported for natural speech.

Dell's model was based on two intersecting systems of interconnected nodes, one for linguistic representation (with levels for words, syllables, phonemes, and phonological features), and another for output sequencing (with levels for rimes and clusters, which are constituents of syllables). Dell's model works by *spreading activation*, or the selective radiation of activation along its connections. Both the linguistic subsystem and the sequencing subsystem provide activation input to a phoneme.

As a phoneme is activated, it activates in turn all of the features and syllables to which it is connected. The activated features and syllables (and words) then activate other phonemes. When applied under certain conditions, this spreading activation allows errors to occur. When they do, they are constrained by some of the same factors that seem to constrain errors in natural speech.

For example, syllable position of a sound is a potent factor in accounting for sequencing errors. A general assumption of the spreading activation theory is that representations of an utterance are constructed simultaneously at various levels, but within the limits of coordinated information that operates across levels. For example, a lexical selection must precede assignment of phonological structure. Activation is modeled as a real variable with the properties of spreading (distributing nonzero levels of activation to all connected nodes), summation (integration or addition of activation at each node), and decay (a temporal, passive loss of activation at each node).

A major attraction of PDP models is that they can permit context sensitivity without increasing the number of degrees of freedom. Rumelhart and Norman developed a PDP model for typing, a task that has interesting similarities to speech, particularly in regard to the goal of a serially ordered output

— alphabet letters for typing and phonetic segments for speech.

Jordan and Rosenbaum and Jordan propose a parallel approach to account for serial order that has special relevance to speech production. It operates as follows: An action is a pattern of activation across the output units. Sequences of actions are generated by changing weights in the network. The network receives an external input in the form of a constant *plan* vector, which specifies the sequence to be executed. The network also receives input from a *state* vector, a time function changing in response to recurrent connections affecting the state units.

The model works by decomposing the serial order problem into two subproblems. The first is how to change the state vector in time; the second is how to map the states to actions. The only requirement of the recurrent connections is that they produce discriminable state patterns at each time step.

Additional discriminability comes from the plan. The other parts of the network learn to map the state patterns to target output patterns at each time step. The single output vector means that all actions are a function of one set of tunable weights. As a particular learned action affects the weights, other actions in the sequence are also affected. That is, context sensitivity arises naturally from the operation of the network.

Connectionist systems have become popular in many fields. The many issues surrounding connectionist systems are discussed further by Massaro, Pinker and Meher, and Hanson and Burr. Some hints of the controversy can be offered here. Fant expresses one of the major sources of uneasiness about the connectionist solution for speech production: "It may prove fruitful, but at the same time it implies a failure. We leave it to the computer to learn what we have failed to understand.

The computer might do the job but can it tell us how?" Fant explains that the connectionist approach reveals neither the system at hand nor invariance criteria. It yields "... only a complex pattern of joint probabilities set by a large number of weighting factors within complex layers of neuron-like units trained for the specific task." Some proponents of connectionist systems have admitted that features such as hidden units may have little or no bearing on the behavioural or cognitive phenomena of interest.

Commenting on this issue, Lamberts and d'Ydewalle observed that hidden-unit nets will be of greater psychological relevance if their features are constrained by knowledge gained from psychological research. They assert that "Hidden-unit nets can be used as tools for generating candidate psychological theories, but unless network features are constrained in a psychologically plausible way, a principled choice among these candidates is impossible."

Chapter 7

Composite Models Production

SUBSYSTEM MODELS

The models addressed to this point have intended to explain how speech movements are regulated to accomplish phonetic objectives. Many modeling efforts have been made at subsystem levels. This section addresses models for individual subsystems such as the larynx or vocal tract. It also considers attempts to model the overall system of speech production by taking together various subsystem models into a model of the complete system. Such endeavors have particular value as models for the articulatory synthesis of speech. The term composite model here refers to models that incorporate several submodels or concepts to arrive at an overall model of the speech production system, or at least several of its components. A great deal of modeling has focused on the vocal tract, that subsystem of the speech production system that extends from the vocal folds to the lips. Many of these models neglect the contributions of the larynx and the pulmonary system.

Other models are devoted exclusively to the laryngeal or pulmonary subsystem. Putting these subsystems into a reasonably complete model of the speech production system is an ambitious task. It is best to begin with a brief assessment of each subsystem — respiratory, laryngeal, and supraglottal. This assessment is aimed at a characterization of each subsystem and a very brief introduction to subsystem models.

A number of models attempt to characterize the operation of specific components of speech production. In recent years separate models have been advanced for the respiratory, laryngeal, and supralaryngeal subsystems. A brief discussion of some of these models will illustrate the complexity of behaviours considered in any complete model of speech production.

RESPIRATORY SUBSYSTEM

During speech, one of the main goals of the respiratory system is to maintain an adequate and fairly constant subglottal pressure over the course of an utterance by the coordination of active muscular forces and passive elastic forces. The passive forces are produced by the elastic properties of the respiratory tissues (e.g. lungs, muscles, and tendons of the rib cage), which attempt to return an inflated or deflated respiratory system to its resting position.

These recoil forces are analogous to the force that causes an inflated balloon to deflate. The muscular forces correspond to the active contraction of various respiratory muscles such as those of the rib cage, diaphragm, and abdomen. These act to modulate the passive recoil forces and to produce the ongoing adjustments in subglottal pressure required for speech. In some early models of speech breathing, the active muscular forces were thought to be turned off whenever the passive recoil forces were sufficient to produce the desired subglottal pressures. However, more recent research has demonstrated that the muscular forces are active throughout the speech breathing cycle.

The continuous muscular activity associated with speech breathing may represent a more efficient control strategy than one in which muscular forces are turned on and off. Hixon et al. suggest that this control strategy involves setting the muscles of the respiratory system into a configuration that is optimal for generating rapid pressure changes without requiring major changes in the shape of the system.

In other words, the respiratory system may be tuned to a posture optimally suited to the rapid and fine-grained changes in subglottal pressure required for speech breathing. For a number of years the muscular forces used during the expiratory phase of speech breathing were thought to be caused primarily by the contraction of the muscles of the rib cage (e.g., internal intercostals). The muscles of the abdomen were thought to contribute to the muscular forces only during loud speech or possibly toward the end of the expiratory phases of speech breathing.

However, recent kinematic and dynamic studies of respiration conducted by Hixon and his coworkers have reinterpreted this traditional view, showing that the abdominal muscles are generally quite active throughout the expiratory phase of speech breathing and thus appear to play an important role in speech production. Weismer has argued that this relatively continuous abdominal activity during speech represents a biologically efficient mode of action. First, the continuous contractions of the abdominal muscles appear to provide a platform that optimizes the expiratory actions of the rib cage during speech.

Without such a platform, the expiratory actions of the rib cage would expand the abdomen, reducing the force available for the expiration of air from the lungs. It is further argued that the ongoing contractions of the abdomen may maintain the muscles of the diaphragm at an optimal length for rapid inspiration. In a sense this may reflect the abdomen's contribution to what was described earlier as the speaker's attempt to maintain a preferred respiratory posture that is most efficient for the demands of speech production.

The foregoing describes in a very general way certain characteristics of chest wall behaviour during speech breathing. However, when speech breathing patterns are examined in more detail, a great deal of variability is observed across subjects and speaking tasks. For example, speech breathing patterns have been found to vary with the subject's age, gender, and body type.

The nature of the spoken material (e.g., conversation versus prolonged vowels), the subject's body position (e.g., standing versus supine), and loudness of speech can also influence chest wall configurations. Furthermore, a certain amount of variability has been noted in an individual subject's breathing pattern across repeated productions of the same utterance. This may reflect a form of motor equivalence whereby the speaker uses a variety of chest wall configurations to accomplish similar respiratory goals during speech. These are just a few of the sources of variation that must be explained in any model of speech breathing.

Both Hixon et al. and Weismer emphasize the need for research to describe the influence of various linguistic factors in speech breathing. Hixon et al. call for studies to quantify the relatively minute chest wall adjustments observed during utterances of varying linguistic content. In addition, Weismer points out the paucity of studies on the organization of speech breathing during connected discourse. He suggests that an indepth analysis of the effects of grammatical structure or passage content on chest wall behaviour is necessary.

Laryngeal Subsystem

Attempts to model laryngeal behaviour during speech production have been approached from a number of perspectives. First, because the vocal folds play such an important role in the generation of sound for speech production, attention has been focused on the mechanisms responsible for vocal fold vibration. Models of vocal fold vibration attempt to explain the biomechanical and aerodynamic forces responsible for different patterns of vibration.

For example, Ishizaka and Matsudaira developed a *two-mass model* of vocal fold vibration in which the upper and lower portions of each vocal fold are characterized as two separate masses connected by elastic components.

This model describes how aerodynamic forces due to subglottal pressure and the flow of air through the glottis (Bernoulli forces) are sequenced with the elastic forces of the vocal fold tissues to produce the continuous vibrations of the vocal folds. The two-mass model also helps to explain certain microaspects of laryngeal kinematics such as the vertical wave in vocal fold vibration, which is characterized by the bottom edge of the vocal fold moving in advance of the top edge throughout the vibratory cycle.

Some theorists have further refined the two-mass model by adding more components (e.g., the 16-mass model by Titze with the result that additional microaspects of laryngeal vibration can be explained.

Anatomical and histological studies of the vocal folds have led to the development of theories to explain some of the prosodic and qualitative aspects of vocal behaviour. For example, the cover-body theory posits that certain aspects of vocal behaviour result from the speaker's explicit control of the mechanical properties of different layers of tissue in the vocal folds.

As a first approximation, the vocal fold is seen to be composed of two separate layers, a cover layer near the surface of the fold and a body layer lying deeper in the vocal fold. Contraction of different laryngeal muscles alters the relative stiffness of these two layers, and this causes different patterns of vocal fold vibration.

For example, Hirano suggests that weak contractions of the vocalis and cricothyroid muscles produce both a slack cover and body layer, resulting in a soft phonatory pattern produced at a low fundamental frequency. In contrast, if the strength of contraction in the vocalis muscle is increased while that of the cricothyroid remains relatively weak, the body layer will become stiffer than the cover layer.

According to the theory, this will result in a louder phonatory pattern at a medium fundamental frequency. Thus, through graduated changes in the relative stiffness of the vocal fold layers, it is hypothesized, the speaker can make a variety of prosodic changes during speech. Vocal fold vibration and its timing relative to supralaryngeal movements are also seen to be critical for certain segmental aspects of speech production.

For example, the coordination of voice onset with lingual and labial releasing gestures has a major contribution to the voicing contrast in obstruent consonants (e.g., [p] versus [b]).

In the case of voiceless obstruents (e.g., [p t s k]), vocal fold vibration is interrupted briefly by what Weismer called the "laryngeal devoicing gesture." This gesture appears to have an immutable and fairly stereotypical topology across a variety of contexts.

A very tight temporal relationship exists between this laryngeal gesture and other oral gestures. For example, the sound/p/is produced with a laryngeal devoicing gesture whose peak in laryngeal abduction coincides with the onset of the bilabial opening gesture. Attempts to explain the mechanisms by which the speaker achieves such precise control in the timing of multiple gestures has been a central issue in the development of many recent models of speech production. This issue will be treated in more detail in subsequent sections.

Supralaryngeal Subsystem

Attempts to characterize the supralaryngeal subsystem form the basis of much theoretical work in speech production. The models discussed here are those that attempt to describe the principles for controlling a single speech articulator or a restricted portion of the supralaryngeal system.

The major task of the supralaryngeal system in speech is to shape and constrict the vocal tract in ways that accomplish specific patterns of acoustic output. For many speech sounds these constrictions are due in large part to the movements of a single supralaryngeal articulator.

For example, the production of an alveolar lingual plosive (e.g., [t]) is due primarily to movements of the front of the tongue. Other parts of the tongue and other articulators (e.g., the jaw) are also involved, but they have a relatively minor or indirect role in the production of this sound.

To a large extent, models of single-articulator movements and of subsystems have intended to explain the variability of speech movements. For example, the quantal theory of articulation explains the variability in speech production in terms of acoustic and perceptual constraints. Drawing on the acoustic theories of speech production, the quantal theory holds that in critical regions of the vocal tract, small articulatory adjustments can have relatively large acoustic consequences.

The sensitivity in these critical regions is seen as a problem for articulatory control because these regions demand a high degree of articulatory precision to produce a specific result. The quantal theory posits that the speech production system employs a control strategy that avoids these critical regions as places of articulation for speech sounds. The quantal theory accounts for certain articulatory-acoustic relations in speech production, but it is not a complete theory for the regulation of speech sounds.

Wood and Perkell and Nelson support the basic conceptions of quantal theory by showing that during vowel productions the articulations of the tongue are least variable in dimensions that are the most critical for acoustic output (e.g., the degree of vocal tract constriction). Thus, in the supralaryngeal system, there may be acoustically driven constraints operating to control the amount of variation in articulatory positions.

Other models describe the variability of movements from one articulatory position to another. For example, Fujimura and Kent have observed that vowel-to consonant and consonant-to-vowel articulatory transitions are produced in a fairly standard manner. Fujimura emphasizes the importance of these stable transitional movements in his *iceberg model* of articulatory invariance. In this model, the transitions are seen as fixed elementary gestures that are free to vary with respect to one another in time.

The metaphor of icebergs continuously shifting their relative positions in currents of water emphasizes the concept of these stable transitional movements in speech production. Kent argues that stereotypical transitional segments may reflect optimized movement patterns for speech produced under normal conditions. He suggests that under certain abnormal circumstances such as neuropathology or possibly during certain prosodic changes (e.g., slow speaking rate), the form of these transitional movements may change.

Presumably this results from some change in the underlying movement variables being controlled or optimized.

Many studies of supralaryngeal articulation describe the variations of specific movement parametres such as the amplitude of a movement, the average or maximum velocity of a movement, and the duration of a movement. Some researchers have modeled the mechanisms of motor control responsible for changes in these variables. Ostry and Munhall model the control of specific movement variables associated with transitional movements produced at various speaking rates.

They found systematic changes in certain movement variables (e.g., peak velocity and movement amplitude) as speakers increased their rates of speech. They interpret their data in the context of a mass-spring model of articulation, in which the transitional movements in speech are likened to the movements of a mass attached to a spring. The speed of movement of the mass can be increased if the stiffness of the spring is increased.

Similarly, the mass-spring model suggests that changes in the speed of transitional movements are accomplished by explicit control of the stiffness of the speech articulators. Ostry, Keller, and Parush and Ostry, Cooke, and Munhall have also applied the mass-spring model to other oral nonspeech transitional movements and transitional movements of the limbs. Thus, it appears that controlling articulatory stiffness to change the rate of movement may reflect a general strategy of motor control that has been incorporated into the speech production system. It seems likely that in a behaviour as complex as speech, there may be a nesting of numerous motor control strategies, some specific to speech and others related to more global aspects of movement control. Determination of the physical economies of movement should underlie an understanding of movement control.

Many models focus on simplifying notions of vocal tract configurations. The work on vowels is illustrative. Stevens and House and Fant developed a three-parametre model of the vocal tract shape for vowels based on:

- Location of the constriction,
- Size of the constriction,
- The ratio of mouth opening to length.

Liljencrants, Harshman, Ladefoged, and Goldstein, Kiritani, and Maeda have taken statistical approaches, especially factor analysis.

Generally, the factor analytical studies agree that vowel articulation can be described with two tongue factors, a lip factor, and perhaps a jaw factor.

Still another direction in modeling is to identify independently controllable functional blocks, or solid articulatory structures, by which the articulatory organs can be represented. Rubin, Baer, and Mermelstein incorporated their model in the gestural patterning model of Saltzman and Munhall.

A basic goal in this work is to reduce the number of degrees of freedom compared with that required for an acoustic tube model of the vocal tract divided into sections 0.5 to 1 cm long. As Scully points out, ideally the number of degrees of freedom in an articulatory model should be identical to that defined by the physiological constraints of the actual articulatory system. We thus return to the fundamental issue of degrees of freedom.

Composite Models

The foregoing illustrates that the speech production system can be viewed as a complex arrangement of multiple subsystems operating in parallel or in series and that each one is fairly complicated. Unfortunately, most models of speech production address only individual subsystems or single levels within a subsystem. One of the great challenges of modeling is to explain the way these subsystems are integrated together in the production of speech. Allwood and Scully and Scully have produced a composite model of the speech production process.

The model identifies parametres at the pulmonary, laryngeal, and supralaryngeal levels. The parametres are divided into three major categories: articulatory, aerodynamic and mechanical. Computer implementation requires three major programmes, one for timing and articulation, another for aerodynamics with acoustic sources, and a third for filtering the acoustic sources by the vocal tract and radiating the sound pressure wave of speech.

Scully describes the application of this model to the study of differences between speakers, with the intent of developing rules to identify types of speakers. In fact, the parametres must be precisely regulated and coordinated. The accuracy of the model depends on the availability of data on the various subsystems of speech production. Therefore, the actual implementation is a highly involved set of computer programmes that reflect much accumulated knowledge about speech production.

LANGUAGE BEHAVIOUR

Although one could become completely occupied in the study of speech as a motor behaviour or a conversion of articulation to sound pattern, speech is, after all, of greatest interest because of its primacy as a language modality. One of the most exciting facets of a speech production model is what it can tell us about language. The study of language generally may also direct research and theory on speech production.

That is, speech is constrained not only by the task dynamics of its production system and the articulatory-acoustic relations of the vocal tract, but also by its service to language. Unfortunately, only a few brave scientists have directly attacked the formidable question of how speech production relates to a more general model or theory of language formulation. A particularly comprehensive source of information on this topic is Levelt, who considers speech from "intention to articulation".

Another valuable source is Bock's 1982 presentation of a model for utterance formulation. Gee and Grosjean have done related work on prosodic patterns as performance structures of language, and Martin has studied the rhythmic structure of spoken language. Eventually speech must be integrated into a fuller understanding of human language and its social utility. One aspect of speech is often taken as an important attribute but is neglected in speech production models.

This aspect, rhythm, may hold particular significance in relating speech to language behaviour. Speech has a rhythmic quality, as is most evident in the recitation of verse. Simply, rhythm is the distribution of various levels of stress across a chain of syllables. The implementation of rhythm involves a complex interaction beginning at the sentence or phrase level and going down to the actuation of individual phonemes. Rhythm also plays a key role in the understanding of speech.

It is thought to provide a listener with the means to anticipate future elements in the speech stream for more efficient perceptual processing. To give credence to the concept of rhythm, researchers have attempted to uncover consistent aspects of stress patterning. Temporal measures, such as the interval between two stressed syllables and the duration of metrical feet (a foot consists of a combination of stressed and unstressed syllables), have been analysed for consistency.

The only positive durational finding was a tendency for constancy (isochronicity) in some types of metrical feet. This difficulty in uncovering the rhythmic units of speech has led some researchers to speculate that the perceptual phenomena of rhythm may be based on some other acoustical aspect of stress besides duration. More recently, metric phonology has set forth a different view of rhythmic organization.

To establish rhythmic constancy, individuals manipulate the placement of stress by avoiding strings of adjoining stressed syllables or adjoining unstressed syllables. That is, speakers alternate strong and weak stress. One means of testing this hypothesis is to observe whether individuals shift syllable stress in phrases where stress clashing (two adjacent strong stress syllables) occurs.

If Selkirk's hypothesis holds true, there is a tendency for a speaker to adjust the metrical pattern of the second stressed syllable. Perceptually, the stressed syllable may provide the beat for which anticipatory perceptual processing can be undertaken. The perceptual salience of the stressed syllable is enhanced by the adjacent unstressed syllable. Cooper and Eady and Kelly and Bock undertook relevant studies. Cooper and Eady measured the duration and pitch change associated with the stress clash.

They did not find an acoustic reduction in stress (reduced duration and pitch) for either syllable of the stress clash pair. Kelly and Bock chose a perceptual means to test for changes in the metrical feet. Their findings indicated that speakers did tend to change the metrical feet so as to impose alternating stress rhythm. These mixed but promising results provide a slightly clearer picture of the rhythmic characteristics of speech, which need to be accounted for in a model of speech.

Rhythm has not been addressed with much satisfaction in the majority of models discussed in this chapter. Indeed, many models ignore it altogether. It will be interesting to observe in the development of speech production models whether rhythm will be a clarifying and organizing influence on models or simply an add-on feature. Edelman, writing on the *theory of neuronal group selection*, gives particular emphasis to rhythm as a potent factor in the evolution of language:

In the evolution of speech systems, the linkage of the means of sound production to the breath period and to the rhythm of speech was probably particularly important. This temporal aspect of the production of speech sounds was, in all likelihood, correlated with the phasic reentrant signaling of cortical systems yielding correlations among various memory systems.

A concept of speech organization with implications for rhythm and other aspects of prosody is known as *slots and fillers* or *frames and contents*. Slots (or frames) are syllable markers embodying information such as speaking rate and stress. Fillers (or contents) are the phonetic segments assigned to slots (or frames). In this view, speech is organized in two channels, one representing syllable markers and the other representing the phonetic content associated with syllables.

Lindblom introduced the *H & H theory*, which has a number of implications for understanding speech behaviour in its communicative function. Basically, this theory holds that speech is controlled along a continuum of *hyperspeech* to *hypospeech*. Hyperspeech is described as output-oriented because this kind of control is purposive and prospectively organized.

Speakers use hyperspeech to ensure that speech sound discriminations can be made by a listener. Hypospeech is system-oriented in the sense that it seeks a low-cost form of regulation. Speakers tend to use hypospeech to minimize the energy costs of speech production. Especially when other factors, such as context and topic familiarity, can be relied on to facilitate transmission of the message, speakers are inclined to use hypospeech.

The output-oriented aspects of hyperspeech (insure speech sound discriminability) are in conflict with the system-oriented aspects of hypospeech (save energy), which is to say that both sets of aspects cannot be completely satisfied at the same time. The theory holds that a speaker selects for a given situation the degree to which hyperspeech or hypospeech will prevail.

In other words, speech production is not undertaken with an invariant regulatory process but rather with a regulatory process that is adjusted to the demands of the situation. It has been suggested that when speakers make adjustments along a certain hypo-hyper continuum, such as intended clarity, there may be an active reorganization of phonetic gestures.

Results from an acoustic study of duration dependent formant undershoot during clear speech have been offered as support for this reorganization hypothesis. (*Formant undershoot* is a formant pattern that falls short of the formant-frequency values observed in an isolated or context-free production of the sound in question; in other words, the speaker falls short of the full movement for a sound.) Moon's results indicate that while clear speech is associated with a certain degree of formant undershoot at shorter vowel durations, the amount of undershoot is much less than that observed during a more casual citation-form of speech.

Thus, for equivalent vowel durations, clear speech appears to show less formant undershoot than more casual styles of speech. A parallel finding was obtained in a kinematic analysis of clear and casual speech. Tongue movements produced during clear speech were found to have larger movement amplitudes and greater peak velocities than movements produced at equivalent durations during a more casual style of speech. However, these kinematic differences were not associated with any fundamental changes in the relationship between peak velocity and movement amplitude or the topology of movements, as measured by the velocity profiles, during clear speech. This led Adams to conclude that although clear speech may be associated with slightly larger movement amplitudes in some speakers, there is little evidence that variations in clarity are associated with a basic reorganization of motor control processes.

At least three drifts of major importance are discernible. Each of these has operated for centuries, each is at work in other parts of our linguistic mechanism, each is almost certain to continue for centuries, possibly millennia. The first is the familiar tendency to level the distinction between the subjective and the objective, itself but a late chapter in the steady reduction of the old Indo-European system of syntactic cases. This system, which is at present bestpreserved in Lithuanian, was already considerably reduced in the old Germanic language of which English, Dutch, German, Danish, and Swedish are modern dialectic forms.

The seven Indo-European cases (nominative, genitive, dative, accusative, ablative, locative, instrumental) had been already reduced to four (nominative, genitive, dative, accusative). We know this from a careful comparison of and reconstruction based on the oldest Germanic dialects of which we still have records. In the group of West Germanic dialects, for the study of which Old High German, Anglo-Saxon, Old Frisian, and Old Saxon are our oldest and most valuable sources, we still have these four cases, but the phonetic form of the case syllables is already greatly reduced and in certain paradigms particular cases have coalesced.

The case system is practically intact but it is evidently moving towards further disintegration. Within the Anglo-Saxon and early Middle English period there took place further changes in the same direction. The phonetic form of the case syllables became still further reduced and the distinction between the accusative and the dative finally disappeared.

The new "objective" is really an amalgam of old accusative and dative forms; thus, *him,* the old dative (we still say *I give him the book,* not "abbreviated" from *I give to him;* compare Gothic *imma,* modern German *ihm*), took over the functions of the old accusative and dative. The distinction between the nominative and accusative was nibbled away by phonetic processes and morphological levelings until only certain pronouns retained distinctive subjective and objective forms.

In later medieval and in modern times there have been comparatively few apparent changes in our case system apart from the gradual replacement of *thou—thee* (singular) and subjective *ye*—objective *you* (plural) by a single undifferentiated form *you*. All the while, however, the case system, such as it is (subjective-objective, really absolutive, and possessive in nouns; subjective, objective, and possessive in certain pronouns) has been steadily weakening in psychological respects.

At present it is more seriously undermined than most of us realise. The possessive has little vitality except in the pronoun and in animate nouns. Theoretically we can still say *the moon's phases* or *a newspaper's vogue;* practically we limit ourselves pretty much to analytic locutions like *the phases of the moon* and *the vogue of a newspaper*. The drift is clearly toward the limitation of possessive forms to animate nouns. All the possessive pronominal forms except *its* and, in part, *their* and *theirs,* are also animate.

It is significant that *theirs* is hardly ever used in reference to inanimate nouns, that there is some reluctance to so use *their,* and that *its* also is beginning to give way to *of it. The appearance of it* or *the looks of it* is more in the current of the language than *its appearance.* It is curiously significant that *its young* (referring to an animal's cubs) is idiomatically preferable to *the young of it.*

The form is only ostensibly neuter, in feeling it is animate; psychologically it belongs with *his children,* not with *the pieces of it.* Can it be that so common a word as *its* is actually beginning to be difficult? Is it too doomed to disappear? It would be rash to say that it shows signs of approaching obsolescence, but that it is steadily weakeningis fairly clear. In any event, it is not too much to say that there is a strong drift towards the restriction of the inflected possessive forms to animate nouns and pronouns.

How is it with the alternation of subjective and objective in the pronoun? Granted that *whom* is a weak sister, that the two cases have been leveled in *you* (in *it, that,* and *what* they were never distinct, so far as we can tell), and that *her* as an objective is a trifle weak because of its formal identity with the possessive *her,* is there any reason to doubt the vitality of such alternations as *I see the man* and *the man sees me?*

Surely the distinction between subjective *I* and objective *me,* between subjective *he* and objective *him,* and correspondingly for other personal pronouns, belongs to the very core of the language. We can throw *whom* to the dogs, somehow make shift to do without an *its,* but to level *I* and *me* to a single case—would that not be to un-English our language beyond recognition? There is no drift toward such horrors as *Me see him* or *I see he.*

True, the phonetic disparity between *I* and *me, he* and *him, we* and *us,* has been too great for any serious possibility of form leveling. It does not follow that the case distinction as such is still vital. One of the most insidious peculiarities of a linguistic drift is that where it cannot destroy what lies in its way it renders it innocuous by washing the old significance out of it. It turns its very enemies to its own uses.

This brings us to the second of the major drifts, the tendency to fixed position in the sentence, determined by the syntactic relation of the word. We need not go into the history of this all-important drift. It is enough to know that as the inflected forms of English became scantier, as the syntactic relations were more and more inadequately expressed by the forms of the words themselves, position in the sentence gradually took over functions originally foreign to it. *The man* in *the man sees the dog* is subjective; in *the dog sees the man,* objective.

Strictly parallel to these sentences are *he sees the dog* and *the dog sees him.* Are the subjective value of *he* and the objective value of *him* entirely, or even mainly, dependent on the difference of form? I doubt it. We could hold to such a view if it were possible to say *the dog sees he* or *him sees the dog.* It was once possible to say such things, but we have lost the power.

In other words, at least part of the case feeling in *he* and *him* is to be credited to their position before or after the verb. May it not be, then, that *he* and *him, we* and *us,* are not so much subjective and objective forms as pre-verbal and post-verbal forms, very much as *my* and *mine* are now pre-nominal and post-nominal forms of the possessive (*my father* but *father mine; it is my book* but *the book is mine)?*

That this interpretation corresponds to the actual drift of the English language is again indicated by the language of the folk. The folk says *it is me,* not *it is I,* which is "correct" but just as falsely so as the *whom did you see?* that we have analysed. *I'm the one, it's me; we're the ones, it's us that will win out*—such are the live parallelisms in English to-day.

There is little doubt that *it is I* will one day be as impossible in English as *c'est je,* for *c'est moi,* is now in French. How differently our *I: me* feels than in Chaucer's day is shown by the Chaucerian *it am I.* Here the distinctively subjective aspect of the *I* was enough to influence the form of the preceding verb in spite of the introductory *it;* Chaucer's locution clearly felt more like a Latin *sum ego* than a modern *it is I* or colloquial *it is me.*

We have a curious bit of further evidence to prove that the English personal pronouns have lost some share of their original syntactic force. Were *he* and *she* subjective forms pure and simple, were they not striving, so to speak, to become caseless absolutives, like *man* or any other noun, we should not have been able to coin such compounds as *he-goat* and *she-goat,* words that are psychologically analogous to *bull-moose* and *mother-bear.*

Again, in inquiring about a new-born baby, we ask *Is it a he or a she?* quite as though *he* and *she* were the equivalents of *male* and *female* or *boy* and *girl.* All in all, we may conclude that our English case system is weaker than it looks and that, in one way or another, it is destined to get itself reduced to an absolutive (caseless) form for all nouns and pronouns but those that are animate.

Animate nouns and pronouns are sure to have distinctive possessive forms for an indefinitely long period. Meanwhile observe that the old alignment of case forms is being invaded by two new categories—a positional category (pre-verbal, post-verbal) and a classificatory category (animate, inanimate).

The facts that in the possessive animate nouns and pronouns are destined to be more and more sharply distinguished from inanimate nouns and pronouns (*the man's,* but *of the house; his,* but *of it*) and that, on the whole, it is only animate pronouns that distinguish pre-verbal and post-verbal forms are of the greatest theoretical interest.

They show that, however the language strive for a more and more analytic form, it is by no means manifesting a drift toward the expression of "pure" relational concepts in the Indo-Chinese manner. The insistence on the concreteness of the relational concepts is clearly stronger than the destructive power of the most sweeping and persistent drifts that we know of in the history and prehistory of our language.

The drift toward the abolition of most case distinctions and the correlative drift toward position as an all-important grammatical method are accompanied, in a sense dominated, by the last of the three major drifts that I have referred to.

This is the drift toward the invariable word. In analyzing the "whom" sentence I pointed out that the rhetorical emphasis natural to an interrogative pronoun lost something by its form variability (*who, whose, whom*). This striving for a simple, unnuanced correspondence between idea and word, as invariable as may be, is very strong in English.

It accounts for a number of tendencies which at first sight seem unconnected. Certain well-established forms, like the present third person singular *-s* of *works* or the plural *-s* of *books.* have resisted the drift to invariable words, possibly because they symbolize certain stronger form cravings that we do not yet fully understand.

It is interesting to note that derivations that get away sufficiently from the concrete notion of the radical word to exist as independent conceptual centres are not affected by this elusive drift. As soon as the derivation runs danger of being felt as a mere nuancing of, a finicky play on, the primary concept, it tends to be absorbed by the radical word, to disappear as such.

English words crave spaces between them, they do not like to huddle in clusters of slightly divergent centres of meaning, each edging a little away from the rest. *Goodness,* a noun of quality, almost a noun of relation, that takes its cue from the concrete idea of "good" without necessarily predicating that quality (e.g., *I do not think much of his goodness*) is sufficiently spaced from *good* itself not to need fear absorption. Similarly, *unable* can hold its own against *able* because it destroys the latter's sphere of influence; *unable* is psychologically as distinct from *able* as is *blundering* or *stupid.* It is different with adverbs in *-ly.* These lean too heavily on their adjectives to have the kind of vitality that English demands of its words. *Do it quickly!* drags psychologically.

The nuance expressed by *quickly* is too close to that of *quick,* their circles of concreteness are too nearly the same, for the two words to feel comfortable together. The adverbs in *-ly* are likely to go to the wall in the not too distant future for this very reason and in face of their obvious usefulness. Another instance of the sacrifice of highly useful forms to this impatience of nuancing is the group *whence, whither, hence, hither, thence, thither.*

They could not persist in live usage because they impinged too solidly upon the circles of meaning represented by the words *where, here* and *there.* In saying *whither* we feel too keenly that we repeat all of *where.* That we add to *where* an important nuance of direction irritates rather than satisfies. We prefer to merge the static and the directive (*Where do you live?* like *Where are you going?*) or, if need be, to overdo a little the concept of direction (*Where are you running to?*).

Now it is highly symptomatic of the nature of the drift away from word clusters that we do not object to nuances as such, we object to having the nuances formally earmarked for us. As a matter of fact our vocabulary is rich in near-synonyms and in groups of words that are psychologically near relatives, but these near-synonyms and these groups do not hang together by reason of etymology. We are satisfied with *believe* and *credible* just because they keep aloof from each other. *Good* and *well* go better together than *quick* and *quickly.*

The English vocabulary is a rich medley because each English word wants its own castle. Has English long been peculiarly receptive to foreign words because it craves the staking out of as many word areas as possible, or, conversely, has the mechanical imposition of a flood of French and Latin loan-words, unrooted in our earlier tradition, so dulled our feeling for the possibilities of our native resources that we are allowing these to shrink by default? I suspect that both propositions are true.

Each feeds on the other. I do not think it likely, however, that the borrowings in English have been as mechanical and external a process as they are generally represented to have been. There was something about the English drift as early as the period following the Norman Conquest that welcomed the new words. They were a compensation for something that was weakening within.

NEURAL MODELS OF SPEECH PRODUCTION

The challenges of modeling loom even larger with the neural regulation of human speech. This chapter does not present detailed models of the neural control of speech or discuss putative differences between the cerebral hemispheres in the processing of various kinds of information for speech and language. Netsell and Kuehn, Lemme, and Baumgartner offer general coverage of neural bases of speech and language.

Instead this brief section considers some general models for the neural control of speech as a voluntary motor behaviour. One of the most frequently reproduced diagrams to represent the motor control of speech is one adapted from Allen and Tsukahara. This diagram, in the original or a modified form, has been presented as a model for speech regulation by Hirose, Netsell, and Barlow and Farley, among others.

The pathways for the planning, programming, and execution of movement are depicted. Obviously, this is a very general conception of the neural control of voluntary movement. The brain structures and pathways are not specific to speech. The model serves primarily to identify parts of the nervous system that control various aspects of movement.

The parietal, frontal, and temporal cortices are thought to be involved in the initial planning for action (or *intent*). In addition, movement is programmed in a system composed of the premotor cortex, supplementary motor area, thalamus, lateral cerebellum, and motor cortex. The medial cerebellum monitors the motor instructions from the motor cortex and may revise them as needed to accomplish the goal.

Somatosensory afference is the primary feedback channel and the feedback is probably plurimodal, involving taction, movement, position, aerodynamic, and other signals. Certain observations on the control of voluntary movement suggest some changes in the picture. First, Eccles has reviewed evidence that the initial neuronal event in all voluntary movements is in the supplementary motor areas of both hemispheres.

Another possible change is motivated by the work summarized by De Long and Alexander showing that the basal ganglia-thalamocortical circuit may consist of segmental circuits, with at least a motor loop and an association loop, if not several such loops. Alexander, De Long and Strick and Miller and De Long have proposed a parallel organization of several such segmental circuits, in which a portion of the striatum, principally the putatem, receives partially overlapping projections from the motor cortex, premotor cortex, supplementary motor area, primary somatosensory cortex, and superior parietal lobule.

The somatopically organized projections are thought to be maintained from putamen to globus pallidus and substantia nigra. The putamen thus represents a convergence of segmental circuits from various cortical regions. The basal ganglia are thought by many neuroscientists to be involved somehow in the programming of movement, one major aspect of which may be the coupling of sensory and motor responses.

One possibility of such coupling for speech is the preparation of sensorimotor trajectories that guide the performance of movement. Edelman wrote that the basal ganglia, by virtue of their connections to prefrontal, premotor, and motor areas, may play an important role in linking motor programmes to behavioural plans.

Another feature that may require modification, or at least essential elaboration, is the interconnections among various cortical and subcortical sites. Edelman proposed that serially-ordered behaviour is based on interconnections among neuronal groups in various regions "that are responsive to moment to-moment sensory input." The importance of these interconnections is that they enable cortical neuronal groups to anticipate the consequences of their own activity and thereby prepare for the next action in a series. Cortical regions may be particularly responsible for longer intervals in the preparation and planning of action. Edelman wrote of "organs of succession," meaning brain structures that participate in the regulation of successive actions.

He ascribed time constants to various structures in the following manner: neocortex — short, medium, and long; basal ganglia-short; and cerebellum — short. With respect to the control of voluntary movements like speech, these time constants can be interpreted to mean that the neocortex maintains the long-term pattern of an action series, while the basal ganglia and cerebellum are responsible for relatively short spans of time.

The basal ganglia participate in aspects of programming and sensorimotor coordination, and the cerebellum engages primarily in the control of timing and synchronization of movements. In this conceptualization, the control of succession is distributed among various parts of the brain according to time constants of activity.

The extension of this idea to language as well as speech may provide some useful hypotheses for the governance of syntactic relationships, semantic associations, and morphologic units. Ideas about the neural control of language are changing rapidly. New data from brain imaging are providing new insights into patterns of brain activity associated with language. In addition, new hypotheses are being formulated about brain structures that have not been clearly represented in extant theories of neural bases of language.

For example, recent speculations attribute important cognitive and language functions to the cerebellum a structure conspicuously lacking in classical accounts of brain systems in language. Research on neural function in oral and vocal behaviour of animals also is a rich source of hypotheses about the neural bases of language. Although humans may be unique in possessing language, some mechanisms related to language may be shared by humans and animals.

Chapter 8

Phonetic English Dictionary

Phonetic dictionaries are special dictionaries that list words by how they sound instead of how they are spelled. English phonetic dictionaries are particularly helpful to people just learning a language, because phonetic dictionaries represent words the way they're meant to be pronounced using the sounds and characters of any language.

STUSY OF PHONETICS

Phonetics is a branch of linguistic study that concerns itself with how words sound-not how they look, what they mean, or where they're from. Phonetics can help people better understand a language through hearing, and better speak a language by providing help with pronunciation.

USE OF PHONETIC DICTIONARY

Just about anyone can use a phonetic dictionary! For example, students who are unfamiliar with the English language might pick up a phonetic dictionary to accustom themselves with the way a word is intended to sound, which helps with pronunciation, identification, and comprehension of English words. These are particularly helpful to non-native English speakers who are proficient in reading and understanding the written language, but have trouble speaking it and comprehending it when it is spoken. Some teachers are beginning to use phonetic dictionaries with pictures as a way to aid younger students who are just learning to read-being able to learn bigger words and understand how those words are put together through phonics can result in better listening comprehension, and can aid the young boy or girl as he or she begins to identify and sound out words. Phonetic dictionaries are very useful tools for writers and poets as well. Alliteration, assonance, rhyme, and consonance refer to the way certain parts of words sound like one another. In addition to rhyme, poets use repetition of other sounds to engage a reader and to express different emotions. Searchable online phonetic dictionaries, and searchable software version, can help to construct more interesting, beautiful-sounding pieces of work.

ABOUT THE IPA

In case you were wondering, there is actually a standardized, prescribed set of phonetic rules known as the International Phonetic Alphabet that anyone can use (in any language) to learn the sounds and pronunciation of another language. When you look inside of a normal dictionary like Webster's or the Oxford English Dictionary, you'll often notice a string of funny symbols next to a word, usually before the definition. These symbols, based in the Latin alphabet, allow for a word to be written and transcribed into any language—and still read the same way aloud! These symbols can be extremely useful, as they demonstrate the proper way of pronouncing a word and offer various alternative pronunciations also considered to be correct.

PROBLEMS AND SOLUTIONS

The problem with the International Phonetic Alphabet, however, is that the symbols are somewhat difficult to learn, almost like trying to learn another whole language on its own. Plus, if a person already knows how to pronounce a word but simply cannot find the definition, they're still stuck. Phonetic dictionaries often do two things: first, they will take the IPA recommended pronunciation of a word and convert it into more common characters. Then, they list the newly spelled (or misspelled!) words in alphabetical order. Take, for example, the common word "fiancée," a woman engaged to be married. "Fiancée" can actually be pronounced in one of two ways—with the accent on the second or third syllable. The IPA lists the pronunciation of this word as either "fiQn'sej" or "fi'Qnsej." To most people, these symbols look quite foreign. Other dictionaries might use still other standardized forms of phonetic pronunciation; for example, "fç'än-sâ'."

However, a phonetic dictionary takes the IPA pronunciation and shows the way the word is pronounced in a particular language. A phonetic dictionary might list the word as being pronounced "fee-ahn-sey" or "fee-ahn-say," with the accent on the bolded portion of the word. These words would be listed in order of pronunciation with other words that have the same beginning sound, whether the word begins with "fee," "fi," "phi" or "fei."

FINDING A PHONETIC DICTIONARY

Phonetic dictionaries are available everywhere. They can be bought from bookstores or universities and online. Many phonetic dictionaries are now run through computers to allow a user to try out different types of phonetic searches with just a few clicks. Software for these dictionaries can sometimes be downloaded for free. And many online phonetic dictionaries exist as well—some for children, some for adults; some for native Spanish or French speakers; and some for parties simply interested in the way a particular word is supposed to sound. Here are some links to online phonetic dictionaries to get you started:This is meant to be a starting point for newbie's to the Korean language. Since most people new to Korea are not familiar with the language at all, and not yet ready to attempt reading or writing the actual Korean language, we have not included any introduction or comparison between the actual Korean characters and the English equivalents.

Keep in mind that the sounds we are used to making in our language are different in the Korean language. This dictionary will give you a starting point to the Korean words, but in order to perfect the actual pronunciation, you should try to practice the words with Koreans or others. that have spent some time in Korea, and are familiar and comfortable with the language.

A

Abalone - Axe

Abalone	Chuhn-bohk
Abdomen	P(B)ae
Abnormal	ee-sahng-hae
Abortion	Yoo-sahn
Absent	Kyuhl-g(k)uuhn
Absent-minded	Muhng-hah-goh-ee-nuuhn
Abundance	Poong-boo
Abundant	Poong-boo-hahn
Academy	Hahg-wahn
Accommodation (lodgings)	Soog(k)-soh
Accomplice	G(K)ohng-bahm-jah
Ache	Ah-puuh-yoh or Ah-puuh-dah
Acorn	D(T)oh-toh-ree
Acquaintance	Ah-nuuhn-sah-rahm
Actor	Nahm-bae-oo
Actress	Yuh-bae-oo
Add	D(T)uh-hah-dah
Address (mail)	J(CH)oo-soh
Adjust	J(CH)uhng-dohn-hah-dah
Administrator	Haeng-juhng-gwahn
Adopted son	Yahng-jah
Adult	Uh-ruuhn
Adventure	Moh-huhm
Adventurer	Moh-huhm-gah
Adversary (enemy)	Wuhn-soo
Adversary (opponent)	Sahng-dae
Advertisement	Kwahng-goh
Advice	Choong-goh
Advise	Choong-goh-hah-dah
Adviser	J(CH)oh-uhn-jah
Airplane	B(P)ee-haeng-gee
Affection (Love)	Ae-Joh-ng
Afraid	Moo-suh-wah

Afternoon	Oh-hoo
Age (years)	Nah-ee
Age (period)	Yuhn-dae
Agree	D(T)ohng-ee-hah-dah
Air (atmosphere)	G(K)ohng-gee
Air Base	G(K)ohng-goon gee-jee
Air Conditioning	Naeng-nahn-bahng
Alarm Clock	J(CH)ah-myuhng-johng
Alcohol	Al-koh-ol
Algebra	D(T)ae-soo-hahk
Alive	Sah-rah-ee-nuuhn
Alligator	Ahg-uh
Alphabet	Al-pah-bet
Aluminum	Al-roo-mee-nyoom
Ambassador	D(T)ae-sah
Ambulance	G(K)oo-goop-chah
America	Mee-gook
American (person)	Mee-gook-een
American (language)	Mee-gook-uh
Anatomy	Hae-boo
Ancestor	J(CH)oh-sahng
Angel	Chuhn-sah
Angry	Shung-nah-soh
Animal	D(T)ohng-mool
Ankle	B(P)ahl-mohk
Anniversary	G(K)ee-nyuhm-eel
Ant	G(K)ae-mee
Apartment	Ah-paht-uh
Room	B(P)ahng
Ape	Wuhn-soong-ee
Apple	Sah-gwah
Apricot	Sahl-goo
April	Sah-wuhl
Aquarium	Soo-johk-gwahn
Archaeology	G(K)oh-goh-hahk
Archery	G(K)oong-sool

Architect	G(K)uhn-chook-gah
Architecture	G(K)uhn-chook-sool
Area (space)	Myuhn-juhk
Arithmetic	Sahn-soo
Arm	Pahl
Army	Yook-goon
Artist	Hwah-gah
Asia	Ah-see-ah
Asthma	Chuhn-seek
Astrology	J(Ch)uhm-suhng-hahk
Astronomer	Chuhn-moon-hahk-jah
Astronomy	Chuhn-moon-hahk
Athlete	oohn-dohng-suhn-soo
Athletics	oohn-dohng-G(K)yuhng-gee
Atlantic	D(T)ae-suh-yahng
Atlas	J(Ch)ee-doh-chaek
Atom	Wuhn-jah
August	Pahl-wuhl
Aunt	Sook-moh
Author	J(Ch)uh-jah Automobile
J(Ch)áh-dohng-chah	Autumn G(K)ah-uuhl
Aviation	B(P)ee-haeng
Aviator	B(P)ee-haeng-sah
Axe	D(T)oh-ggee

B

Baby - Buy

Baby	Ah-gee
Back (of body)	D(T)wee
Backbone	Chuhk-choo
Bacon	B(P)eh-ee-kuhn
Baggage	Soo-hah-mool
Bake	G(K)oop-dah
Bald	D(T)ae-muh-ree
Balloon	Poong-suhn
Bamboo	D(T)ae-nah-moo
Banana	B(P)ah-nah-nah
Band (music)	Ahk-dae

Bandage	B(P)oong-dae
Bank	Uuhn-haeng
Barber shop	Ee-bahl-gwahn
Base (of operations)	B(P)oo-dae
Baseball	Yah-goo
Basketball	Nohng-goo
Bat (animal)	B(P)ahk-jee
Bath	Mohk-yohk
Bathe	Mohk-yohk-hah-dah
Bathroom	Hwah-Jahng-s(sh)eel
Beach	Hae-beeuhm
Bear	G(K)ohm
Beard	Soo-yuhm
Beautiful	Ah-ruuhm-dah-oon
Beauty parlor	Mee-jahng-wuhn
Bed	J(Ch)eem-dae
Bed clothes	J(Ch)ahm-oht
Bedding	J(Ch)eem-goo-reeyoo
Bedroom	J(Ch)eem-s(sh)eel
Bee	Kkool-buhl
Beef	Soh-goh-gee
Beehive	Kkool-buhl-jeep
Beer	Maek-joo
Beginner (novice)	J(Ch)oh-boh-jah
Bible	Suhng-geeuhng-chaek
Bicycle	J(Ch)ah-juhn-guh
Big	Kuuh-dah
Billiards	D(T)ahng-goo
Bill	G(K)ae-sahn-suh
Binoculars	Ssahng-ahn-gee-uhng
Biography	J(Ch)uhn-gee
Biology	Saeng-mool-hahk
Bird	Sae
Birthday	Saeng-ell
Birthplace	J(Ch)ool-saeng-jee
Blackboard	J(Ch)eel-pahn
Black market	Ahm-s(sh)ee-jahng
Blanket	D(T)ahm-yoh

Bleach	Peeyo-baek-hah-dah
Blood	Pee
Bloo	Kkoh-chee pee-dah
Blossom	Kkoht
Blouse	B(P)uuhl-rah-oo-suuh
Blue	Poo-ruuhn
Blueprint	J(Ch)uhng-sah-jeen
Boar (wild)	Meht-twae-jee
Boat 1	J(Ch)ahk-uhn g(k)ee-suhn
Boat 2	B(P)oh-oo-tuuh
Body	Yook-cheh
Boil	Gg(Kk)uuhl-tah
Bone	Bb(Pp)ee-uh
Book	Chaek
Bookstore	Suh-juhm
Bottle	B(P)ee-uhng
Bottom	Meet-bah-dahk
Bottomless	Meet-bah-dahk-ee uhp-nuuhn
Bouquet	Gg(Kk)oht-dah-bahl
Bow (the head)	J(Ch)uhl-hah-dah
Bowl	Sah-bahl
Boy	Nahm-jah-ah-ee
Bracelet	Pahl-jjee
Brain	Nwae
Branch (of tree)	G(K)ah-jee
Bread	Bb(Pp)ahng
Bride	S(Sh)een-boo
Bridegroom	S(Sh)eel-lahng
Bridesmaid	S(Sh)een-boo d(t)uuhl-ruh-re
Brides man	S(Sh)eel-lahng d(t)uuhl-ruh-ree
Bring (of things)	G(K)ah-jeeuh-oh-dah
Broadcasting station	B(P)ahng-sohng-gook
Broil	G(K)oop-dah
Broken	B(P)oo-suh-jeen
Bronchitis	G(k)ee-gwahn-jee-yuhm
Broom	B(P)ee-chah-roo
Bucket	Yahng-dohng-ee
Buddha	B(P)oo-chuh

Buddhism	B(P)ool-gee-oh
Buddhist	B(P)ool-gee-oh-doh
Buddhist temple	J(Ch)uhl
Bull (animal)	Hwahng-soh
Bull frog	S(Sh)eek-yohng G(K)ae-goo-ree
Bus	B(P)uh-suuh
Butcher	Poo-joo-hahn
Butter	Buh-tuh
Butterfly	Nah-bee
Button	D(T)ahn-choo
Button hole	D(T)ahn-choo G(K)oo-muhng
Buy	Sah-dah

C

Cabbage - Customs

Cabbage	Yahng-bae-choo
Cake	Keh-eek-uh
Calculate	G(K)ae-sahn-hah-dah
Calculation	G(K)ae-sahn
Calendar	D(T)ahl-yuhk
Calf	Sohng-ah-jee
Camel	Nahk-tah
Camera	Sah-jeeng-gee
Camping	Yah-yuhng
Campus	Hahk-geeyoh G(K)oo-naeCandle
Yahng-choh	
Candle light	Choht-bool
Candle stick	Choht-dae
Candy	Sah-tahng
Car	J(Ch)ah-dohng-chah
Career (occupation)	J(Ch)eek-Jahng-een
Carpenter	Mohk-soo
Carrot	D(T)ahng-guuhn
Cat	G(K)oh-yahn-gee
Caterpillar	Pool-sswae-gee
Cave	G(K)ool
Celery	Sehl-ruh-ree
Cemetrey	G(K)ohng-dohng-mee-oh-jee

Centipede	J(Ch)ee-neh
Ceremony	Yeh-S(sh)eek
Chair	Uuhee-jah
Chalk	B(P)oon-peel
Change (money)	J(Ch)ahn-dohn
Checker board	J(Ch)ahng-gee-pahn
Checkers	Suh-yahng-jahng-gee
Cheek	Bb(Pp)ee-ahm
Cheese	Chee-ee-juuh
Chemistry	Hwah-hahk
Cherry	B(P)uh-jjee
Chess	Cheh-suuh
Chestnut	B(P)ahm
Chewing gum	Gg(Kk)uhm
Chicken	D(T)ahk
Chicken meat	D(T)ahk-goh-gee
Child	Uh-reen-ee
Chin	Tuhk
China (country)	J(Ch)oong-gook
China (porcelain)	D(T)oh-jah-gee
Chinese (language)	J(Ch)oong-gook-uh
Chinese (people)	J(Ch)oong-gook-een
Chocolate	Chohk-uhl-reet
Chopsticks	J(Ch)uht-gah-rahk
Christian	G(K)ee-dohk-geeoh-een
Church	G(K)eeoh-hey
Cider	Sah-ee-dah
Cigarette	D(T)ahm-bae
City	D(T)oh-s(sh)ee
Classmate	D(T)ohng-guuhp-saeng
Classroom	G(K)ee-oh-s(sh)eel
Clock	D(T)aht-dah
Closet	B(P)ee-uhk-jahng
Clothes	Oht
Coat	Wae-too
Coconut	Yah-jah-yuhl-mae
Coffee	Koh-oh-pee
College	D(T)ahn-gwah-dae-hahk

Comb	B(P)eet
Community	Sah-wey
Company (firm)	Hey-sah
Competition	G(K)eeuhng-jaeng
Concert	Uuhm-ahk-hey
Congratulation	Chook-hah
Consonant	J(Ch)ah-uuhm
Contagious	J(Ch)uhn-yuhm-suhng
Contaminate	Oh-yuhm-s(sh)eek-ee-dah
Contraband	Meel-soo
Contract	G(K)ae-yahk
Contribution	G(K)ee-boo
Convert (money)	D(T)ohn pahk-oo-dah
Cook	Yoh-ree-hah-dah
Cook (person)	Yoh-ree-sah
Cookie	G(K)wah-jah
Copy	B(P)eh-ggee-dah
Corn	Ohk-soo-soo
Cost (price)	G(K)ahp
Cotton	Sohm
Cough	G(K)ee-cheem
Courthouse	B(P)uhp-whun
Cousin	Sah-chuhn
Crab	G(K)eh
Cracker (biscuit)	Kuuh-rae-kuh
Crane (bird)	Hahk
Crane (machine)	G(K)ee-joong-gee
Crayon	Kuuh-reh-yohng
Cream	kuuh-ree-eem
Cricket (insect)	G(K)wee-ddoo-rah-mee
Crime	J(Ch)ey
Criminal	B(P)uhm-j(ch)ey-chah
Crocodile	Ahg(k)-uh
Cruise (sail)	Soon-hahng-hah-dah
Cucumber	Oh-ee
Cup 1	J(Ch)ahn
Cup 2	Kuhp
Cupboard	Chahn-jahng

Curfew	Tohng-haeng-guuhm-jee
Cushion	B(P)ahng-suhk
Customer	G(K)oh-gaek
Customs (import duties)	G(K)wahn-seh

D

Daffodil - Dysentery

Daffodil	Soo-suhn-hwah
Dairy products	Yoo-jeh-poom
Daisy	S(sh)eel-gook-hwah
Dam	D(T)aem
Dance	Choom
Dancer (professional)	Moo-yohng-gah
Dandelion	Meen-duuhl-reh
Danger	Wee-huhm
Dangerous	Wee-huhm-hahm
Dark	Uh-doo-oon
Daughter	Ddahl
Daughter-in-law	Meeuh-nuuh-ree
Dawn	Sae-bee-yuhk
Day	Nahl
Dead	J(Ch)ook-uuhn
Deadly	Chee-meeyuhng-juh-keen
Deaf	G(K)wee-muhk-uuhn
Dean (college)	Hahk-jahng
Death	J(Ch)ook-uuhm
December	S(Sh)eep-ee-wuhl
Decorate	Gg(Kk)oo-mee-dah
Decoration	J(Ch)ahng-s(sh)eek
Deer	Sah-suuhm
Degree (school)	Hahk-wee
Delicious	Mah-s(sh)ee-nuuhn
Democracy	Meen-joo-joo-uuhee
Democratic	Meen-joo-juhng-cheh-uuhee
Dentist	Chee-gwah-uuhee-sah
Depart	Dd(Tt)uh-nah-dah
Department store (mall)	B(P)aek-hwah-juhm
Departure	Chool-bahl

Desert	Sah-mahk
Desk	Chaek-sahng
Dessert	D(T)ee-juh-uh-tuuh
Detain (keep waiting)	G(K)ee-dah-ree-geh hah-dah
Dew	Ee-suuhl
Diametre	J(Ch)ee-ruuhm
Diamond	G(K)uuhm-gahng-suhk
Diaper	G(K)ee-juh-gwee
Diarrhea	Suhl-sah
Diary	Eel-gee
Dice	J(Ch)oo-sah-wee
Dictatorship	D(T)ohk-jae
Dictionary	Sah-juhn
Diet (loose weight)	Sahl-pae-dah
Diet (menu)	S(Sh)ee-gee-yuhp-puhp
Digestion	Soh-hwah
Dimple	B(P)oh-joh-gae
Dining	S(Sh)eek-sah
Dining room	S(Sh)eek-dahng
Dining table	S(Sh)eek-tahk
Dinner	J(Ch)uhng-chahn
Diploma	J(Ch)oh-ruhp-jahng
Direction	B(P)ahng-heeahng
Dirty	D(T)uh-ruh-oon
Disaster	J(Ch)ae-nahn
Discount	Hah-reen
Disease	B(P)ee-uhng
Dish	J(Ch)uhp-s(sh)ee
Distance	G(K)uh-ree
Dizzy	Uh-jee-ruh-oon
Doctor	Uuhee-sah
Dog	G(K)ae
Donkey	D(T)ahng-nah-gwee
Door	Moon
Dormitory	G(K)ee-sook-sah
Downtown	D(T)oh-s(sh)eem-jee
Dozen	Yuhl-doo-gae
Dragonfly	J(Ch)ahm-jah-ree

Dress (put on)	Eep-dah
Dresser	Hwah-jahng-dae
Drink	Mah-S(Sh)ee-dah
Duck (animal)	Oh-ree
Dusk	Dd(Tt)ahng-guh-mee
Dust	Muhn-jee
Dusty	Muhn-jee too-suhng-ee
Duty	Uuhee-moo
Dye	Mool-gahm
Dysentery	Ee-jeel

E

Eagle - Eyesight

Eagle	D(T)ohk-soo-ree
Ear	G(K)wee
Early	Ee-ruuhn
Earring	G(K)wee-goh-ree
Earth	Ee-seh-sahng
Earthquake	J(Ch)ee-jeen
Earthworm	J(Ch)ee-ruhng-ee
East	D(T)ohng-jjohk
Easter	B(P)oo-hwal-juhl
Eat	Muhk-dah
Eclipse (lunar)	Wuhl-S(Sh)eek
Eclipse (solar)	Eel-s(Sh)eek
Eclipse (total)	G(K)ae-gee-s(sh)eek
Economics	G(K)ee-uhng-jeh-hahk
Economy	G(K)ee-uhng-jeh
Editor	Pee-uhn-jeep-jah
Educate	G(K)eeoh-yook-hah-dah
Education	G(K)eeoh-yook
Eel	B(P)aem-jahng-uh
Egg (chicken)	G(K)ae-rahn
Eggplant	G(K)ah-jee
Egypt	Ee-jeep-tuuh
Elastic	G(K)oh-moo-jool
Elbow	Pahl-ggoom-chee
Electrician	J(Ch)uhn-gee G(K)ee-sah

Electricity	J(Ch)uhn-gee
Elementary school	G(K)oog(k)-meen-hahk-geeyoh
Elephant	Koh-ggee-ree
Elevator	Suuhng-gahng-gee
Embark (board)	B(P)ae-ruuhl-tah-dah
Embark (start)	Chool-bahl-hah-dah
Embassy	D(T)ae-sah-gwahn
Emerald	Eh-muh-rahl-duuh
Emergency	B(P)ee-sahng-sah-tae
Employee	G(K)oh-yohng-een
Employer	G(K)oh-yohng-joo
Employment	G(K)oh-yohng
Encyclopedia	B(P)aek-gwah-sah-juhn
Engine	G(K)ee-gwahn
Engineer	G(K)ee-sah
England	Yuhng-gook
English (language)	Yuhng-uh
Englishman	Yuhng-gook-sah-rahm
Enter (go into)	D(T)uuh-ruh-gah-dah
Entertainment	J(Ch)uhp-dae
Entrance (door)	Eep-goo
Envelope	Pee-uhn-jee-b(p)ohng-too
Environment	Hwahn-geeuhng
Equator	J(Ch)uhk-doh
Eraser	J(Ch)ee-oo-gae
Estimate (of cost)	G(K)eeuhn-juhk
Estimate (written)	G(K)eeuhn-juhk-suh
Europe	Yoo-ruhp
European	Yoo-ruhp-een
Evening	J(Ch)uh-neeuhk
Evil	Nah-bbuuhn
Evolution	J(Ch)een-hwah
Examination	(Sh)ee-huhm
Examine	S(Sh)ee-huhm-hah-dah
Example	B(P)oh-gee
Exchange	G(K)eeoh-hwahn
Exercise	Oon-dohng
Exit	Chool-goo

Expedition	Wuhn-Juhng
Expensive	B(P)ee-sah-dah
Experience	G(K)eeuhng-huhm
Experiment	S(Sh)eel-huhm
Expert	Eek-sook-hahn
Exploration	Tahm-huhm
Explore	Tahm-huhm-hah-dah
Explorer	Tahm-huhm-gah
Exterior	B(P)ah-ggah-tuuhee
Eye	Noon
Eyebrow	Noon-ssuhp
Eyelash	Sohk-noon-ssuhp
Eyelid	Noon-gguh-pool
Eyesight	S(Sh)ee-reeuhk

F

Face - Future

Face	Uh-guhl
Factory	G(K)ohng-jahng
Faith	S(Sh)een-ahng
Faithful	S(Sh)eel-ley-hahl-soo eet-nuuhn
Fall (Autumn)	G(K)ah-uuhl
Family	G(K)ah-johk
Famous	Yoo-meeyuhng-hahn
Fan (electric)	Sahn-poon-gee
Fan (hand)	B(P)oo-chae
Farm	Nohng-jahng
Farm house	Nohng-gah
Farmer	Nohng-boo
Farming	Nohng-uhp
Fashion	Yoo-haeng
Fashionable	Yoo-haeng-eh maht-nuuhn
Father	Ah-buh-jee
Fawn	Sae-ggee sah-suuhm
Feather	G(K)eet-tuhl
February	Ee-wuhl
Female	Yuh-jah
Fence	D(T)ahm

Fern	G(K)oh-sah-ree
Ferry	Yuhl-lahk-suhn
Festival	Chook-jeh
Fiction (novel)	Soh-suhl
Fig	Moo-hwah-gwah
Fight	Ssah-oom
Film	Peel-ruuhm
Filter	G(K)uh-ruuh-dah
Finger	Sohn-gah-rahk
Finger nail	Sohn-tohp
Finger print	J(Ch)ee-moon
Fire	B(P)ool
Fire escape	B(P)ee-sahng-goo
Fire extinguisher	Soh-hwah-gee
Fireman	Soh-bahng-gwahn
Fish	Saeng-suhn
Fisherman	Uh-boo
Fishing	G(K)oh-gee-jahp-ee
Flag	G(K)ee
Flavour	Maht
Flea	B(P)eeuh-rook
Float	Dd(Tt)uuh-dah
Floor	Meet-dah-dahk
Flour	Meel-gah-roo
Flower	Gg(Kk)oht
Flower pot	Hwah-boon
Flu	Yoo-haeng-suhng kahm-gee
Fly (flight)	B(P)ee-haeng
Fly (insect)	Pah-ree
Fog	Ahn-gae
Foil	Uuhn-bahk-jee
Food	Uuhm-s(sh)eek
Foot	B(P)ahl
Football	Poot-boh-ohl
Forehead	Ee-mah
Foreigner	Wey-gook-een
Forest	Soop
Fork	Sahm-chahng

Fox	Yuh-oo
Fraction (math)	B(P)oon-soo
Fragrance	Heeahng-gee
Free	Moo-ree-oh
Freedom	Chah-yoo
Freeze	Uhl-dah
Friday	G(K)uuhm-yoh-eel
Friend	Cheeng-goo
Frog	G(K)ae-goo-ree
Frost	Suh-ree
Frozen	Ah-ruuh-soom
Fruit	G(K)wah-eel
Fry	Twee-gee-dah
Frying pan	Puuh-rah-ee-paen
Full moon	B(P)oh-ruuhm-dahl
Fume	Yuhn-gee
Fun	J(Ch)ae-mee
Funeral	J(Ch)ahng-nae-s(sh)eek
Funny	J(Ch)ae-mee-eet-nuuhn
Fur	Moh-pee
Furnishings	Seh-gahn
Furniture	G(K)ah-goo
Fuse	Peeyoo-juuh
Future	Mee-rae

G

Gallery - Gymnastics

Gallery	Hwah-rahng
Gamble	Toh-bahk
Game	Oh-rahk
Garbage	Ssuuh-reh-gee
Garden	J(Ch)uhng-wuhn
Gardener	J(Ch)uhng-wuhn-sah
Garlic	Mah-nuhl
Garnish	J(Ch)ahng-S(sh)eek
Gas (natural)	Chuhn-yuhn-gah-suuh
Gasoline	Hwee-bahl-yoo
Gauze	G(K)ah-ah-jeh

Gem	B(P)oh-suhk
Gentleman	S(Sh)een-sah
Geography	J(Ch)ee-ree-hahk
Geology	J(Ch)ee-jeel-hahk
Geometry	G(K)ee-hah-hahk
German (language)	D(T)ohk-ee-ruh
German (people)	D(T)ohk-eel-sah-rahm
Germany	D(T)ohk-eel
Ghost	Yoo-ree-uhng
Gift	Suhn-mool
Ginger	Saeng-gahng
Ginseng	Een-sahm
Giraffe	G(K)ee-reen
Girl	Soh-neeuh
Glass (drinking)	Yoo-ree kuhp
Glasses (spectacles)	Ahn-gee-uhng
Glove	J(Ch)ahng-gahp
Glue	Pool
Go	G(K)ah-dah
Goat	Yuhm-soh
Gold	G(K)uuhm
Goldfish	G(K)uuhm-boong-uh
Golf	G(K)ohl-puuh
Goose	G(K)uh-wee
Government	J(Ch)uhng-boo
Governor	Tohng-chee-jah
Grand daughter	Sohn-nyuh
Grand father	Hah-rah-buh-jee
Grand mother	Hahl-muh-nee
Grand son	Sohn-jah
Grape	Poh-doh
Grapevine	Poh-doh-duhng-gool
Grasshopper	Meh-ddoo-gee
Grave	Moo-duhm
Gravestone	Meeoh-bee
Graveyard	Meeoh-jee
Gravy	G(K)oh-gee g(k)ook-mool
Great granddaughter	J(Ch)uuhng-sohn-nyuh

Great grandfather	J(Ch)uuhng-joh-boo
Great grandmother	J(Ch)uuhng-joh-moh
Great grandson	J(Ch)uuhng-sohn-jah
Green (colour)	Choh-rohk
Greenhouse	Ohn-s(sh)eel
Grey/gray	Hwey-saek
Groceries	S(Sh)eek-neeoh-poom
Grow	J(Ch)ah-rah-dah
Guard	Pah-soo-goon
Guest	Sohn-neem
Guide	Ahn-nae-jah
Guidebook	Yuh-haeng ahn-nae-suh
Gum (chewing)	Gg(Kk)uhm
Gymnasium	Cheh-yook-gwahn
Gymnastics	Cheh-joh

H

Habit - Husband

Habit (reoccurrence)	B(P)uh-ruuht
Hair	Tuhl
Hairbrush	Muh-ree-sohl
Half-moon	B(P)ahn-dahl
Ham	Haem
Hammer	Mahng-chee
Hand (of the body)	Sohn
Handbag	Sohn-gah-bahng
Handkerchief	Sohn-soo-guhn
Handshake	Ahk-soo
Handsome	J(Ch)ahl-saeng-geen
Hangar	G(K)ee-ohk-nahp-goh
Hanger	Oht-guh-ree
Happy	Haeng-bohk-hahn
Harp (Korean)	G(K)uh-moon-goh
Harvest	Soo-hwahk
Hat	Moh-jah
Hawk	Mae
Hay	G(K)uhn-choh
Haystack	G(K)uhn-choh g(k)ah-ree

Hazy (weather)	Huuh-reen-nahl-sshi
Head	Muh-ree
Headache	D(T)oo-Tohng
Healthy	G(K)uhn-gahng-hahn
Hear	D(T)uuht-dah
Hearing	D(T)uuht-gee
Heart	S(Sh)eem-jahng
Heart disease	S(Sh)eem-Jahng-beeuhng
Heartburn	G(K)ah-suuhm-ah-ree
Heater	Nahn-bahng-jahng-chee
Heaven	Chuhn-gook
Heavenly	Chuhl-lae-uuhee
Heavy	Moo-guh-oon
Heel	D(T)wee-ggoom-chee
Height	Noh-pee
Heirloom	G(K)ah-boh
Helicopter	Hehl-ree-kohp-tuh
Hello (telephone)	Yuh-boh-seh-yoh
Help	D(T)oh-oom
Hemisphere	B(P)ahn-goo
Hen	Ahm-tahk
Henhouse	D(T)ahk-jahng
Herb	Choh-bohn
Herb (medicinal)	Yahk-choh
Hiccup	Dd(Tt)ahl-ggook-jeel
Highway	G(K)oh-sohk-toh-roh
Hike	D(T)oh-boh yuh-haeng
Hill	Uhn-duhk
Hire	G(K)oh-yohng
History	Yuhk-sah
Hives	D(T)oo-duuh-ruh-gee
Hobby	Chwee-mee
Hoe	G(K)waeng-ee
Hole	G(K)oo-muhng
Holiday	Hyoo-eel
Home	G(K)ah-juhng
Home (native land)	B(P)ohn-gook
Homesick	Hee-ahng-soo-bee-uhng

Homework	Sook-jeh
Honey	Gg(Kk)ool
Honeymoon	Meel-wuhl
Horse	Mahl
Horse race	G(K)ee-uhng-mah
Hospital	B(P)ee-uhng-wuhn
Hot (spicy)	Mae-oon
Hot (temperature)	D(T)oh-oon
Hot spring	Ohn-chuhn
House	J(Ch)eep
Hundred	B(P)aek
Hungry	B(P)ae-goh-poon
Hurricane	Pohk-poong
Hurry	Bb(Pp)ah-lee
Husband	Nahm-pyuhn

I

Ice - Ivy

Ice	Uh-ruuhm
Ice cream	Ah-ee-suuh-kuuh-reem
Ice house	Uh-ruuhm chahng-goh
Ice water	Uh-ruuhm-mool
Iceberg	B(P)eeng-sahn
Icebox (refrigerator)	Naeng-jahng-goh
Icicle	G(K)oh-duuh-ruuhm
Identification card	S(Sh)een-boon-juuhng
Ill (sick)	B(P)eeuhng-duuhn
Illegal	B(P)ool-buhp
Immigrant	Ee-meen
Immigrate	Ee-joo-hah-yuh-oh-dah
Import	Soo-eep-hah-dah
Important	J(Ch)oong-yoh-hahn
Incense	Heeahng
Inch	Een-chee
Incline (angle)	G(K)ee-ool-dah
Income	Soo-eep
Incubator	B(P)oohwah-gee
India	Een-doh

Indigestion	Soh-hwah-b(p)ool-yahng
Industrial	Sahn-uhp-uuhee
Industry	Sahn-uhp
Infant	Yoo-ah
Infantry	B(P)oh-beeuhng
Infect	J(Ch)uhn-yuhm-sheek-ee-dah
Infection	J(Ch)uhn-yuhm
Influenza	Yoo-haeng-suhng gahm-gee
Information	J(Ch)ee-s(sh)eek
Ingredient	Suhng-boon
Inhabit	G(K)oh-joo-hah-dah
Inhabitant	J(Ch)oo-meen
Inherit	Sahng-sohk-hah-dah
Injection	J(Ch)oo-sah
Injure	D(T)ah-chee-dah
Ink	Eeng-kuuh
Inlet (entrance)	Eep-goo
Inoculate	Yeh-bahng-junp-johng
Inoculation	J(Ch)uhp-johng
Insect	G(K)ohn-choong
Insecticide	Sahl-choong-jeh
Inspect	J(Ch)oh-sah-hah-dah
Inspection	G(K)uhm-sah
Inspector	G(K)uhm-sah-gwahn
Institute	Heeuhp-hae
Instructor	G(K)eeoh-sah
International	G(K)ook-jeh-juhk-een
Interpret	Hae-suhk-hah-dah
Interpreter	Hae-suhl-jah
Interrogation	J(Ch)eel-moon
Invent	B(P)ahl-meeuhng-hah-dah
Invention	B(P)ahl-meeuhng-poom
Inventor	B(P)ahl-meeuhng-gah
Invitation	Choh-dae
Invite	Choh-dae-hah-dah
Ironing	D(T)ah-ree-mee-jeel
Irrigation	Mool-daem
Island	Suhm

Itch	G(K)ah-reeuh-oom
Itinerary	Yuh-haeng eel-juhng
Ivy	D(T)ahm-jaeng-ee

J

Jacket - Jungle

Jacket	J(Ch)ah-keht
Jade	B(P)ee-chwee
January	Eel-wuhl
Japan	Eel-bohn
Japanese (language)	Eel-bohn-mahl
Japanese (people)	Eel-bohn-sah-rahm
Jaw	Tuhk
Jazz	J(Ch)ae-juuh
Jelly	J(Ch)ehl-ree
Jellyfish	Hae-pah-ree
Jesus	Yeh-soo
Jet plane	J(Ch)eht-uuh-gee
Jewel	B(P)oh-suhk
Jeweler	B(P)oh-suhk-sahng
Job	J(Ch)eek-uhp
Journal (diary)	Eel-gee
Journalist	G(K)ee-jah
Juice	J(Ch)oo-oo-suuh
July	Cheel-wuhl
June	Yoo-wuhl
Jungle	J(Ch)uhng-guuhl

K

Kangaroo - Korean

Kangaroo	Kaeng-guh-roo-oo
Keepsake	Yoo-poom
Kerosene	D(T)uuhng-yoo
Key	Yuhl-sey
Keyhole	Yuhl-sey g(k)oo-muhng
Key money	B(P)oh-juuhng-guuhm
Kidnap	Yoo-gey-hah-dah
Kidney	S(Sh)een-Jahng

Kimchi	Keem-chee
Kilometre	Keel-roh-meet-uh
Kindergarten	Yoo-chee-wuhn
King	G(K)ook-wahng
Kingdom	Wahng-gook
Kiss	Kee-suuh
Kitchen	J(Ch)oo-bahng
Kite	Yuhn
Kitten	G(K)oh-yahng-ee sae-gggee
Knapsack	B(P)ae-nahng
Knee	Moo-ruuhp
Knife	Kahl
Korea	Hahn-gook
Korean (people)	Hahn-gook-sah-rahm
Korean (language)	Hahn-gook-mahl

L

Laboratory - Luxury

Laboratory	Yuhn-goo-soh
Lace	Reh ee-suuh
Lady	Sook-neeuh
Lake	Hoh-soo
Lamb	Uh-reen yahng
Lamp	D(T)uuhng
Landlady	Yuh-jah-joo-een
Landlord	J(Ch)eep-joo-een
Landowner	J(Ch)ee-joo
Lantern	Choh-rohng
Latrine	B(P)eeuhn-soh
Laundry	Seh-tahk-mool
Lavatory	Hwah-jahng-s(sh)eel
Lawyer	B(P)eeuhn-hoh-sah
Leaf (tree)	Nah-moot-eep
Leak	Sae-dah
Learn	B(P)ae-oo-dah
Learning	Hahk-suuhp
Lease	Eem-dae
Leash	G(K)ah-jook-gguuhn

Leather	G(K)ah-jook
Left	Wehn-jjohk
Left-handed	Wehn-sohn-jahp-ee
Leg	D(T)ah-ree
Lemon	Reh-mohn
Lemonade	Reh-mohn-soo
Lens	Rehn-juuh
Leopard	Peeoh-buhm
Lesson (school)	Soo-uhp
Letter (message)	Peeuhn-jee
Letter (alphabet)	Moon-jah
Lettuce	Sahng-choo
Librarian	D(T)oh-suh-gwahn-wuhn
Library	D(T)oh-suh-gwahn
Lifeboat	G(K)oo-joh-suhn
Life preserver	G(K)oo-meeuhng-goo
Light	B(P)ool-keeuh-dah
Lighthouse	D(T)uuhng-dae
Lightning	B(P)uhn-gaet-bool
Lilac	Rah-eel-rahk
Lily	B(P)aek-hahp
Lion	Sah-jah
Lip	Eep-sool
Lipstick	Reep-suuh-teek
Lipstick	Eep-sool-yuhn-jee
Liquid	Aek-cheh
Liquor	Ahl-koh-ohl
Literature	Moon-hahk
Liter	Reet-uh
Little (size)	J(Ch)ahk-uuhn
Little (amount)	J(Ch)uhk-uuhn
Liver	G(K)ahn-jahng
Lizard	D(T)oh-mah-baem
Lobby	Hyoo-geh-s(sh)eel
Lobster	B(P)ah-dah-gah-jae
Locomotive	G(K)ee-gwahn-chah
Locust	Meh-ddoo-gee
Lodging house	Hah-sook-jeep

Lose (defeated)	J(Ch)ee-dah
Lost (items)	Ee-ruuhn
Lotion	Hwah-jahng-soo
Lounge	Sah-gyoh-s(sh)eel
Love	Sah-rahng
Lucky	Haeng-oon
Luggage	Yuh-haeng-hah-mool
Lukewarm	Mee-jee-guuhn-hahn
Lullaby	J(Ch)ah-jahng-gah
Lunch	J(Ch)uhm-s(sh)eem
Lung	Huh-pah
Luxurious	Sah-chee-suuh-ruh-oon
Luxury	Sah-chee

M

Machine - Myself

Machine	G(K)ee-gey
Mackerel	G(K)oh-duuhng-uh
Mad (angry)	Hwah-gah-nahn
Magazine (periodical)	J(Ch)ahp-jee
Maggot	G(K)oo-duh-gee
Magnet	J(Ch)ah-suhk
Magnetic	J(Ch)ah-suhk-uuhee
Magnolia	Mohk-reeuhn
Maid (servant)	Hah-nyuh
Mail	Oo-pyuhn-mool
Mainland	B(P)ohn-toh
Make-up	Hwah-jahng-poom
Malaria	Hahk-jeel
Male	Nahm-suhng
Mamma	Uhm-mah
Mammal	Poh-yoo tohng-mool
Man	Nahm-jah
Management	G(K)wahl-lee
Manager	J(Ch)ee-bae-een
Manicure	Mae-nee-kyoo-uh
Mansion	D(T)ae-juh-taek
Manual (book)	Soh-chaek-jah

Manufacture	J(Ch)eh-joh
Manufacturer	J(Ch)eh-joh-uhp-jah
Map	J(Ch)ee-doh
Maple	D(T)ahn-poong
Maple tree	D(T)ahn-poong-nah-moo
Marble	D(T)ae-ree-suhk
March	Sahm-wuhl
Marine Corps	Hae-beeuhng-dae
Market	S(Sh)ee-jahng
Mask	G(K)ah-meeuhn
Massage	Mah-sah-ah-jee
Mathematics	Soo-hahk
Mattress	Cheem-dae-yohng
May	Oh-wuhl
Mayor	S(Sh)ee-jahng
Maze	Mee-goong
Mealtime	S(Sh)eek-sah s(sh)ee-gahn
Measles	Hohng-yuhk
Meat	G(K)oh-gee
Medicine	Yahk
Melon	Mehl-rohn
Melt	Nohk-dah
Menstruation	Mehn-suuh
Merchandise	Sahng-poom
Merchant	Sahng-een
Metre (measure)	Meet-uh
Microphone	Hwahk-suhng-gee
Microscope	Hyuhn-mee-gyuhng
Midnight	Yah-bahn
Military	G(K)oon-een
Milk	Oo-yoo
Million	B(P)aek-mahn
Millionaire	B(P)aek-mahn-jahng-jah
Minister	Mohk-sah
Mirror	G(K)uh-ool
Missionary	Suhn-gyoh-sah
Mist	Ahn-gae
Mistake	S(Sh)eel-soo

Molasses	Tahng-meel
Mole (on body)	Sah-mah-gwee
Monday	Wuh-ryoh-eel
Money	D(T)ohn
Money changer	Hwahn-juhn-sahng
Monk	Soo-doh-suuhng
Monkey	Wuhn-soong-ee
Monsoon	J(Ch)ahng-mah-chuhl
Month	D(T)ahl
Moon	D(T)ahl
Moonlight	D(T)ahl-beet
Mosquito	Moh-gee
Mosquito net	Moh-gee Jahng
Moth	Nah-bahng
Mother	Uh-muh-nee
Motorcycle	Oh-oh-toh-bye
Mountain	Sahn
Mouse	Saeng-jwee
Mouth	Eep
Movie	Yuhng-hwah
Mule	Noh-sae
Multiplication	G(K)ohp-sehm
Multiply	G(K)ohp-sehm-hah-dah
Murder	Sah-reen
Museum	B(P)ahk-mool-gwahn
Mushroom	B(P)uh-suht
Music	Uuhm-ahk
Musician	Uuhm-ahk-gah
Mustache	Koht-soo-yuhm
Mustard	G(K)yuh-jah
Myself	Nah-cha-s(sh)een

N

Nail - Nut

Nail	Moht
Name	Ee-ruuhm
Nap	Naht-jahm
Napkin	Naep-keen

National anthem	G(K)ook-gah
Nationality	G(K)ook-juhk
Nature	J(Ch)ah-yuhn
Navigate	Hahng-hae-hah-dah
Navigation	Hahng-hae
Navy	Hae-goon
Nearsighted	G(K)uuhn-s(sh)ee
Neck	Mohk
Necklace	Mohk-guh-ree
Necktie	Nehk-tah-ee
Needle	B(P)ah-nuuhl
Needle work	B(P)ah-nuuhl-jeel
New Year	Sae-hae
News	Nyoo-oo-suuh
Newspaper	S(Sh)een-moon
Nickname	B(P)yuhl-mee-uhng
Night	B(P)ahm
Nightgown	J(Ch)ahm-oht
Nightmare	Ahk-mohng
No	Ah-nee-oh
Noisy	S(Sh)ee-gguuh-ruh-oon
Noodles	G(K)ook-soo
North	B(P)ook-jjohk
Northeast	D(T)ohng-book
Northwest	Suh-book
Nose	Koh
Nostril	Koht-goo-muhng
Notebook	G(K)ohng-chaek
Notepaper	Pyuhn-jee-jee
November	S(Sh)eep-ee-wuhl
Now	J(Ch)ee-guuhm
Nurse	G(K)ahn-hoh-wuhn
Nursery	Uh-reen-ee-b(p)ahng
Nursery rhyme	J(Ch)ah-jahng-gah
Nut (food)	G(K)yuhn-gwah

O

Oak tree - Oyster

Oak tree	Chahm-nah-moo
Oatmeal	Oh-oo-tuuh-meel
Observatory	Chuhn-moon-dae
Occupation	J(Ch)eek-uhp
Ocean	B(P)ah-dah
October	S(Sh)eel-wuhl
Octopus	Moon-uh
Office	Sah-moo-s(sh)eel
Oil	G(K)ee-ruuhm
Ointment	Yuhn-goh
Old (item)	Nahl-guuhn
Old (person)	Nuuhl-guuhn
Olive	Ohl-ree-buuh
Onion	Yahng-pah
Opal	D(T)ahn-baek-suhk
Open	Yuhl-dah
Opera	Oh-peh-rah
Opera house	Oh-peh-rah Ġ(K)uuhk-jahng
Operation (surgery)	Soo-sool
Orange	Oh-rehn-jee
Orchard	G(K)wah-soo-wuhn
Orchestra	Oh-keh-suuh-tuuh-rah
Orchid	Nahn-choh
Organ (body part)	G(K)ee-gwahn
Organ (music)	Oh-ruuh-gahn
Orient	D(T)ohng-yahng
Oriental	D(T)ohng-yahng-een
Orphan	G(K)oh-ah
Orphanage	G(K)oh-ah-wuhn
Ostrich	Tah-joh
Outing	Nah-duuh-ree
Outside	B(P)ah-ggaht
Owl	B(P)oo-uhng-ee
Owner	Eem-jah
Ox	Hwahng-soh
Oyster	Saeng-gool

P

Pacific ocean - Puzzle

Pacific ocean	Tae-pyuhng-yahng
Package	Soh-poh
Padlock	J(Ch)ah-mool-sey
Pain	G(K)oh-tohng
Pain killer	J(Ch)een-tohng-jeh
Paint	Peh-een-tuuh
Paint brush	G(K)uuh-reem poot
Palm (hand)	Sohn-bah-dahk
Palm (tree)	Yah-jah-soo
Pan	Nahm-bee
Pansy	Paen-jee
Panther	Pyoh-buhm
Pants	B(P)ah-jee
Papa	Ah-bbah
Paper	J(Ch)ohng-ee
Parachute	Nahk-hah-sahn
Parade	Haeng-ree-uhl
Paralysis	Mah-bee
Parasol	Yahng-sahn
Parent	B(P)oo-moh
Park	G(K)ohng-wuhn
Parrot	Aeng-moo-sae
Party	Pah-ah-tee
Passenger	Suuhng-gaek
Passport	Yuh-gwuhn
Pastor	Mohk-sah
Pastry	Saeng-gwah-jah
Pasture	Mohk-jahng
Patient	Hwahn jah
Pay	J(Ch)ee-bool
Pea	Wahn-doo-kohng
Peach	B(P)ohk-soong-ah
Peacock	G(K)ohng-jahk
Peanut	DD(TT)ahng-kohng
Pear	B(P)ae

Pearl	J(Ch)een-joo
Pen	Pehn
Pencil	Yuhn-peel
People	Sah-rahm-duuhl
Pepper (black)	Hoo-choo
Pepper (red)	G(K)oh-choo
Peppermint	B(P)ahk-hah
Perfume	Hyahng-soo
Persimmon	G(K)ahm
Person	Sah-rahm
Pesticide	Sahl-choong-jeh
Pestilence	Huuhk-sah-byuhng
Pet	Ae-wahn-dohng-mool
Pharmacist	Yahk-jeh-sah
Pharmacy	Yahk-gook
Pheasant	Gg(Kk)wuhng
Philosophy	Chuhl-hahk
Phone	J(Ch)uhn-hwah
Photograph	Sah-jeen
Physician	Uuhee-sah
Physics	Mool-ree-hahk
Pickle	Oh-ee J(Ch)ahng-ah-jjee
Pickpocket	Soh-mae-chee-gee
Picnic	Pee-kuuh-neek
Picture	G(K)uuh-reem
Pier	B(P)oo-doo
Pig	D(T)wae-jee
Pigeon	B(P)ee-dool-gee
Pillow	B(P)eh-gae
Pillowcase	B(P)eh-gaet-eet
Pilot	J(Ch)oh-johng-sah
Pimple	Yuh-duuh-ruuhm
Pine tree	Soh-nah-moo
Pineapple	Pah-een-ae-puuhl
Ping Pong	Tahk-goo
Pink	B(P)oon-hohng-saek
Pipe (smoking)	D(T)ahm-baet-dae
Plane (aircraft)	B(P)ee-haeng-gee

Planet	Yoo-suhng
Plate	Chuhp-s(sh)ee
Playground	Noh-ree-tuh
Playmate	Noh-ree cheen-goo
Pliers	Bb(Pp)ehn-jjee
Plum	J(Ch)ah-d(t)oo
Plumber	Yuhn-gohng
Pneumonia	Pae-ryuhm
Poem	S(Sh)ee
Poet	S(Sh)ee-een
Poetry	S(Sh)ee
Poison	D(T)ohk-yahk
Poisonous	Yoo-dohk-hahn
Police	G(K)yuhng-chahl
Police station	G(K)yuhng-chahl-suh
Policeman	G(K)yuhng-chahl-gwahn
Politician	J(Ch)uhng-chee-gah
Politics	J(Ch)uhng-chee
Pond	Yuhn-moht
Pony	J(Ch)oh-rahng-mahl
Popcorn	Twee-geem ohk-soo-soo
Porcelain	Sah-gee Guuh-ruuht
Pork	D(T)wae-jee goh-gee
Portrait	Choh-sahng-hwah
Post office	Oo-cheh-gook
Postage	Oo-pyuhn-yoh-guuhm
Postcard	Yuhp-suh
Pot (jar)	D(T)ahn-jee
Potato	G(K)ahm-jah
Poultry	G(K)ah-guuhm
Pray	G(K)ee-doh-hah-dah
Preacher	Suhl-gyoh-jah
Pregnant	Eem-s(sh)een-hahn
Presbyterian	J(Ch)ahng-roh-gyoh
Prescription	Chuh-bahng
Priceless	Mohp-s(sh)ee Kwee-joong-hahn
Priest (minister)	Mohk-sah
Priest (monk)	Soo-doh-jah

Principal (school)	G(K)yoh-jahng
Prison	G(K)yoh-doh-soh
Privacy	Sah-saeng-hwahl
Professor	G(K)yoh-soo
Promise	Yahk-sohk
Pronunciation	B(P)ah-ruuhm
Proprietor	Soh-yoo-jah
Protestant	S(Sh)een-gyoh-doh
Psychology	S(Sh)eem-ree-hahk
Pumpkin	Hoh-bahk
Puppy	G(K)ahng-ah-jee
Purple	J(Ch)ah-joo-beet
Purse	J(Ch)ee-gahp
Puzzle	Soo-soo-ggeh-ggee

Q

Quail - Quilt

Quail	Meh-choo-rah-gee
Quality	Poom-jeel
Quantity	Yahng
Quarantine	G(K)uhm-yuhk
Quarter (1/4)	Sah-boon-uuhee-eel
Queen	Yuh-wahng
Quick	B(P)ah-lee
Quiet	G(K)oh-yoh-hahn
Quilt	Noo-bee-ee-bool

R

Rabbit - Ruler

Rabbit	Toh-ggee
Race (contest)	G(K)yuhng-joo
Radio	Rah-dee-oh
Radish	Moo-oo
Railroad	Chuhl-doh
Rain	Pee
Rainbow	Moo-jee-gae
Raincoat	B(P)ee-oht
Rainstorm	B(P)ee-bah-rahm

Rainy	**B(P_ee-oh-nuuhn**
Raisin	**G(K)uhn-poh-doh**
Ranch	**Nohng-jahng**
Rape	**G(K)ahng-gahn-hah-dah**
Raspberry	**Ddahl-ggee**
Rat	**J(Ch)wee**
Rat poison	**J(Ch)wee-yahk**
Ravine	**G(K)ee-puuhn-kae-gohk**
Raw	**Nahl-guh**
Razor	**Meeuhn-doh-kahl**
Read	**D(T)ohk-suh-hah-dah**
Receipt	**Yuhng-soo-juuhng**
Reception (party)	**Hwahn-yuhng-hey**
Recess (school)	**S(Sh)wee-nuuhn s(sh)ee-gahn**
Recipe	**J(Ch)oh-ree-buhp**
Rectangle	**J(Ch)eek-sah-gahk-heeuhng**
Red	**Bb(Pp)ahl-gahn**
Reef	**Ahm-choh**
Reel	**G(K)ahm-dah**
Refresh	**Sae-rohp-geh-hah-dah**
Refrigerate	**Naeng-gahk-s(sh)eek-ee-dah**
Refrigerator	**Naeng-jahng-goh**
Register	**D(T)uuhng-rohk-hah-dah**
Registration	**D(T)uuhng-rohk**
Regulation	**G(K)yoo-cheek**
Reindeer	**Mahl-sah-suuhm**
Relative (family)	**Cheen-chuhk**
Religion	**J(Ch)ohng-gyoh**
Religious	**J(Ch)ohng-gyoh-juhk-een**
Rent	**J(Ch)eep-seh**
Repair	**Soo-suhng-hah-dah**
Repay	**G(K)ahp-dah**
Replacement	**G(K)yoh-cheh**
Report card	**Suhng-juhk-pyoh**
Reporter	**G(K)ee-jah**
Representative	**D(T)ae-pyoh-jah**
Reproduce	**B(P)ohk-sah-hah-dah**
Rescue	**G(K)oo-joh-hah-dah**

Research	J(Ch)oh-sah-yuhn-goo-hah-dah
Reservation (of...)	Yee-yahk
Residence	J(Ch)oo-taek
Resident	G(K)uh-joo-jah
Resort (vacation)	Hyoo-yahng-jee
Restaurant	Uuhm-s(sh)eek-juhm
Retail	Soh-mae
Reunion	J(Ch)ae-hey
Rice (cooked)	B(P)ahp
Rice (raw)	Ssahl
Rich	D(T)ohn-mahn-uuhm
Right (direction)	Oh-ruuhn
Ring (finger)	B(P)ahn-jee
River	G(K)ahng
Robber	G(K)ahng-do
Robbery	Yahk-tahl
Robe	G(K)ah-oon
Roommate	Hahn-bahng cheen-goo
Rooster	Soo-tahk
Rope	B(P)aht-jool
Rose	J(Ch)ahng-mee
Rotate	D(T)ohl-dah
Rotation	G(K)yoh-dae
Rubber	G(K)oh-moo
Ruby	Roo-oo-bee
Ruler (measurer)	J(Ch)ah

S

Safe - Sword

Safe (lockbox)	G(K)uuhm-goh
Safe guard	B(P)oh-hoh
Safety	Ahn-juhn
Sail boat	(T)oht-bae
Salad	Sael-ruh-duuh
Salary	Wuhl-guuhp
Sale	Pahn-mae
Saloon	Sool-jeep
Salt	Soh-guuhm

Salty	Jjah-dah
Sanctuary	G(K)uh-rook-hahn-koht
Sand	Moh-rae
Sandwich	Saen-duuh-wee-chee
Sandy	Moh-rae-uuhee
Sapphire	Sah-pah-ee-uh
Sardine	J(Ch)uhng-uh-ree
Satellite	Wee-suhng
Satin	G(K)ohng-dahn
Saturday	Toh-yoh-eel
Sauce	Soh-oh-suuh
Saucepan	Suuh-tyoo-oo nahm-bee
Saucer	B(P)aht-cheem chuhp-s(sh)ee
Sausage	Soh-s(sh)ee-jee
Scarf	Mohk-doh-ree
Scenery	G(K)ee-uhng-chee
Schedule	S(Sh)ee-gahn-pyuh
Scholarship	J(Ch)ahng-hahk-guuhm
School	Hahk-gee-oh
Schoolmate	Hahk-oo
Science	G(K)wah-hahk
Science fiction	G(K)ohng-sahng
Scientific	G(K)wah-hahk-juhk-een
Scientist	G(K)wah-hahk-jah
Scissors	G(K)ah-wee
Scorpion	J(Ch)uhn-gahl
Screwdriver	(T)uh-rah-ee-buh
Sculptor	J(Ch)oh-gahk-gah
Sculpture	J(Ch)oh-gahk
Sea	B(P)ah-dah
Seagull	G(K)ahl-mae-gee
Seal (animal)	B(P)ah-dah-pyoh-buhm
Seashore	B(P)ah-daht-gah
Seasickness	B(P)aet-muhl-mee
Seaweed	Mee-yuhk
Secret	B(P)ee-meel
Security	Ahn-juhn
Sell	Pahl-dah

Seller	Pah-nuuhn sah-rahm
Semester	Hahk-gee
Seminar	Seh-mee-nah-ah
Send	B(P)oh-nae-dah
September	G(k)oo-wuhl
Sergeant	Hah-sah-gwahn
Serpent (snake)	B(P)aem
Seventh-day-Adventist	Ahn-s(sh)eek-gee-oh
Sew (by hand)	B(P)ah-nuuh-jeel-hah-dah
Sew (by machine)	J(Ch)ae-bohng-hah-dah
Sewing (by hand)	B(P)ah-nuuh-jeel
Sewing (by machine)	J(Ch)ae-bohng
Shade	G(K)uuh-nuuhl
Shadow	G(K)uuh-reem-jah
Shady	G(K)uuh-nuuhl-jeen
Shampoo	S(Sh)yaem-poo-oo
Shark	Sahng-uh
Sharp	Nahl-kah-roh-oon
Shave	Mee-uhn-doh
Sheep	Yahng
Ship	B(P)ae
Shipwreck	Nahn-pah-suhn
Shipyard	J(Ch)oh-suhn-soh
Shirt	Oo-d(t)oh-ree
Shoe	G(K)oo-doo
Shoe brush	G(K)oo-doot-sohl
Shoe horn	G(K)oo-doot-joo-guhk
Shoe lace	G(K)oo-doo-gguuhn
Shoe polish	G(K)oo-doo-yahk
Shoe shine	G(K)oo-doo-dahk-ggee
Shopping	Chahng-boh-gee
Shorts	B(P)ahn-bah-jee
Shoulder	Uh-ggae
Shower	S(Sh)yah-oo-uh
Shrimp	Sae-oo
Shrine	Sah-dahng
Sick	B(P)ee-uhng-duuhn
Sightseeing	G(K)oo-gee-uhng

Silk	Mee-uhng-joo
Silkworm	Noo-eh
Silver	Uuhn
Sin	J(Ch)wae
Sing	Noh-rae-hah-dah
Singer	G(K)ah-soo
Sink	Suhl-guh-jee-tuhng
Sit	Ahn-dah
Skate	Suuh-keh-ee-tuuh
Skating	Suuh-keh-ee-ting
Ski	Suuh-kee-ee
Skirt (dress)	Chee-mah
Sky	Hah-nuuhl
Sleep	J(Ch)ahm
Sleeping car	Cheem-dae-chah
Sleepy	J(Ch)ohl-ree-nuuhn
Smart	D(T)ohk-d(t)ohk-hah-dah
Smell	Naem-sae
Smile	Mee-soh
Smiling	Mee-soh-hah-nuuhn
Snail	D(T)ahl-paeng-ee
Snake	B(P)aem
Sneeze	J(Ch)ae-chae-gee
Snore	Koh-ruuhl g(k)ohl-dah
Snow	Noon
Snowball	Noon-moong-chee
Snowdrift	Noon-duh-mee
Snowflake	Noon-sohng-ee
Snowing	Noon-ee-ohn-dah
Snowman	Noon-sah-rahm
Snow slide (avalanche)	Noon-sah-tae
Snowstorm	Noon-boh-rah
Snowy	Noon-ee-mahn-uuhn
Soap	B(P)ee-noo
Socks	Yahng-mahl
Soda	Soh-oh-dah
Sofa	Soh-pah
Soldier	G(K)oon-een

Son	Ah-duuhl
Song	Noh-rae
Soup	G(K)ook
South	Nahm-jjohk
Southeast	D(T)ohng-nahm
Southern	Nahm-jjohk-uuhee
Soy sauce	G(K)ahn-jahng
Spain (country)	Suuh-peh-een-uh
Spain (people)	Suuh-peh-een-sah-rahm
Sparrow	Chahm-sae
Spice	Yahng-nee-uhm
Spider	G(K)uh-mee
Spinach	S(Sh)ee-guuhm-chee
Spine	Chuhk-choo
Sponge	Suuh-puhn-jee
Spoon	Soot-gah-rahk
Spouse	B(P)ae-oo-jah
Squadron	J(Ch)oong-dae-bohn-boo
Square	Neh-moh
Squash	Hoh-bahk
Squirrel	D(T)ah-rahm-jwee
Stadium	G(K)ee-uhng-gee-jahng
Staircase	G(K)ae-dahn
Star	B(P)ee-uhl
Starry	B(P)ee-uhl-beet pahl-guuhn
Stationery	Pee-uhn-jee-jee
Steak	Suuh-teh-ee-kuuh
Steam	Chuuhng-gee
Stepchild	Uuhee-boot-jah-s(sh)eek
Stomach	Wee
Stomach (belly)	B(P)ae
Store (market)	Sahng-juhm
Store (stow)	J(ch)uh-jahng-hah-dah
Storm	Pohk-poong
Stove	Nahl-loh
Straw	Bb(Pp)ahl-d(t)ae
Strawberry	Dd(Tt)ahl-gee
Stream (creek)	G(K)ae-ool

String	Gg(Kk)uuhn
Stroke (illness)	J(Ch)oong-poong
Student	Hahk-saeng
Substitute (item)	D(T)ae-yohng-poom
Substitute (person)	D(T)ae-ree
Subtraction (math)	Bb(Pp)ae-gee
Subway	J(Ch)ee-hah-chuhl
Sugar	Suhl-tahng
Sugar cane	Sah-tahng-soo-soo
Sum (calculation)	G(K)ae-sahn
Sum (total amount)	Hahp-g(k)ae
Summer	Yuh-ruuhm
Sun	Hae
Sunburn	Haet-beeuh-teh tah-dah
Sunday	Ee-reeoh-eel
Sunflower	Hae-bah-rah-gee
Sunrise	Hae-doh-jee
Sunset	Hae-jeel-nee-uhk
Sunshine	Haet-bee-uht
Supper	J(Ch)uhn-yuhk-s(sh)eek-sah
Surname	Suhng
Swan	B(P)aek-joh
Sweet potato	G(K)oh-goo-mah
Swimming	Soo-yuhng
Swine	D(T)wae-jee
Sword	Kahl

T

Table - Typhoon

Table (dining)	S(Sh)eek-tahk
Table (in general)	Tahk-jah
Tablecloth	S(Sh)eek-tahk-boh
Tailor	J(Ch)ae-bohng-sah
Tank (army)	Taeng-kuuh
Tape	Teh-ee-puuh
Tape measure	J(ch)ool-jah
Taxi	Taek-s(sh)ee
Tea	Chah

Teach	G(K)ah-ruuh-chee-dah
Teacher	Suhn-saeng
Teacup	Chah-jahn
Teapot	Chah-joo-juhn-jah
Telephone	J(Ch)uhn-hwah
Telescope	Mahng-wuhn-gee-uhng
Television	Tehl-ree-bee-jee-uhn
Temperature	Cheh-ohn
Tennis	Teh-nee-suuh
Tent	Tehn-tuuh
Terminal (transportation)	J(Ch)ohng-chahk-yuhk
Textbook	G(K)ee-oh-gwah-suh
Thank you	G(K)ahm-sah-hahp-nee-dah
Theater	G(K)uuhk-jahng
Theft	J(Ch)uhl-doh
Thermometre	Ohn-doh-g(k)ae
Thief	D(T)oh-dook
Thimble	G(K)ohl-moo
Thirsty	Mohk-mah-ruuhn
Thread	S(Sh)eel
Throat	Mohk-goo-muhng
Thumb	Uhm-jee
Thunder	Chuhn-doong
Thunderstorm	Ney-oo
Thursday	Mohk-yoh-eel
Tick	J(Ch)een-duuh-gee
Tiger	Hoh-rahng-ee
Tiny	J(Ch)ahk-uuhn
Toad	D(T)oo-gguh-bee
Tobacco	D(T)ahm-bae
Today	Oh-nuuhl
Toe	B(P)ahl-gah-rahk
Toilet	B(P)ee-uhn-soh
Toilet paper	Hyoo-jee
Tomato	Toh-mah-toh
Tomb	Moo-duhm
Tombstone	Mee-oh-bee
Tomorrow	Nae-eel

Tongs	J(Ch)eep-geh
Tongue	Hee-uh
Tonight	Oh-nuuhl-bahm
Tooth	Ee-bahl
Toothache	Chee-tohng
Toothbrush	Cheet-sohl
Toothpick	Ee-ssoo-s(sh)ee-gae
Tortoise	G(K)uh-book
Tourist	G(K)wahn-gwahng-gaek
Towel	Tah-wuhl
Toy	Jahng-nahm -gahm
Toyshop	Jahng-nahm-gahm gah-gae
Train	G(K)ee-chah
Translate	B(P)uhn-yuhk-hah-dah
Translation	B(P)uhn-yuhk
Transport	Soo-sohng-hah-dah
Transportation	Soo-sohng
Trash	Ssuuh-reh-gee
Travel	Yuh-haeng
Traveller	Yuh-haeng-jah
Tree	Nah-moo
Triangle	Sahm-gahk-hee-uhng
Tricycle	Seh-bahl chah-juhn-goh
Tropical	Yuhl-dae
Tropics	Yuhl-dae chee-bahng
Trout	Sohng-uh
Truck	Tuuh-ruhk
Trumpet	Tuuh-ruhm-peht
Trunk (box)	Tuuh-ruhng-kuuh
Trunk (tree)	J(Ch)ool-gee
Tub (bath)	Mohk-yohk-tohng
Tuberculosis	G(K)ee-uhl-haek
Tuesday	Hwah-yoh-eel
Tug boat	Yeh-een-suhn
Tuition	Soo-uhp-ree-oh
Tumor	J(Ch)ohng-yahng
Tuna	D(T)ah-rahng-uh
Turkey	Cheel-mee-uhn-joh

Turnip	Soon-moo
Turtle	B(P)ah-dah-guh-book
Tutor	G(K)ah-juhng-gyoh-sah
Tweezers	J(Ch)ohk-jeep-geh
Typhoid	J(Ch)ahng-tee-poo-suh
Typhoon	Tae-poong

U

Ulcer - Urgent

Ulcer	Wee-kae-yahng
Umbrella	Oo-sahn
Underwear	Sohk-oht
Unhappy	B(P)ool-haeng-hahn
Uniform	J(Ch)eh-bohk
Universe	J(Ch)uhn-seh-gae
University	D(T)ae-hahk-gyoh
Unlucky	Oon-ee nah-bbuuhn
Unpack	J(Ch)eem-uuhl-pool-dah
Untie	Gg(Kk)uuh-ruuh-dah
Upstairs	Ee-chuuhng
Urgent	G(K)een-guuhp-hahn

V

Vacation - Vulture

Vacation	Hyoo-gah
Vaccination	Oo-doo
Vase	Gg(Kk)oht-bee-uhng
Vegetable	Yah-chae
Vehicle	Chah-ree-ahng
Vein	Hee-uhl-gwahn
Venom	D(T)ohk-aek
Ventilate	Hwahn-gee-hah-dah
Ventilation	Hwahn-gee
Vest	J(Ch)oh-ggee
Village	Mah-uuhl
Vine	Nuhng-gool
Vinegar	S(Sh)eek-choh
Violet	J(Ch)eh-bee-ggoht

Violin	B(P)ah-ee-uhl-reen
Visit	B(P)ahng-moon
Visitor	B(P)ahng-moon-gaek
Volcano	Hwah-sahn
Volleyball	B(P)ae-goo
Volunteer	J(Ch)ee-wuhn-jah
Vomit	G(K)oo-toh
Vulture	D(T)ohk-soo-ree

W

Waist - Writer

Waist	Guh-ree
Waiter	Weh-ee-toh
Waiting room	D(T)ae-hahp-s(Sh)eel
Waitress	Weh-ee-tuuh-reh-suuh
Wallet	J(Ch)ee-gahp
Walnut	Hoh-doo
War	J(Ch)uhn-jaeng
Warehouse	Chahng-goh
Warm	Dd(Tt)ah-dduuht-hahn
Warning	G(K)ee-uhng-goh
Wash (clothes)	Seh-tahk-hah-dah
Wash (self)	Ss(Sh)eet-dah
Washing machine	Seh-tahk-gee
Washroom	Yohk-s(sh)eel
Wasp	Mahl-buhl
Water	Mool
Water lily	Soo-ree-uhn
Waterfall	Pohk-poh
Watermelon	Soo-bahk
Wave (water)	Mool-gyuhl
Wealthy	Poo-yoo-hahn
Weapon	Moo-gee
Weather forecast	Eel-gee yeh-boh
Web (spider)	G(K)uh-mee-jool
Wedding	G(K)yuhl-hohn
Wedding ring	G(K)yuhl-hohn-bahn-jee
Wednesday	Soo-yoh-eel

Weekend	J(Ch)oo-mahl
Weekly	Mae-joo
Weigh	Moo-geh-ruuhl-tahl-dah
Weight	Moo-geh
Welcome	Hwahn-yuhng
West	Suh-jjohk
Wet	J(Ch)uh-juuhn
Whale	G(K)oh-rae
Wharf	B(P)oo-doo
Wheat	Meel
Wheel	B(P)ahk-wee
Whistle (by mouth)	Hwee-pah-rahm
Whistle (object)	Hoh-gahk
White	Huuh-een
Widow	G(K)wah-boo
Widower	Hoh-rah-bee
Wife (other's)	Boo-een
Wife (own)	Ah-nae
Wig	G(K)ah-bahl
Windmill	Poong-chah
Window	Chahng-moon
Windpipe	Soom-tohng
Wine	Poh-doh-joo
Wing (bird)	Nahl-gae
Winner	Suuhng-ree-jah
Wolf	Nuuhk-dae
Woman	Yuh-jah
Wood (timber)	Mohk-jae
Woodpecker	Dd(Tt)ahk-dah-goo-ree
Wool	Yahng-moh
World	Seh-gae
Worm (earth)	J(Ch)ee-ruhng-ee
Wreck (destroy)	Pah-gey-hah-dah
Wrench	Rehn-chee
Wrist	Sohn-mohk
Wristwatch	Shee-gae
Writer	J(Ch)ahk-gah

X

Xmas - Xylophone

Xmas (Christmas)	Suhng-tahn-juhl
X-ray	Ehk-suuh-reh-ee
Xylophone	S(Sh)eel-roh-pohn

Y

Yacht - You

Yacht	Yoh-tuuh
Yam	G(K)oh-goo-mah
Yardstick	Yah-ah-duuh chah
Yarn	Tuhl-s(sh)eel
Yes	Yeh or Neh
Yesterday	Uh-jeh
Yolk	Noh-ruuhn-jah
Yo	Tahng-s(sh)een

Z

Zebra - Zoology

Zebra	Uhl-rook-mahl
Zero	Yuhng or Cheh-roh
Zipper	Chah-kuuh
Zoo	D(T)ohng-mool-wuhn
Zoology	D(T)ohng-mool-hahk

STANDARD USAGE

Phonetic Spelling	Pronounced
Simple vowels	Simple vowels
ah	f*a*ther
ae	p*a*y (soft)
ai	*eye*
eh	l*e*t
uh	f*u*n
uuh	brok*e*n
ee	*i*ncubator
oh	hone

ey	h*ey*
oo	*to*

Compound vowels	Compound vowels
uuhee	broken + we
wah	*wa*nder
wae	*whey* (soft)
weh	*wed*
wuh	*wo*nder
wee	*wie*ner
yah	*ya*rn
yae	*yea* (soft)
yeh	*ye*sterday
yuh	*yea*rn
yoh	*yo*del
yoo	*You*

Chapter 9

International Phonetic Alphabet

TABLES

The International Alphabet was invented by the International Phonetic Association in 1888 and has undergone constant revision since. Here isthe official chart.

The tables shown here follow the manner of the official chart with the addition of an "epiglottal" column in the consonants table because there is no reason not to do so (there are as many symbols in the epiglottal as in the glottal locations, and it is interesting to parallel the pharyngeal, epiglottal and glottal consonants), and similarly an "implosives" row. When the consonants' table shows two characters in a square, the first is the voiceless sound and the second is voiced; when only one character is shown, it is voiced, except for the glottal and epiglottal plosives, which are voiceless (it is — probably — not possible to pronounce a voiced pharyngeal, glottal or epiglottal plosive). A grey rectangle (if your browser displays it, that is) means that the corresponding sound is impossible to pronounce, or meaningless; the voiceless pharyngeal plosive is possible (only the voiced counterpart is not), it just doesn't have a symbol.

An empty square means that the sound is (presumably) possible, but no symbol has been defined (because no language uses it, or because it is just as convenient to use diacritics over an existing symbol). Dentals, alveolar and postalveolar consonants use the same symbols except forfricatives: if necessary, diacritics can be used to mark them apart; the standard version is alveolar (though in my opinion, the approximant used to mark the English 'r' (lowercase turned r, number 151) is distinctly postalveolar, even slightly retroflex). The vowels' table attempts to map the vowel symbols.

However, when used phonemically, their value varies greatly from language to language, much more than consonants. When two vowels are shown in a square, the first is unrounded and the second is rounded (though it is by no means true that all "unrounded" vowels are equally unrounded, or even that all "rounded" vowels are equally rounded). When a single vowel is shown, it varies in roundedness, being generally of somewhat neutral value; however, the ash (lowercase ae ligature, number 325) is a distinctly unrounded front semi-open vowel, and the upsilon (number 321, which looks like a turned small capital omega) is a distinctly rounded back-centre semi-closed vowel.

REGULAR IPA

The following tables show the regular IPA symbols.

DISPLAYED WITH GRAPHICS

These tables show one small (PNG) graphics file for each character. These graphics file were prepared from the "TIPA" TeX/LaTeX fonts written by Rei Fukui (*fkr@tooyoo.l.u-tokyo.ac.jp*) using an ad hoc Perl script to convert the METAFONT output to individual PNG files.

The images are numbered using the International Phonetic's Association standard numbering of IPA symbols. If your browser is text-only, you will see the corresponding numbers in place of the images.

Consonants	Bilabial	Labiodental	Dental	Alveolar	Postalveolar	Retroflex
Plosive	pb			td		td
Nasal	m	ɱ		n		ɳ
Trill	ʙ			r		
Flap				ɾ		ɽ
Fricative	ɸβ	fv	θð	sz	ʃʒ	ʂʐ
Lateral fricative				ɬɮ		
Approximant		ʋ		ɹ		ɻ
Lateral approximant				l		ɭ
Implosive	ɓ			ɗ		

GENERAL PHONETIC

SEGMENTS

One of the fundamental (but perhaps debatable) postulates behind the International Phonetic Alphabet is that speech, or, at any rate, the meaningful and "abstract" content of speech, can be divided in atomic sound utterances called *phones* or *segments*. For example, the English word "dog" consists of three segments, which happen to be represented by one letter each; the middle one is a *vowel* (a rounded back vowel that is relatively open, though the degree of openness depends on the variant of English being considered) and the first and last are *consonants* (avoiced alveolar plosive, and a voiced velar plosive, respectively). Another important postulate is that some phones are common between languages. For example, the segment [v], corresponding to the first consonant ('v') in the English word "view" is the same as that which starts the French word "ver", the German word "weg" or the Russian word "âîäà".

Naturally, the validity of these hypotheses is not complete. First, spectral analysis of sounds show that dividing a continuous utterance into well-delimited segments is hopeless: there exists all sorts of complicated transition patterns, and a sound only makes sense in a certain phonetic context. Second, phones do not fall in neatly defined little bins, and there exists a continuum of possibilities (this is even more true for vowels than for consonants). Third, no two phones are exactly identical: within a same language, people pronounce things differently, and between different languages, no two sounds are ever *exactly* identical. Still, despite all these limitations, the hypotheses we have formulated are a useful basis that works well in practice.

Although there is a slight correspondance between letters and segments, it is by no means true that every letter corresponds to a single segment or *vice versa*. In English, this is "particularly false", in fact. In the name "Vaughan", the letter sequence 'augha' corresponds to a single segment; in the word "music", the letter 'u' corresponds to two segments (the first being a consonant and the second a vowel). Furthermore, a given letter or letter sequence can correspond to several different segments or segment sequences according to context, and a given segment or segment sequence can be represented by several different letters or letter sequences in various words. Again, English is particularly badly behaved in this respect: compare "laughter" and "daughter" or "how" and "low" on the one hand, "bury" and "berry" or "son" and "sun".

All segments are pronounced using the vocal tract, from the larynx to the lips, including the nose. Sounds which could be produced by other parts of the body (such as by snapping one's fingers) are not included in phonetic studies: it seems that no language uses them for articulated communication, though there is no reason why they should not be. (Of course, body *gestures* are used by the hearing impaired, but the language in question is visual and not phonetic, its very *ratio operandi* in fact.)

KINDS OF SEGMENTS

Voiced and Voiceless Phones

During normal speech, in particular when one is not whispering, the vocal cords are vibrating part, but not all, of the time. Phones which are pronounced with the vocal cords vibrating are called *voiced*, and the others are called *voiceless*. This is illustrated by the difference between the English words "view" [vju:] and "few" [fju:]: the initial segment (a labiodental fricative) is voiced in the former and voiceless in the latter. This should be perfectly clear if you put your hand to your throat: you should feel your vocal cords vibrating when saying "view" whereas when saying "few" they start vibrating only after the 'f'.

Or, to say things differently: voiced segments are pronounced with a simultaneous "humming" sound (vibration of the cords) whereas voiceless segments are pronounced without it.

Despite this, even when whispered, the [v] and [f] segments do not sound exactly identical (though the differences is *much* slighter than in normal speech): this is presumably because the vocal cords, although not vibrating, are not quite in the same position when [v] is pronounçed as when [f] is pronounced; if the difference between a devoiced [v] and an [f] is to be emphasized, the former can be called a *lenis* and the latter a *fortis*.

CONSONANTS AND VOWELS

Vowels are sounds which are produced with the vocal tract unobstructed, whereas consonants are those which are produced with some obstruction to the flow of air. For example, if the mouth is opened widely, with the tongue kept at rest, completely out of the way of the air, while the vocal cords are made to vibrate, the sound [a] is produced: it is a vowel (not found in English, but in French, as in the word"ami"), and it is the furthest removed from any consonant. On the other hand, if the lips are closed so as to interrupt the flow of air, and then opened again, all while the vocal cords are vibrating, the sound [b] is produced: it is a consonant, and specifically a bilabial plosive.

Vowels are voiced except when they are whispered. Consonants, on the other hand, can be voiced or voiceless.

The distinction between vowels and consonants is not always clear-cut, and there exists a fuzzy boundary region. First note that any consonant (except perhaps a plosive) can be used as a syllable nucleus just as if it were a vowel: this is particularly common in English for the consonants [l] and [n]. For example, in way the word"bottle" is usually pronounced, the second syllable consists of the consonant [l] all by itself (though it is always possible to add a weak schwa vowel before it to serve as syllable nucleus in its stead). This does not concern the sound of the segment itself but rather its duration and phonetic environment.

Second, there exists sounds which are just in between vowels and consonants. In the English word"yeast", the'y' is clearly a consonant (a voicedpalatal fricative, number 139). In"year", it is still a consonant, but it is much more open: it has changed from a fricative to an approximant. On the other hand, the'e' in"Seattle" is ever so slightly more open, and, this time, it is a vowel.

KINDS OF CONSONANTS

Plosives (also called"occlusives" or"stops") are consonants which are produced by completely interrupting the flow of air by obstructing it in some way. For example, the two consonants in the English word"copy" are (voiceless) plosives. A plosive consists of three parts: first, the flow is interrupted (this is the attack), then for some time there is no flow (and thus no sound if the plosive is voiceless), and finally comes the releasewhich terminates the plosive.

If the plosive is the first phone pronounced, then there is no attack: if the plosive is voiced, it starts with a vibration of the vocal cords, and if it is voiceless it simply starts with the release. The release is usually the most audible part of the plosive, and it is for this reason that final plosives tend to vanish, especially voiceless ones (their release is suppressed, and then the entire plosive is reduced to very little).

The release might not be complete. If the plosive is the last segment, the release might simply be omitted or inaudible. If the next segment is anasal consonant articulated in the same place, the release is nasal: the air is allowed to flow through the nose. If the next segment is a lateral consonant articulated in the same place, the release is lateral: the air is allowed to flow around the obstacle. The English words"button" and"bottle" show examples of nasal and lateral release respectively, if the final segment is pronounced syllabically: once the tip of the tongue is in place against the alveolar ridge (when pronouncing the't' sound), it remains there, and the release of air is made either through the nose or by the sides of the tongue.

Note that if a plosive is lengthened, it is the period between attack and release which is lengthened. In the case of a voiceless plosive, this is merely a period of silence.

This section for a detailed segment-by-segment discussion of plosives. Nasals are very much like plosives, except that the air is allowed to escape through the nose: the attack diverts the flow of air through the nose rather than interrupting it. The sound commonly represented by the letter'n' in English is a nasal consonant. A detailed description of nasals is found in this section.

Trills (or"rolled consonants") are produced by repeatedly interrupting the airstream. The"rolled r" of various languages are trills; but in practice, trills, being rather hard to produce, are often simplified to flaps or approximants. We will say more about trills and how to articulate them further on.

Flaps (or"taps") are obtained by shortening trills to a single interruption, which therefore comes very close to a"light" plosive (but it is much shorter, and the interruption is usually not complete). Some British speakers will pronounce intervocalic'r' (of such words as"very") as a flap; Americans, on the other hand, will pronounce some intervocalic't"s (such as that of"butter") as a kind of (voiced) flap. More about this later.

Fricatives (also called"spirants" or"constrictives") are probably the most important kind of consonants, in that it permits the greatest number of easily producible and distinguishable places of articulation. A fricative is obtained by narrowing the airstream so as to make the flow turbulent and produce a kind of hissing sound (frication). A fricative does not usually have a clear attack and release; it can be arbitrarily prolonged. The two consonants in the English word"fuss" are fricatives.

When the airflow is no longer turbulent, fricatives becomes approximants (also called"continuants" or"semivowels" - although the latter term is better reserved for non-lateral approximants). This can be because there is less narrowing, or because the air flows more slowly (fluid dynamics teaches us that the Reynolds number, which determines how turbulent the flow is, is proportional to the speed of the fluid).

Although approximants are classified as consonants, there is no real distinction with vowels (at least for non-lateral approximants between the palatal and pharyngeal regions): any vowel that is sufficiently close or back can be made into an approximant. The letter'y' in the English words"year","you" or"yet" is a palatal approximant (on the other hand, in the word"yeast" it comes closer to a voiced fricative); similarly, the letter'w' in"worm" or"wet" is a labio-velar approximant (on the other hand, in some American pronunciations of"where", the'wh' is realised as a voiced fricative). The letter'u' in the French word"nuit" is a labio-palatal approximant, and the letter'w' in the Dutch word"wind" is a labio-dental approximant (whereas in the corresponding German word it is a voiced labio-dental fricative). Note that the letter'r' found in most American and some British pronunciations of English is also an (alveolar) approximant; but analysis of the English'r' is by no means easy. Finally, the'l' of English and French (the two are not the same) are lateral approximants.

One sequence commonly found in many languages is the succession of a plosive by the corresponding fricative. It then often happens that the release of the plosive merges with the attack of the fricative to form an affricate. In other words, an affricate pair is a plosive with constrictive release. Whether an affricate consists of a single segment or two is a theological question. Examples of affricates found in English are the'ch' sequences in the word"church" (voiceless postalveolar affricates) and the'j' and'dg' sequences in"judge" (the voiced counterpart). Further, an affricate can lead to an approximant instead of a fricative: the'dr' sequence in some English words is of this kind, at least in some pronunciations.

The voiced/voiceless distinction is mainly found in plosives and fricatives (and affricates). Nasals and approximants are voiced (except when whispered), because it is hard to hear them when they are not: a laminar (the opposite of turbulent) flow of air not accompanied by a vibration of the vocal cords is all but inaudible. In fact, voiceless approximants tend very strongly to be replaced by the corresponding fricative: for instance, when the word"wet" is whispered, or when the word"when" is pronounced by those speakers who make a difference between voiced'w' and voiceless'wh', the voiced (labio-velar) approximant is changed to a voiceless (labio-velar) fricative; even the approximant'r' tends to turn into a fricative (not unlike'sh') when whispered, at least in initial and post-consonantal positions. Trills and flaps are, also, generally voiced (although there is no real reason for this).

ARTICULATION

Bilabials refer to consonants that are produced using the lips, by narrowing or closing them. For example, the sounds usually represented in English by the letters 'p', 'b' and 'm' are bilabials (the first two are plosives, voiceless and voiced respectively, and the third is a nasal).

Labiodentals are consonants which are formed with the upper teeth against the lower lip. English has two such consonants, [f] and [v], both being fricatives; since it knows no bilabial fricatives and the only labiodentals are fricatives, we can say that English does not distinguish bilabials and labiodentals. There also exists a *linguolabial* kind of sounds, made with the tongue against the upper lip; but apart from some Austronesian languages, I don't think they ever occur.

Dentals, alveolars and postalveolars are all made with the tongue in the front of the mouth: dentals use the tip of the tongue against the teeth, alveolars are articulated with the tip or blade of the tongue against the alveolar ridge (that is, the ridge of the gums of the upper teeth), and postalveolars are articulated with the tip or blade of the tongue a little behind the ridge. The'th' sounds of English (both the"soft", i.e. voiced, one, and the"hard" or voiceless one) are dental fricatives. The sounds [s], [z] such as found in English for example are alveolar. The approximant'r', the fricative'sh' (as well as its voiced counterpart) and the affricate'ch', in English, are all postalveolar.

One difficulty of dentals, alveolars and postalveolars is that the tongue, being very mobile in its front, has much freedom of placement, so there are many subtle differences between one sound and another. For example, the [t] and [d] found in French are clearly alveolar, perhaps even dental, whereas those in English are articulated further back, and could be classified as postalveolars. The sound can also be made with the tip or the blade of the tongue: in the formar case it is called apical and in the latter, laminal.

Retroflex consonants are articulated with the tongue's tip curled back against the soft palate. Retroflex sounds are not found in English as such, but some postalveolar consonants tend to have a certain retroflex quality about them, for example the'r'.

Lateral consonants are pronounced with the air escaping on the side of the tongue rather than on the front. The lateral quality is not really a"place of articulation" and can be combined with other prcperties of the consonants: for example, [l] is a (laminal or apical) alveolar lateral approximant (which is further velarized in some cases in English).

Palatals are articulated by bringing together the front of the tongue and the hard palate (i.e. the front part of the palate). The sound [j] found at the start of the English word"yet" is a palatal approximant; the soft'ch' in German (found in such words as"ich") is a (voiceless) palatal fricative; thesound represented in Italian by'gli' (for example in the word"figlio") is a palatal lateral approximant; the sound represented in French by'gn' (such as in"mignon") is a palatal nasal.

Velars are articulated further back than palatals: this time, the back of the tongue approaches the soft palate (i.e. the back of the palate, sometimes called its"veil", or velum, hence the name). The term"guttural" is also sometimes found. The letters'k','g' and'ng' in the English words"key","get" and"ring" represent respectively a voiceless velar plosive, a voiced velar plosive and a velar nasal.

Uvulars are articulated even further back, with the very back of the tongue coming up to the uvula (the uvula is"that thing which hangs down at the back of our throats"). There are no uvular sounds in English, but the French'r' sound is uvular (generally it is a voiced fricative, but it can be an approximant in certain contexts, and a trill if spoken carefully).

Pharyngeals are produced by constricting the pharynx, which is the region extending from the uvula down to the larynx (where the vocal cords are found). A strictly pharyngeal sound is produced with the root of the tongue, whereas an epiglottal is made with the epiglottis, i.e. that cartilage which prevents food from entering the trachea when one swallows. Finally, glottals or"laryngeals" are made at the level of the glottis. There are no pharyngeals (let alone epiglottals) in English, but there are some glottal sounds: the normal'h' sound is a voiceless glottal fricative, and, although it is not really part of the English phonemic system, one finds some glottal stops (plosives) in certain circumstances in many varieties of English.

Chapter 10

Acoustic Phonetics

SOUN

Sound is the result of the disturbance of air by some kind of movement. These disturbances of the air are called sound waves. Examples of the types of movement that cause this disturbance of air are the vibrations of a tuning fork, a guitar string, or a rubber band.

Let's take the guitar string as an example. The disturbance in the air is the movement of air molecules as a result of the movement of the string back and forth. When a guitar string is plucked, the string quickly moves back and forth. As it goes in one direction, the string pushes the air molecules closest to it. These air molecules then get closer to the air molecules surrounding it. This is called compression.

Here's a little note about air molecules. They prefer to be equidistant from each other. If an air molecule gets too close, the surrounding air molecules move away, attempting to reestablish the status quo.

So, when the air molecules closest to the string are compressed against the surrounding molecules, a chain reaction is set up, in which the surrounding air molecules move away from the first ones, and are then compressed against other air molecules, which then move away, and so on, and so on.

But that's not the end of it. As stated above, the guitar string moves back and forth. So, after the guitar string moves in the first direction, causing compression, it then moves in the opposite direction. As it does so, it pulls away from the surrounding air molecules. When this happens, those air molecules are now farther away from the air molecules on the other side of the string. This is called rarefaction. Since air molecules prefer to be equidistant from each other, they will move towards the molecules that are too far away. This, in turn, pulls them away from the surrounding air molecules, which then move to restablish the correct distance.

Then, the guitar string moves back again, causing compression, and the whole thing starts over again.

The following animation is an illustration of compression and rarefaction.

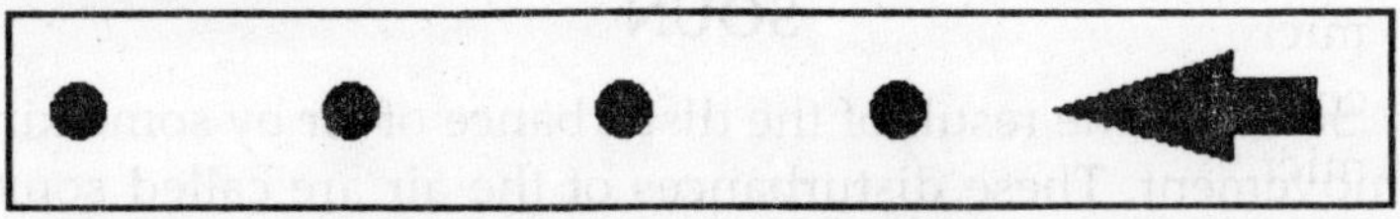

The arrow represents the movement of the guitar string, and the individual circles represent air molecules. The chain reaction through the surrounding air caused by compression and rarefaction is the sound wave.

As the guitar string vibrates at a certain number of times within a second, the surrounding air molecules within a certain distance from the string will move back and forth at that same number of times within a second.

The next section discusses the parts of a sound wave and how to calculate them.

DETERMINING THE FORMANTS OF VOWEL

A vowel's formants are the frequencies at which it resonates; that is, the frequencies which are particularly loud in an acoustic signal. Each vowel has its own set of signature formants. Vowels in different dialects also have different formant patterns. This tutorial is intended to show you how to determine vowel formants in your own speech.

Extracting formants is no simple task. It involves recording your sample and creating a spectrogram. Fortunately, there is software that allows a user to do all of these. The Language Samples Project uses Praat, a shareware product created by the linguist Paul Boersma. When using

Praat, there is an intermediate step, which is to convert the recorded sample into a Praat object.

RECORDING YOUR SAMPLE

To analyse your speech, Praat first needs to have a sound file to work with. Choose the"Record Sound..." option under the"New" menu. This calls up the SoundRecorder window.

Make sure the Sample rate is set at 44100. The Input Source may be either External Mic (recommended) or Sound In. You will know that the programme can detect your speech because the Metre will react to any sound picked up by your microphone, even if it is not recording. If you do not see colours spiking in the Metre, double check to make sure your microphone is plugged in.

To obtain your sample, click the Record button and speak into the microphone. When you have finished, click Stop. You may listen to the recording again by clicking Play.

You may need to try more than once to get a good sample. Holding the microphone too close to your mouth will result in the signal having loud puffs and hisses. If this happens, try holding the microphone a few inches farther away. If you are satisfied with your sample, you can now save it as a.WAV file. Do not click the Close button! Instead, open the"File" menu in the SoundRecorder window, and choose"Write left channel to WAV file." This will let you save your recording as a digital file. Give your sample a name and remember which folder you're saving it in. Once the file has been saved, you may close the SoundRecorder window.

Prevent future hassles by choosing an easily identifiable name. For example, if your name is Norma and the word you recorded is"thing", name the file"NormaThing.wav" instead of just"sample.wav","Norma.wav", or"thing.wav". Otherwise, if Norma and Nicole both had files named simply"sample.wav" or"thing.wav", either one of them might be analyzing the wrong sample at a later date!

MAKING AN OBJECT

Praat is designed to create different"objects" from sound

files, and it can only work with these objects. Objects are normally listed in the Praat Objects window. The first object you need to add is the sound file itself. To do so, open the"Read" menu and choose"Read from file...". This will allow you to open your.WAV file as an object. Choose your sound file as you would choose any other document, by finding the proper folder and locating the file. When you click Open, Praat will add the file as a'Sound' object.

You can rename and edit (clip, trim) this object without affecting the original.WAV file. So if you mess up, don't worry! You can higllight an unwanted Sound object and click Remove at the bottom of the window. Then read the.WAV file over again as a new object.

Your Sound object is now something that Praat can apply various functions to, creating more objects in the process. Some of these other objects include spectrograms. You can examine each object in a separate window, but the commands for doing so differ, diepending on the nature of the object.

VIEWING A SPECTROGRAM

There are two ways of getting spectrograms in Praat. One way is to examine your Sound object itself, by clicking the Edit button in the Praat Objects window.

If you don't see an Edit button, make sure your Sound object is highlighted.

a. The Edit button opens another window, named for the Sound object. You should see a waveform in this window, as well as several drop-down menus.. To see the spectrogram, open the"Spectrogram" menu and choose"Show". The window should now be a split screen, with a waveform on top and a spectrogram on the bottom. The spectrogram is a graph that plots frequency (y-axis) and amplitude (darkness) over time (x-axis).

   Make sure you choose"Spectrogram > Show" and not"Spectrogram > View".

   To have a better view of the spectrogram, delete the empty space that is probably found before and after your sample. Highlight those areas and choose"Edit > Cut".

b. You should now be able to see formants in the window, as dark, mainly horizontal bands. The horizontal cursor in this window can give you an idea of the frequencies of these formants. If you click anywhere on the spectrogram, you will see a time value at the bottom and a frequency value at the left. You should also see the intersection of a vertical and horizontal red line at the point on which you clicked. So if you click in the vertical centre of a formant, you can determine its frequency very easily.

   Another way to view a spectrogram is to create a Spectrogram object. Instead of pursuing Step (3a), you would have your Sound object highlighted in the Praat Objects window. Click on the Spectrum - button and choose"to Spectrogram...".

   You will see a window appear that gives you several options about the specifications of the spectrogram. Clicking the Defaults button will give you decent settings, but you may want to try reducing the Maximum Frequency to anywhere between 5000 and 7000 Hz. This will reduce the amount of empty space on the ensuing spectrogram, but it will also widen the formants, making it harder to determine their centre with precision. Increasing the Analysis Width to 0.05 s will create a wide-band spectorgram.

c. You will see a new object in the Praat Objects window, called Spectrogram [name]. When this object is highlighted, click the View button to see the spectrogram. A window will appear with the Spectrogram plotted againts time and frequency, just like in Step (3b). However, this spectrogram will not give you precise frequency values; you would need to estimate a frequency using the scale on the y-axis. So while this way of obtaining a spectrogram gives you the option of viewing it to your specifications, it is harder to get a precise formant value.

Index